GLOBALIZING EDUCATIONAL ACCOUNTABILITIES

Globalizing Educational Accountabilities analyzes the influence that international and national testing and accountability regimes have on educational policy reform efforts in schooling systems around the world. Tracing the evolution of those regimes, with an emphasis on the OECD's PISA, it reveals the multiple effects of policy as numbers in countries with different types of government and different education systems. From the effect of Shanghai's PISA success on nations trying to compete economically to the perverse effects of linking funding to performance targets in Australia, the analysis links testing and accountability to new modes of network governance, new spatialities, and the significance of data infrastructures. This highly illustrative text offers scholars and policy makers a critical policy sociology framework for doing education policy analysis today.

Bob Lingard is a Professorial Research Fellow in the School of Education at The University of Queensland, Australia.

Wayne Martino is a Professor of Education in the Faculty of Education at the University of Western Ontario, Canada.

Goli Rezai-Rashti is a Professor of Education at the University of Western Ontario, Canada.

Sam Sellar is a Postdoctoral Research Fellow in the School of Education at The University of Queensland, Australia.

Education in Global Context

Series editor: Lois Weis

Social Class and Education: Global Perspectives
Edited by Lois Weis and Nadine Dolby

Confucius and Crisis in American Universities
Amy Stambach

Globalizing Educational Accountabilities
Bob Lingard, Wayne Martino, Goli Rezai-Rashti and Sam Sellar

GLOBALIZING EDUCATIONAL ACCOUNTABILITIES

*Bob Lingard,
Wayne Martino,
Goli Rezai-Rashti, and
Sam Sellar*

NEW YORK AND LONDON

First published 2016
by Routledge
711 Third Avenue, New York, NY 10017

and by Routledge
2 Park Square, Milton Park, Abingdon, Oxon, OX14 4RN

Routledge is an imprint of the Taylor & Francis Group, an informa business

© 2016 Taylor & Francis

The right of Bob Lingard, Wayne Martino, Goli Rezai-Rashti and Sam Sellar to be identified as authors of this work has been asserted by them in accordance with sections 77 and 78 of the Copyright, Designs and Patents Act 1988.

All rights reserved. No part of this book may be reprinted or reproduced or utilised in any form or by any electronic, mechanical, or other means, now known or hereafter invented, including photocopying and recording, or in any information storage or retrieval system, without permission in writing from the publishers.

Trademark notice: Product or corporate names may be trademarks or registered trademarks, and are used only for identification and explanation without intent to infringe.

Library of Congress Cataloging-in-Publication Data
Lingard, Bob.
  Globalizing educational accountabilities / by Bob Lingard, Wayne Martino, Goli Rezai-Rashti, and Sam Sellar.
    pages cm. — (Education in global context)
  Includes bibliographical references and index.
  1. Educational accountability. 2. Educational tests and measurements. I. Martino, Wayne. II. Rezai-Rashti, Goli.
III. Sellar, Sam. IV. Title.
  LB2806.22.L56 2016
  371.14'4—dc23
  2015009704

ISBN: 978-0-415-71024-4 (hbk)
ISBN: 978-0-415-71025-1 (pbk)
ISBN: 978-1-315-88513-1 (ebk)

Typeset in Bembo
by Apex CoVantage, LLC

*This book is dedicated to our friend and colleague,
Gregory James Dimitriadis
1969–2014*

CONTENTS

List of Tables ix
Series Editor Introduction xi
    Lois Weis
Acknowledgements xiii
List of Abbreviations xvii

1 Introduction 1

2 Global Educational Accountabilities 19

3 Politics of Mutual Accountability 40

4 Catalyst Data 63

5 PISA and the Invisibility of Race 90

6 PISA and the Politics of "Failing Boys" 121

7 Conclusion 146

References 163
Index 179

TABLES

4.1 2010 reward frameworks, New South Wales, Victoria,
     and Queensland   76
4.2 Mandated measure 1: New South Wales, targets and performance 76
4.3 Mandated measure 1: Victoria, targets and performance   77
4.4 Mandated measure 1: Queensland, targets and performance   77

SERIES EDITOR INTRODUCTION
Lois Weis

Globalizing Educational Accountabilities analyzes the influence that international and national testing and accountability regimes have on educational policy reform efforts in schooling systems around the world. Tracing the evolution of those regimes, with an emphasis on the OECD's PISA, it reveals the multiple effects of policy as numbers in countries with different types of government and different education systems. From the effect of Shanghai's PISA success on nations trying to compete economically to the perverse effects of linking funding to performance targets in Australia, the analysis links testing and accountability to new modes of network governance, new spatialities, and the significance of data infrastructures. This highly illustrative text offers scholars and policy makers a critical policy sociology framework for doing education policy analysis today.

The changing nature of transnational migration patterns holds significant implications for this broad intellectual project. In a context where migrants—here defined as immigrants across class, race/ethnic, and religious background; refugees who comprise a range of national origins; and international students who similarly hail from a wide range of "sending nations"—are positioned and work to reposition themselves inside new global circumstances, we can expect notable change in the nature of and engagement with knowledge, educational practices, and outcomes across the globe. This works to alter social structural arrangements both within and between nations.

ACKNOWLEDGEMENTS

During the completion of this book, our dear colleague and friend, Professor Greg Dimitriadis of the State University of New York at Buffalo, sadly passed away. We dedicate this book to him and his memory. He talked with all of us about the ideas contained in this book. Indeed, we had some time together in Toronto discussing the effects of testing and new modes of educational accountability. He is sadly missed, but we are better persons for having known him and his quiet dignity and intelligence. We acknowledge his contributions to educational research.

We also acknowledge the support of Canadian and Australian research councils for funding the projects that form the basis of this book. In Canada, we acknowledge the support of the Social Sciences Humanities Research Council of Canada (SSHRC) for funding the project entitled, *Beyond the crisis of failing boys: Investigating which boys and which girls are underachieving* (410–2010–059). In Australia, we acknowledge funding support from the Australian Research Council (ARC) for the Discovery project (DP1094850), *Schooling the nation in an age of globalization: National curriculum, accountabilities and their effects*, and for the Linkage project (100200841), *Pursuing equity in high poverty rural schools: Improving learning through rich accountabilities*. We also wish to thank most sincerely all of the research participants in these projects for their generous contribution to these studies.

In 2013, three of the authors of this book—Bob, Wayne, and Goli—edited a special number of the *Journal of Education Policy* on testing regimes, accountabilities, and education policy (28,3) and the fourth author—Sam—contributed to papers included in that special number. This editorial work and the development of papers contained in the special number enhanced and advanced our thinking on the topic of the book. We also need to mention the time the four of us had together in Muskoka, Canada, working on this book. This was a wonderful place to think and write and at the same time to encounter the natural beauty of Canada.

Dr. Aspa Baroutsis has worked on this book with us through her editing, general support, and oversight. We thank her most sincerely for her contribution. The book is better for her involvement.

We thank Professor Lois Weis, the editor of the Series in which this book is published, for commissioning the book. Our very special thanks go to Catherine Bernard, our commissioning editor at Routledge, New York. We appreciate her forbearance in waiting for this manuscript to appear. We hope it was worth the wait, Catherine. And thanks also for your quiet dignity and intelligence, even when we failed to deliver the manuscript at the second submission date.

Bob and Sam would like to thank their doctoral students, Anna Hogan and Steven Lewis, for contributing to their learning about and understanding of edu-businesses and PISA for schools, respectively. They would also like to thank Steven for the annotated bibliography that he developed on new modes of educational accountability. They also thank Angelique Howell, another of their doctoral students, for her research on the impact of NAPLAN on primary students in Catholic schools. Bob would also like to thank former doctoral students, Greg Vass and Sue Creagh, for contributing to his understanding of testing and accountability regimes in education. Working with other doctoral students, Stephen Heimans, David Peacock, Faridah Awang, Khalaf Al'Abri, and Yu-Chih Li, has also contributed to our thinking about educational policy today. Working on an edited book for Routledge on NAPLAN in Australia with Greg Thompson has also advanced our thinking.

We note that our names on the authorship of this book are in alphabetical order. We all contributed equally to the thought behind it and to the production of the text.

Bob, as always, would like to thank with all his heart his beloved partner, Carolynn, for all her support for everything he does, including spending too much time on the computer (and in art galleries).

Wayne would like to acknowledge the ongoing love and support of his partner, Jose. He would also like to acknowledge Western University and the funds made available through his Faculty Scholar Award that contributed to making the writing of this book possible.

Goli is grateful to her partner Nibaldo Galleguillos for his love and ongoing support for everything including the writing of this book.

Sam would like to thank Julie for her support throughout a busy period of research, in both of our lives, during which this book was written.

We acknowledge that some of this book has been derived from our earlier journal articles. These include:

Chapter 2 draws on two articles: Sellar, S., & Lingard, B. (2014). The OECD and the expansion of PISA: New global modes of governance in education. *British Educational Research Journal, 40*(6), 917–936; Sellar, S., & Lingard, B. (2013). The OECD and global governance in education. *Journal of Education Policy, 28*(5), 710–725.

Chapter 3 draws on: Sellar, S., & Lingard, B. (2013). Looking East: Shanghai, PISA 2009 and the reconstitution of reference societies in the global education policy field. *Comparative Education, 49*(4), 464–485.

Chapter 4 draws on: Lingard, B., & Sellar, S. (2013). "Catalyst data": Perverse systemic effects of auditand accountablity in Australian schooling. *Journal of Education Policy, 28*(5), 634–656.

Chapter 6 draws on: Martino, W., & Rezai-Rashti, G. (2013). "Gap talk" and the global rescaling of educational accountability in Canada. *Journal of Education Policy, 28*(5), 589–611.

ABBREVIATIONS

ACARA	Australian Curriculum Assessment and Reporting Authority
AITSL	Australian Institute of Teaching and School Leadership
CERI	Centre for Research and Innovation
CMEC	Council of Ministers of Education, Canada
COAG	Council of Australian Governments
DEELSA	Directorate for Education, Employment, Labour and Social Affairs
DFES	Department for Education and Skills
ELL	English language learners
EQAO	Education Quality and Accountability Office
ESL	English as a second language
GERM	Global Education Reform Movement
GTA	Greater Toronto Area
IAFFR	Intergovernmental Agreement on Federal Financial Relations
ICSEA	Index of Community Socio-Economic Advantage
IEA	International Association for the Evaluation of Educational Achievement
INES	Indicators of Education Systems
KPI	Key performance indicators
LBOTE	Language Background other than English
LSA	Large-scale assessment
MOOC	Massive open online courses
NAEP	National Assessment of Educational Progress
NAP	National Assessment Program
NAPLAN	National Assessment Program—Literacy and Numeracy

NASSP	National Association of Secondary School Principals
NGO	Nongovernmental organization
NPM	New public management
OECD	Organisation for Economic Co-operation and Development
PCAP	Pan-Canadian Assessment Program
PIAAC	Programme for International Assessment of Adult Competencies
PIRLS	Progress in International Reading and Literacy
PISA	Programme for International Student Assessment
SCSEEC	Standing Council on School Education and Early Childhood
TALIS	Teaching and Learning International Survey
TDSB	Toronto District School Board
TIMSS	Trends in International Mathematics and Science Study
UNESCO	United Nations Educational, Scientific and Cultural Organization

1
INTRODUCTION

Introduction

What is counted affects what counts in schooling today and is central to how educational accountability is framed. Globally, but particularly in Anglo-American and Asian nations, testing of various kinds has become an instrument for steering schooling systems in particular directions using accountability regimes. Rizvi and Lingard (2010) have argued that what Bernstein (1971) called the evaluation message system of schooling, in the form of testing, now steers schooling systems as meta-policy, with significant implications for the work of schools and teachers (see Lingard, Martino, & Rezai-Rashti, 2013). Such steering through testing has had great effects on each of the three message systems described by Bernstein—pedagogies, curricula, and assessment—as well as upon student learning and experiences of schooling. This is in stark contrast to a recent recommendation by the Organisation for Economic Co-operation and Development (OECD; 2013a) that effective forms of educational accountabilities should limit negative effects on teacher practices and professionalism. Central to the evaluation message system is high-stakes testing, which has witnessed the rise of top-down accountabilities linked to test performance and their use to hold schools, principals, and teachers accountable for school and student outcomes. Such high-stakes testing is now operative in the form of large-scale assessments (LSAs) conducted at provincial, national, and international scales.

LSAs and related accountabilities must be seen as part of the contemporary phenomenon of "policy as numbers" (Ozga & Lingard, 2007; Ozga, 2009; Lingard, 2011) and the growing "datafication" of social life. Data are central to new modes of governance linked to, and imbricated in, new public management

(NPM), network governance, and contemporary governmentalities. Rose (1999) provides a clear description of the phenomenon of policy as numbers and the functioning of metrics, statistics, databases, rankings, comparisons, and so on within these mundane technologies of governance:

> Democratic mentalities of government prioritise and seek to produce a relationship between numerate citizens, numericised civic discourse and numerate evaluations of government. Democracy can operate as a technology of government to the extent that such a network of numbers can be composed and stabilized. In analyses of democracy, a focus on numbers is instructive for it helps us turn our eyes from grand texts of philosophy to the mundane practices of pedagogy, of accounting, of information and polling, and to the mundane knowledges and "grey sciences" that support them.
> (Rose, 1999: 232)

This is not simply a new analytical demand on sociologists, but also a description of contemporary practices of social analysis beyond academia. The "grey sciences" come to the fore here in our era of politics and policy as managerialist incrementalism devoid of "big ideas," but replete with "big data." This is in the political context of what Lyotard (1984) has referred to as the death of meta-narratives. Data become central to structuring the system and keeping it operative.

Data-driven rationalities and technologies of governmentality are tied to a form of biopower mobilized through numbers as *inscription devices* (devices both constitute and target specific populations as a basis for identifying policy concerns); Rose (1988: 187) speaks about the role of numbers as a function of biopolitics that establishes both "a regime of visibility" and "a grid of codeability," thereby constituting a navigable space of commensurability, equivalence, and comparison that renders the population amenable to administration, statistical mapping, and governance. The codes and grids of visibility produced by LSAs have disciplining and controlling effects for ranking and comparing education systems, which often incite politically motivated reforms within national systems. Often such incitement works through what has been called "externalization" (Bendix, 1978; Schriewer, 1990), rather than through policy learning, whereby poor national comparative performance on international tests is used to legitimize and strengthen politically driven domestic reform agendas (Sellar & Lingard, 2013a). Educational measurements, and the systems of accountability they enable, are thus an integral feature of the political technologies of governance "with their techniques for achieving subjugations of bodies" and the management or "control of populations" under the global panoptic gaze of other nations, systems, and capital itself (Foucault, 1998: 140).

There has been a specific global aspect to this emergence of policy as numbers and testing as systemic meta-policy. The development of the OECD's Programme for International Student Assessment (PISA) and the International Association for the Evaluation of Educational Achievement's (IEA's) Trends in International Mathematics and Science Study (TIMSS) and Progress in International Reading and Literacy Study (PIRLS) has ushered in a new era of international LSAs. These programs now function as a mode of global educational accountability for national systems of schooling, complemented by national testing programs. There is a real articulation and symbiosis between national and international testing as part of the "respatialization" of educational politics and policymaking, linked to globalization (Amin, 2002) and the enhanced capacity for the "datafication" of schooling facilitated by advances in computational capacities. These interwoven global and national developments have given rise to what has been called the "the infrastructure of accountability" in education (Anagnostopoulos, Rutledge, & Jacobsen, 2013).

The educational accountabilities we examine in this book are linked to changes in the functioning of contemporary capitalism globally, particularly the spread of information infrastructure (Bowker, Baker, Millerand, & Ribes, 2010) as a key technology for monitoring and managing education systems in connection with national economies. In this respect, Thrift (2005: 1) has argued that contemporary capitalism has begun "to consider its own practices on a continuous basis" through the collection and analysis of data by governments, nongovernment organizations, and private companies. Thrift calls this condition "knowing capitalism." New information or data infrastructures associated with globalizing educational accountabilities are part of this phenomenon of capitalism seeking to know and modulate itself in order to sustain productivity and economic growth and to function more effectively and efficiently. We have entered a newly intensified phase of performative accountability in education (Lyotard, 1984; Ranson, 2003).

We see the "audit explosion" and the rise of "audit culture," documented and analyzed by Power (1997), as part of the phenomenon of "knowing capitalism." The proliferation of new sources and quantities of data produced by the everyday infrastructures of capitalism—the phenomenon of "big data" that is well-advanced in certain educational applications (Mayer-Schonberger & Cukier, 2013, 2014)— raises questions about the place and efficacy of an empirical sociology that has long valorized the collection and analysis of data through sample surveys and substantive in-depth interviews as its distinctive modus operandi and raison d'être (Savage & Burrows, 2007). In this context, Savage and Burrows suggest that contemporary sociology must renew itself through an agenda that focuses on analyzing and "challenging current practices in the collection, use, and deployment of social data" (896). Rose (1999), Hacking (1990), and Latour (1987) have also written about the complex classificatory and technical work that goes into the constitution of the numbers that both drive and create contemporary policy, and these arguments have relevance for policy sociology approaches to studying new modes of educational accountability. Examining practices of data collection, analysis, and representation, in relation to international and national testing and associated accountability regimes, is a central aim of this book.

We focus to a large extent on the educational assessment, testing, and accountability work of the OECD and the growth of its role in global governance (Woodward, 2009; Sellar & Lingard, 2013b, 2014). The OECD's PISA and related testing developments (for example, the Programme for International Assessment of Adult Competencies [PIAAC] and the Teaching and Learning International Survey [TALIS]) help to constitute the globe as a commensurate space of measurement, enabling comparative measures of the performance of schooling systems, individual schools, skills development, universities, and national stocks of "human capital." We might see the success of this "commensurative work" (Espland, 2000) as reflecting the rise, or perhaps resurrection, of neopositivist epistemologies and ontologies (Lather, 2013) and a discourse of evidence-based policymaking (Luke, Green, & Kelly, 2010; Wiseman, 2010) that reframes the purposes and methods of educational research in new ways. As Luke and Hogan (2006) remind us, "the centrality of data and numbers to contemporary modes of governance mean that current debates over what counts as evidence in state policy formation are indeed debates over what counts as educational research" (170). However, given that policy is the "authoritative allocation of values" (Easton, 1953), and is constituted through an assemblage of research evidence, political values, and professional knowledges (Head, 2008), we can only really speak of "evidence-informed policy." We might see new evidence-informed policy, data-driven rationalities, and big data analytics as "creating a new ontological 'epoch' as a new historical constellation of intelligibility" (Berry, 2011: 16) that requires new tools for critical sociological analysis.

The context of globalizing educational accountabilities is one in which social research is increasingly conducted beyond academia, and policymaking is increasingly being undertaken beyond the state and beyond the nation (Appadurai, 2001). Here we see the enhanced policy significance of both international organizations and edu-businesses. This book constitutes an engagement with these emergent intellectual, commercial, and policy spaces, evidenced in new imbrications of the local, national, and global, specifically as they relate to educational data and accountabilities. In the concluding chapter, we talk about the enhanced role of edu-businesses in policy work in education today. This development is reflected in the contribution to these methodological debates about new social data analytics by researchers attached to private companies (for example Boyd & Crawford, 2012). We might see these researchers as academic "boundary spanners" (Williams, 2002), working in interstitial spaces with policy analysts and other technical experts, such as secretariat staff at the OECD (described internally as a "non-academic university"), to focus on research *for* policy. In contrast, in this book we undertake research *of* policy (Gordon, Lewis, & Young, 1977), paying attention to the movement of policy actors involved in new modes of network governance, which work across national and global spaces and public and private sectors (see Ball & Junemann, 2012). As a consequence, Ball (2012: 93) suggests that policy analysis today must extend beyond the nation state and that such analysis should include international organizations, NGOs, and edu-businesses.

Throughout the book, we take a policy sociology in education approach (Ozga, 1987) to understanding the rise, functioning, and effects of globalizing educational accountabilities, new policy spaces, and network governance. Policy sociology draws on social science theories, methodologies, and data of various kinds, including interview data, document analysis, and historical work. In this book we engage with data from three government-funded research projects, two in Australia and one in Canada. The originality of the book lies in the utilization of these intellectual resources and their application to our topic, and we believe this extends the canon of work in policy sociology in education. The book might also be seen a response to the challenges Savage and Burrows (2007) have proffered to contemporary social sciences, both in terms of research topics and the intellectual resources, both theoretical and methodological, that are needed to understand data and society in our contemporary moment.

Globalizing Educational Accountabilities is then distinctive both in terms of its topic and the concepts that we bring to bear in our analyses. We see international comparative testing of the performance of schooling systems as constituting new spatialities of educational accountability, with effects on national policy production, the politics of education, and the work of systems, schools, principals, and teachers. To understand this new phenomenon, we draw on a range of intellectual resources derived from emergent theories within the social sciences. These "big ideas" include the related concepts of datafication, "big data," and data infrastructures; new theorizing about post-Euclidean spatialities associated with what has been described as the "becoming-topological" of culture (Lury et al., 2012); and the emergence, post-NPM, of networked or heterarchical modes of governance in schooling, including the growing role of edu-businesses in education policy communities and processes (Ball, 2012; Ball & Junemann, 2012; Au & Ferrare, 2015). Of course, the concept of accountability in education and its contemporary reworking is also central.

Contexts

Globalization has led to enhanced interconnectivity between nations and greater flows of people (including policy makers, politicians, researchers, academics, students) and policy ideas (knowledge economy, lifelong learning, human capital, accountabilities, testing) across the globe. Indeed, we might speak of global "policyscapes" in education (Ball, 1998). Sahlberg (2011) has written of the Global Education Reform Movement (GERM), which has spread through schooling systems around the world. This movement focuses on high-stakes testing, educational accountability, sometimes national curriculum (for example in England and Australia), an emphasis on literacy and numeracy (for example in Ontario and Australia), new managerialism, and marketizations and privatizations of various kinds (Ball & Youdell, 2008; Ball, 2008, 2012), including school choice policies and competition between schools as a putative means to drive up standards. We might more accurately speak of GERMS, given that the features of this reform movement always play out in vernacular ways within different nations and systems, mediated by local histories, politics, and cultures, leading to path dependency for policy in specific systems (Simola, Rinnie, Varjo, & Kauko, 2013; Takayama, 2015). When GERM reaches non-Anglo-American nations, we might also see it as an example of a "globalized localism" (de Sousa Santos, 2006); that is, the spread of an Anglo-American policy ideas globally.

Rizvi and Lingard (2010) have discussed the globalizing education policy discourses emanating from international organizations such as the OECD, World Bank, and UNESCO, which have helped to build convergence at the level of meta-policy discourses in education across nations. Stronach (2010), in this context, has spoken of global "hypernarratives" in education policy, a manifestation in a sense of GERM, which also push policy reform in national systems in particular directions. These are associated with a global respatialization of politics and political relations since the end of the Cold War and a reworking of the nation-state, including the strengthened influence of international organizations, new regionalisms, supranational bodies such as the EU, and so on. The latter have contributed to the creation of an emergent global education policy field (Lingard & Rawolle, 2011), associated with the emergence of global epistemic policy communities (Kallo, 2009) and related policy habitus (Lingard, Sellar, & Baroutsis, 2015), with effects in national schooling systems. In a sense, we see international testing and global accountability in education as helping to constitute the "global" in education, rather than simply being an effect of it (Sobe, 2015).

New educational accountabilities are one manifestation of this policy convergence at the meta-policy level. Novoa and Yariv-Mashal (2003) have written of how the "global eye" and the "national eye" in education govern together today through complementary international and national testing regimes for schools. Comparing the performance of education systems has become a new mode of educational governance, which involves a global politics of mutual accountability and the translation of educational performance into an international "spectacle" (Novoa & Yariv-Mashal, 2003). The latter might be thought about in Foucauldian terms as a "global panopticism," linked to what Lather (2013) has referred to as "metrics mania" in contemporary educational policy and research. This phenomenon is most evident in the references of politicians and policy makers to a global "education race," which is made possible through international assessments and rankings of performance. What has come to count in education is how nations and systems are seen to perform in these rankings, rather than more substantive interrogations of the data generated by LSAs.

Based on our research on the OECD (Sellar & Lingard, 2013a, 2013b, 2014), we see global panopticism in education as coconstituted through value consensus among member nations and the Secretariat of the OECD, given the significant influence of PISA. We must remember that nations pay to participate in PISA and set the agenda for the OECD's work. The OECD thus functions as a node in a network of complex relations between the Secretariat, OECD committees, experts, member nations, nonmember nations, policy discourses, data infrastructures, and commercial and nongovernmental organizations—in effect a complex, heterogeneous assemblage of administrative apparatuses. The resulting regulatory synergy needs to be understood in terms of the interweaving of multiple scales and spaces of governance and governmentalities: a policy "dispositif" (Foucault, 1980; Bailey, 2013) that cuts across these scales and spaces. For Foucault (1980), a dispositif is:

> [A] thoroughly heterogeneous set consisting of discourses, institutions, architectural forms, regulatory decisions, mores, administrative measures, scientific statements, philosophical, moral, and philanthropic propositions—in short, the said as much as the unsaid. Such are the elements of the apparatus. The apparatus itself is the network that can be established between these elements.
>
> (194)

We argue that the OECD's work in education is helping to instantiate new modes of global governance in education, which we have characterized as *epistemological* and *infrastructural* governance, constituted and administered through new quantitative LSAs (Sellar & Lingard, 2013b, 2014). The OECD (2012) recognizes this in its approach to human capital assessment, arguing that any attempt to measure the skills of national labor forces requires the development of agreed definitions of skills and a metric that can be overlaid across the globe as a commensurate space of measurement. This is the technical work that Rose (1999) suggests goes into the mundane practices of policy as numbers. The concept of dispositif captures the complex assemblage of discursive and material elements in a policy network. We also recognize the need to historicize our analytical account of the emergence of global educational accountabilities and associated technologies of governance in the contemporary moment. This emergence is a response to the urgency felt within nations to compete in the global education race, especially after the global financial crisis and European sovereign debt crises, when knowledge capitalism has come to be considered the only game in the networked global village.

The nation-state and subnational political units work in different ways in this global context. Associated with the new individualism and self-responsibilization of neoliberalism, there has been a decline in consensus values underpinning policy. However, there has been a global circulation of policy discourses, which position policy makers in particular ways—this is the contemporary global education policy dispositif. In this setting, the rise of policy as numbers, both globally and nationally in education (Lingard, 2011), functions to keep schooling systems going according to a technical criterion of efficiency, which, set against the decline of meta-narratives, gives meaning to processes of policy production (Lyotard, 1984). As Lyotard observed decades ago, education systems are becoming increasingly performative and oriented towards achieving the best possible input/output equation. In education, with this rise of performativity, the question in schooling systems is "who controls the field of judgment" (Ball, 2003b). In answer to this question, we aver that the field of judgment is now controlled by policy makers and technicians who manage and invoke the results of global and national testing regimes, rather than teachers who are instead held accountable at a distance for the performance of their students and schools. Indeed, a particular fraction of the professional middle class has benefitted from the new demand for data and symbolic analysis (Apple, 2001; Lingard et al., 2015). This shift in control of the field of judgment has had reductive and de-professionalizing impacts in schooling, and particularly on the work of teachers and schools (Nichols & Berliner, 2007).

While the book takes a global view, we recognize that nations have continued importance in an era of globalization and we examine the effects of global educational accountabilities in two national contexts: Australia and Canada. While we now see growing global policy convergence at the meta-policy level, we would argue strongly that these discourses are articulated in vernacular ways within specific nations and subnational political units, manifesting what Appadurai (1996) described as "vernacular globalization." A given nation's politics, political structures (for example federal versus unitary forms of government), culture, and histories combine to mediate and recontextualize these global discourses. For example, Australia's federal political structure and high degree of vertical fiscal imbalance (the federal government has strong revenue raising capacity, while the states have large areas of policy responsibility) gives the federal government much opportunity to constitute "national polices" in schooling, despite schooling being a Constitutional responsibility of the states and territories. Thus, an evident response to globalization in Australia has been the emergence of a national curriculum and national testing (the National Assessment Program—Literacy and Numeracy [NAPLAN] has been in place since 2008), which is used as a form of educational accountability for state systems, schools, and teachers. We have seen the emergence in Australia of a quasi-national schooling system as human capital and productivity discourses reconstitute education policy as a central arm of national economic policy in the context of economic globalization.

Canada also has a federal political structure, but in stark contrast to Australia, there is a much weaker national presence in schooling with provinces retaining policy control of education. Nonetheless, Canada has seen the emergence of the Council of Ministers of Education, Canada (CMEC), founded in 1967, consisting of the Education Ministers of all provinces and territories, with an explicit directive to steer education policy across the nation. In Canada, the provinces control testing and each province has its own and distinct testing regime. Unlike Australia, there is no federal minister for education, no federal department, and thus no federal participation in CMEC and no national testing as in Australia. CMEC functions as a policy mechanism to steer national policy in conjunction with Statistics Canada, particularly in relation to PISA, which works differently in relation to the rescaling of contemporary education politics in Canada. This policy architecture means that any national agendas are driven politically and that the relation to the global policy field works differently from the situation in Australia and elsewhere.

In the USA, for example, there is not the same degree of vertical fiscal imbalance in its federal structure that Australia has, thus limiting the extent of federal involvement in schooling. Nonetheless, there is a stronger federal political and bureaucratic presence in USA schooling than is the situation in Canada (see Savage & O'Connor, 2014). Under President Obama, we have witnessed the states agreeing to Common Core standards in mathematics and English. President Obama's Race to the Top initiative has attempted, through a federal funding regime, to impact employment conditions for teachers at the state level, with tenure and pay increases linked to performance management based on test results. This has occurred at a time when Shanghai-China's outstanding performance on PISA 2009 has precipitated a PISA shock in the USA, a matter dealt with in Chapter 3 of this book. President Obama said this was the 21st-century "Sputnik moment" for the USA, which is now looking outwards again in terms of directions for schooling policy (Luke, 2011).

While we focus on Australia and Canada, considerable references will be made to the educational effects of new accountabilities in other nations, including in particular the USA, China, and England. We will also consider the ways in which these accountability regimes have rearticulated social justice and equity policies globally and within nations in reductive ways (see Lingard, Sellar, & Savage, 2014; Martino & Rezai-Rashti, 2012; Rezai-Rashti, 2009; Rezai-Rashti, Segeren & Martino (in press)). The focus on Australia and Canada, each with very different forms of federalism, allows for consideration of the respatialization of educational politics and policies within and beyond the nation in the context of globalization, and for an analysis of the complex respatialization of educational accountabilities. We pay particular attention to complementarity between international and national LSAs and consider the ways that such testing functions in relation to multiple modes and layers of accountability for teachers, principals, schools, systems, and nations. In this way, following Sobe (2015), we might see these multiple modes of accountability as the "monitoring of monitoring" that is characteristic of audit culture.

Big Ideas

There are four sets of big ideas that inform the analysis provided in this book: data, space, governance, and accountability.

Datafication, Big Data, and Data Infrastructures

The use of quantitative data to monitor and manage the work of schools and systems is not a new phenomenon. However, as Mayer-Schonberger and Cukier (2013) observe, capacities to routinely collect, analyze, and act upon social data are growing rapidly and we find ourselves in a new era of data analytics—the era of "big data." Education is already being profoundly changed by these developments, most obviously in the area of adaptive learning, where new software applications are being developed to collect and analyze data in real time, enabling the modulation and customization of learning experiences based on student differences. Central to this development are new capacities to subject diverse aspects of learning to "datafication" (Mayer-Schonberger & Cukier, 2013): the conversion of information about learning processes and outcomes into quantified formats. The continual evolution of educational testing, including recent developments in international LSAs such as PISA, is helping to enhance capacities for datafication, for example by expanding the scale of assessments, the scope of what is measured, and the types of analyses that can be conducted (Sellar & Lingard, 2014).

Datafication is one aspect of "big data," which can be differentiated from previous approaches to data analytics based on the size, speed, resolution, completeness, and flexibility of big data analytics. Kitchin (2014) has argued that "Big Data is characterized by being generated continuously, seeking to be exhaustive and fine-grained in scope, and flexible and scalable in its production" (2). Big data works with census data rather than samples and is concerned more with correlations and probabilities than with testing hypotheses. The databases generated by retail and credit card companies on customer consumption patterns provide a good example of big data at work. Clearly, LSA data do not qualify as big data defined in these terms, because they are generated periodically, they are often (but not always) sample-based, and they represent a small fraction of the data that could be produced in relation to learning. However, with the shift to online testing, the development of adaptive learning programs, and the spread of massive open online courses (MOOCs), big data is quickly finding its way into education and, in the process, creating lucrative opportunities for edu-businesses to develop applications and analyze data.

While we do not want to suggest that global educational accountabilities are part of the phenomenon of big data, even though others have made this link (Schleicher, 2013), we do suggest that the social and technical contexts in which big data has emerged and which it is now shaping are relevant to the functioning of these accountabilities. Most notably, global educational accountabilities require the development of data infrastructures, which we can define, following Bowker et al. (2010), as *"pervasive enabling resources in network form."* Data infrastructure comprises a diverse assemblage of ideas (for example, evidence-based policy), practices (for example, accountability), and technical objects (for example, databases) that enable data to be generated, analyzed, and used to monitor and modulate education policy settings and practices in education systems and schools. The emergence of globalized educational accountabilities is coterminous with the development of articulated national and international data infrastructures in education (Sellar, 2014). We take up the discussion of this expansion, and its implications for what we describe as infrastructural governance, in Chapter 2.

New Spatialities and the Becoming-Topological of Culture

In order to understand the globalizing of educational accountabilities, we must understand the new non-Euclidean or topological spaces through which educational governance now operates. The "topological turn" refers to two simultaneous phenomena: the changes in the character of space and culture in the contemporary word and developments in approaches to theorizing and understanding that world. On this point, Lury et al. (2012) argue that we are experiencing an "epochal transformation in the intersection between the form and content of cultural expression," which they describe as the becoming-topological of culture:

> [T]opology is now emergent in the practices of ordering, modelling, networking and mapping that co-constitute culture, technology and science. In short, a distributed, dynamic configuration of practices is organizing the forms of social life in ways that supplement and extend those of Euclidean geometry.
>
> (5)

We note that there has been earlier work in education policy concerned with the rescaling of politics and education policy processes (Brenner, 2004; Robertson et al., 2002; Gulson & Symes, 2007; Beech & Larsen, 2014). This works with a "nested" view of the new spatial relations of globalization, which is still aligned with a Euclidean geometry. In contrast, topology shifts attention from fixed spaces to a more thoroughly relational understanding of space. As such, a topological approach challenges a view of power as operating within and across fixed spaces at different scales (for example nations, regions, supranational units such as the EU, international organizations) to instead focus on how power constitutes new kinds of space. From a topological perspective then, Allen (2011: 284) observes, "power relationships are not so much positioned in space or extended across it, as compose the spaces of which they are a part."

In terms of the topological changes within culture, Lury et al. (2012) discern a contemporary evolution of cultural expression paralleled by the emergence of new conceptual vocabularies in social and cultural theory, arguing that "culture is becoming topological" at the same time as we are seeing an increase in the "use of topology as a way of analysing culture" (6). We recognize that there are multiple fields of topology in mathematics and the application of the concept in cultural analysis is nascent and not unproblematic (Phillips, 2013). However, this so-called topological turn does suggest a convergence of multiple threads of contemporary social theory around a concern to understand "topological cultural forms (or constantly changing deformations)" such as "lists, models, networks, clouds, fractals, and flows" (Lury et al., 2012: 4).

One precursor of this shift in contemporary theory is Appadurai's (1990) concept of "scapes," which he uses to describe multiple, intersecting global spaces across which flows of people, ideas, money, policy, etc. pass, can be seen in terms of this topological perspective. We are wary of fashion in social theory, but see merit in adopting topological perspectives, not because they are in vogue, but because they provide a generative conceptual vocabulary that draws together a number of convergent trends in social theory concerning space and mobility, new relational infrastructures, and cultural globalization.

Specifically, topological insights can be used for understanding governmental and policy uses of social data of multiple kinds. Ruppert (2012) provides an illustrative example here of how "topological analytics" can be applied. She examines New Labour's "big data" analyses in the UK (see Mayer-Schonberger & Cukier, 2013, 2014) and the joining-up of various databases in ways that constitute new populations and subjects (what Hacking has called "making up people"), arguing that this produces new "governmental topologies." Ruppert draws here on Foucault's concept of dispositif and theoretical resources from actor-network theory to examine how new governmental and "commercial, social and political practices involve the enacting of multiple forms of association and identification that are more variable, unstable and modulating than 'older' forms of identity" (131). We believe that the topological turn in theory allows for great insights for understanding global educational accountabilities that are the focus of this book.

Network Governance and Heterarchy

Network or heterarchical governance can be seen as an emergent topological configuration of power (Lingard & Sellar, 2013b). The rise of new forms of network governance developed out of NPM principles that were imported from the private to the public sector. NPM challenged old hierarchical bureaucratic structures and instead thinned-out state structures and attempted to steer policy at a distance through a focus on outputs and outcomes rather than inputs, which was central to the earlier Keynesian policy settlement. The emergence of policy as numbers accompanied the move to NPM, and witnessed a new significance of key performance indicators (KPIs) and other data-based outcome measures as the new mode of public sector accountability. Network governance is a subsequent emergence that complements, but does not replace NPM.

Network governance is part of the evolution of the state restructuring and involves relationships between multiple partners, in which governments assume the role of facilitator, to address difficult policy problems "through the 'informal authority' of diverse and flexible networks" (Ball & Junemann, 2012: 3). Ball and Junemann (2012: 138) define network or heterarchical governance as: "An organizational form somewhere between hierarchy and network that draws upon diverse horizontal and vertical links that permit different elements of the policy process to cooperate (and/or compete)." They focus on the relationships between, and the new influence of, individuals and organizations that span the boundaries between governments, philanthropies, and businesses (especially finance capital and edu-businesses). The emergence of these new policy networks has led to "the boundaries and spatial horizons and flows of influence and engagement around education ... being stretched and reconfigured in a whole variety of ways" (Ball & Junemann, 2012: 25); in other words, "the topology of policy is changed" (Ball & Junemann, 2012: 78).

Policy networks are woven from "a kind of connective tissue that joins up and provides *some* durability to these distant and fleeting forms of social interaction" (Ball & Junemann, 2012: 12), but they are also contingent, experimental, and exist in combination with "older" forms of government and bureaucratic authority. We have also suggested that the alignment between the habitus of policy makers and technical experts within international organizations like the OECD, and within nations, facilitates such policy networking. What we see with this transition to network governance are hybrid modes of vertical, hierarchical, and horizontal networked governance relations across public and private organizations (Ball, 2012). There are echoes here of Appadurai's (2006) distinction between vertebrate, top-down relations and cellular networked relations stretching within and across nations globally. Thus we see these hybrid relations also cutting through various spatial scales from the global to the regional to the national and to the local with complex imbrications between each of these spaces. Additionally and importantly, there is an admixture in policy processes of public, state located actors and private business and philanthropic actors; in effect resulting in the partial privatization of policy producing communities in education (Mahony, Menter, & Hextall, 2004). There is also greater involvement of edu-businesses in various aspects of the policy cycle in education (Burch, 2009; Ball, 2012; Au & Ferrare, 2015; Hogan, Sellar, & Lingard, 2015).

Given this networked mode of governance, as pointed out above, Ball (2012: 93) notes presciently that, "education policy analysis can no longer sensibly be limited to within the nation state—the fallacy of methodological territorialism."

He goes on to "argue that policy analysis must also extend its purview beyond the state and the role of multilateral agencies and NGOs to include transnational business practices." Our analysis of globalizing educational accountabilities takes account of these new imperatives for educational policy analysis. We will return to a consideration of the place of edu-businesses in global educational accountabilities and network governance in the concluding chapter of the book.

Educational Accountability

In this book, we focus on the globalizing of top-down, test-based modes of accountability, whether the tests be international comparative ones, national ones, or those at provincial or state and local levels. As we have suggested, these modes of accountability are part of the audit culture, policy as numbers, the datafication of social life, and governance through comparison that is reflective of the new topological governance structures in education. This book is about documenting how these new accountabilities work in education and with what effects. However, as a way of thinking about appropriate political responses to some of the negative impacts of these new modes of accountability, we also need to think about accountability differently and conceptualize it in multiple ways.

At its simplest, "accountability" refers to either giving an account or being held to account (see Epstein, 1996; Ranson, 2003; Biesta, 2004; Sahlberg, 2010; Webb, 2011; O'Neill, 2013). The current modes of accountability are top-down; the gaze is largely on the work of schools and teachers and that work is made calculable through its datafication. Here "answerability" is from those at the base of the system to those at the top (Ranson, 2003). Test-data performance is used as the proxy for measuring the quality of schooling. Thus our attention is largely drawn to accountability understood as holding systems, schools, and teachers to account, but we also see more productive and democratic possibilities for accountability. It is important to consider who should give accounts, and to whom and about what, in relation to the work and goals of schools and schooling systems. This would challenge accountability as only constructed through metrics and numbers, through data. Such a broader construction would also tap into the widest purposes of schooling systems and of the work of principals, teachers, and schools.

We would suggest that in more democratic and effective modes of accountability that the gaze would also go in the other direction, that is, from school communities to schools and from schools back to policy makers and politicians. Here, those who provide the education in schools, along with young people, and with schools' multiple communities, would be able to demand of policy makers and politicians the supply of the necessary resources of all kinds (financial and human) to achieve the expectations held of them. This has been called the demand for "opportunity to learn standards" (Darling-Hammond, 2010). The gaze would go in both directions, top-down and bottom-up, as would answerability. The school would also have to establish two-way horizontal accountability relationships with their communities. Further, in addition to test-based data, other forms of qualitative data would be used and linked to the fulsome sets of goals that systems and schools are attempting to achieve.

We acknowledge that with the datafication of schooling, there is a chance that the call for the recognition of schooling outcomes other than test-results in practices of accountability might well precipitate the development of more metrics measuring quality of life and well-being in schools. Indeed, there are moves in the education work of the OECD to expand the scope of tests such as PISA. There is also the question of how top-down, test-based accountability linked to international large-scale testing ought to be used in schooling systems. Currently it seems to be used to drive current reform strategies and policies. This is the legitimation usage of globalized educational accountabilities, in which there tends to be no productive policy learning. We would argue that there ought to be a much more intelligent and sophisticated reading of these data to frame policy learning, rather than the legitimation of currently existing policy directions. For example, much can be learnt from the OECD's equity and funding data in respect of PISA.

We also argue that we cannot reject the need for accountability in education; rather, what we need to do is reconceptualize it, so that systems and schools are held accountable for their educative and social justice purposes, but in ways that are productive, democratic, and socially just. It has been shown how social justice in education constituted around test performance data alone has very reductive effects on its meaning and possibilities (Lingard et al., 2014). We will return to a fuller consideration of these matters in the conclusion to the book.

Chapters

We see the OECD's education work as central to contemporary modes of global educational accountability and we turn next, in Chapter 2, to an examination of the changing nature of the OECD's education work across multiple contexts. First, we provide an historical and contextual account of the work of the OECD. We next consider the changing place of education work within the OECD's organizational structure, particularly since the 1990s. This entails analysis of the rise of international LSAs with a focus on the changing role and significance of PISA within the OECD and globally, as well as its influence on other global performance measurement programs (for example PIAAC and PISA Tests for Schools). The empirical basis for this chapter includes data collected through more than fifty interviews conducted with policy actors located at the OECD, the IEA, and in national education systems (Australia and England), as well as analysis of OECD documents, media reporting, political press releases, and research reports. Overall, the chapter argues that quantitative LSAs in education, with PISA as the leading and most significant example, are expanding capacities for the datafication of schooling and driving a new politics of mutual accountability globally. PISA has given education a new prominence within the OECD and with this rise come new opportunities and risks in terms of its influence on education policy globally.

In Chapter 3 we turn to Shanghai's outstanding performance on PISA 2009 and its effects on other national systems and within the global education policy field. We begin by considering how the OECD's PISA is helping to create this policy field through constituting the globe as a commensurate space of measurement of national school system performance. We see this as a manifestation of Sassen's (2007) argument that globalization is, in effect, the creation of a new global infrastructure and we consider international LSAs to be an important component of that infrastructure. The chapter traces the rise of China, through the 2009 PISA performance of Shanghai, and the repositioning of this system as a significant new "reference society" for other national schooling systems. We also note how China uses international comparative performance measures to inform internal educational development and to strategically position the nation within changing global economies and labor markets. The chapter provides three cases of responses to China's performance in England, Australia, and the USA. The USA case focuses on President Obama's 2011 State of the Union address and other public statements, where he likens the impact of Shanghai's performance on USA schooling with that of the 1957 Sputnik moment, which pushed the Soviet Union ahead of the USA in the space race. The England case draws on research interviews with senior policy makers and contextualizes these data against the Coalition government's use of comparative international performance data to pressure the schooling system for reform. The Australian case draws on the then Australian Prime Minister's view of the significance to Australian schooling of the high performance of a number of Asian countries on PISA 2009, as well as research reports and media coverage. We argue that responses in each case are indicative of the shifting global gaze in education from Finland to East Asia, particularly China, set against the so-called Asian century and related shifts in the balance of geopolitical and economic relations.

In Chapters 4, 5, and 6 we consider vernacular expressions of globalized accountability discourses in Australia and Canada. Chapter 4 examines the perverse effects of the accountability regime that was central to the Australian government's national reform agenda in schooling (2007–2013). The focus is on NAPLAN results that now act as "catalyst data" and are pivotal to school and system accountability. We offer a case study, with two embedded units of analysis, in which NAPLAN has become high-stakes testing for systems. The first involves the relationships between the Australian federal government and three states (Victoria, New South Wales, Queensland) in negotiating performance targets on NAPLAN for reward payments in respect of a national agreement to improve literacy and numeracy. We show how Victoria used 2009 data as a baseline, set ambitious targets, and failed to meet them, while Queensland set much less ambitious targets, met them, and was rewarded. New South Wales created targets that combined literacy and numeracy scores, thus obfuscating the evidence, and met their targets. The second unit of analysis focuses specifically on Queensland and the ramifications of the poor performance of the state on the 2008 NAPLAN. This resulted in a review commissioned by the then Premier, a report on how to improve performance, and the introduction of Teaching and Learning Audits and state-wide targets for improvement on NAPLAN. This analysis focuses on the perverse effects of this highly politicized agenda. The chapter shows how states seek to protect their "reputational capital" and as such, "game" the system. The data for the analysis draw upon interviews with relevant senior policy makers and on analysis of documents and media coverage. We suggest that the concept of "catalyst data" has broader applicability as a way to encapsulate the multiple effects of LSA data and performative accountability regimes.

In Chapter 5, we provide a critical analysis of the promotional videos of high-performing school systems produced by the OECD and the Pearson Foundation. In these videos, "poster" nations such as Canada (Ontario) are held up, alongside Finland and Shanghai, China, as having high-quality education systems and are marketed as offering lessons for other nations across the globe that are not performing as well. Such high-performing nations are represented as "having succeeded over the last few years in raising their students' performance substantially" and as "displaying some important common features," in spite of the specificities of their varying economic contexts and inequalities. Using a visual sociology approach, we draw attention to the important role of these promotional videos in constituting a global education policy field and a culture of performativity in which benchmarks and spaces of commensurability are set for competing nations within the context of the global marketplace. This is an example of the use today of various media for policy dissemination. Specifically, we are concerned to illustrate how the marketing of Ontario's education system as a special case misrepresents the reality and persistence of racial inequality for particular visible minority populations. Our emphasis is on the decracinated strategy of deploying immigrant as a proxy for race, thereby making invisible the persistence of racial inequality (Goldberg, 2009). Particular attention is given to comparisons that are drawn between Canada (as well as other high-performing nations, such as Finland) and the United States in terms of how education in the USA is viewed "through the prism of PISA." In showing the deracination that is part of the OECD's dealing with migrant student performance, we are exemplifying a specific case of a broader reality in terms of how OECD performance data are used to emphasize policy and school effects, while denying the effects of context and structural inequality (Meyer & Schiller, 2013).

In Chapter 6 we undertake a policy critique and analysis of the gender achievement gap discourse in Ontario and Canada. The OECD represents and celebrates Canada, and specifically Ontario, as a *high-performing, high-quality* education system and one that achieves equitable outcomes for diverse student populations. In contrast, we illustrate how the "failing boys" discourse and achievement "gap talk" have functioned to produce a misrecognition of boys as a disadvantaged category. We focus on the articulation of "gap" talk as it relates to the analysis of outcomes by gender in the Pan-Canadian Assessment Program (PCAP) and the role of OECD's PISA as technology for further steering equity policy in Ontario and within the Ontario Ministry of Education. This is particularly the case with regard to the inclusion of the category of "boys" as a disadvantaged group, alongside students with disabilities, visible minorities, and students from economically disadvantaged backgrounds. In this context, we draw attention to the rescaling effects of political authority in terms of highlighting the role of OECD and the Canadian media in the steering of such policy articulations of misrecognition. We conclude with a cautionary note for education policy makers regarding their uncritical reliance on PISA data as a basis for educational reform.

The final chapter provides a summative account of the arguments presented throughout and will return to a discussion of the big ideas informing our policy sociology analysis. We speculate on the emerging impact of global educational accountabilities on schooling reforms in nation states and provincial systems. We also consider the rearticulation of equity policy discourses through test-based accountabilities and sketch out some possibilities for richer forms of educational accountability, particularly in terms of more sophisticated use of educational data. Finally, we briefly discuss the emerging roles of both edu-business and policy entrepreneurs in the spaces opened up by the policy developments examined throughout the book.

2
GLOBAL EDUCATIONAL ACCOUNTABILITIES

Introduction

Tuesday, December 4, 2001, was an important date in the history of the emergence of global educational accountabilities. On this day, the Organisation for Economic Co-operation and Development (OECD) released the first results from its Programme for International Student Assessment (PISA). The results showed that, in the global rankings produced by PISA, Germany's education system placed 22nd in reading and 21st in mathematics and science amongst OECD member countries, the wealthy economies of the world. For Germany, this ranking came as a shock and challenged established views that the nation's schooling system had long been a world leader. Consequently and subsequently, PISA changed the educational landscape in Europe and globally, initiating a process of soul-searching in Germany and directing new attention to Finland, which topped the reading assessment and was catapulted into the international spotlight as the world's "best" education system. Finland were genuinely surprised at the top ranking of their education system, which resulted in much subsequent educational tourism to Finland, with Finland becoming the "PISA poster child" globally. The salience now given to PISA performance by national education policy makers means there is pressure on all systems, either to improve or to retain their high ranking.

PISA was not the first international large-scale assessment of school students; indeed, under the auspices of UNESCO, work to develop such assessments began in the 1950s and the first International Association for the Evaluation of Educational Achievement (IEA) study was conducted in the 1960s. The PISA methodology drew important lessons from previous national testing programs, such as the National Assessment of Educational Progress (NAEP) in the USA. The shock caused by the release of PISA in 2001 also had precedents, such as the publication of *A Nation at Risk* in 1983, which referenced poor rankings of US performance in IEA assessments conducted during the 1970s. So why settle on Tuesday, December 4, 2001, and the first release of PISA results as the definitive event in the emergence of global educational accountabilities?

To answer this question, we must consider the role of the OECD and PISA in education policy globally, which is the focus of this chapter. As Rinne, Kallo, and Hokka (2004) observed a decade ago, "the OECD has become established as a kind of 'éminence grise' of the education policy of industrialized countries" (456), and the growing influence of PISA since that time has consolidated this position (Sellar & Lingard, 2014). However, it would be a mistake to see the OECD as a homogenous policy actor that imposes policy settings on nations. The OECD is an intergovernmental organization with an economic focus, constituted by its 34 member countries, and exerts its influence on education or other policy areas through the political will of governments to monitor and compare their performance, with a view to improving social and economic well-being. The OECD rarely imposes binding commitments on member countries; rather, it generates data and analyses that change the way people think about policy issues. In other words, the OECD exerts a form of "soft power" (Nye Jr, 2004) by shaping the perspectives of politicians and policy makers (Carroll & Kellow, 2011). Moreover, this capacity to steer educational policy making processes is understood in terms of both its productive capacity vis-à-vis networked governance and regulatory potential in a panoptic sense, as outlined in the introduction to the book.

Prior to 2001, Germany considered their schooling system to be a top performer, but this perception began to change with the release of PISA results. As the OECD explains, the purpose of programs like PISA is to dramatically alter perceptions in this way:

> The exogenous shock involved is likely to be something that radically and abruptly alters perceptions of the system rather than an event that suddenly affects its ability to function. For example, the release of a highly publicised report on disappointing education outcomes or performance may engender a sense of crisis, not because educational outcomes have suddenly changed, but because *assessments* of those outcomes have.
>
> (OECD, 2010d: 161, emphasis added)

It is important to note what did *not* change with the announcement of the PISA results in December 2000: the performance of Germany's schools, teachers, and students. While reforms provoked by PISA have since had considerable effect on the German educational landscape, this followed from the initial dramatic shift in perceptions. Understanding the effects that educational assessments, comparisons, and rankings have on perceptions is of primary importance for understanding how global educational accountabilities function. However, the production and analysis of data, and the ability to compare performance across nations and subnational schooling systems, is not sufficient to produce PISA shocks.

Analyzing the reception of PISA results in 21 OECD countries, Martens and Niemann (2013) argue that for the assessment to have a significant impact two conditions must be met: "a substantial gap between national self-perception and the empirical results ('perception') can be observed, and the evaluated topic is framed as crucial for state purposes ('framing')." In other words, the production and publication of educational data must meet with particular conditions of reception in a nation in order for it to "count" and have policy impact. In 2001, Germany performed worse than expected and strong educational performance was framed as a matter of national pride and economic strength. We must examine the rise and changing role of educational assessments such as PISA *in conjunction with* broader changes in education policy discourse that affect how performance on international large-scale assessments and other educational indicators is perceived and framed.

Comparison is clearly an important factor in this regard. Novoa and Yariv-Mashal (2003) have described "a global trend . . . that perceives comparison as a method that would find 'evidence' and hence legitimise political action" (427); nations look to the performance of other nations as a benchmark and, when being out-performed, use this as a rationale for policy reform, including borrowing policy ideas from "top performers" (see Chapters 5 and 6 for a further critique of such comparative regimes). There are two important aspects to this trend, as analyzed by Novoa and Yariv-Mashal: the rise of "the society of the 'international' spectacle" and the move towards a global "politics of mutual accountability" (427). The society of the international spectacle describes extension, from the nation to a global space, of modes of governance that rely on the production of social data as source of "evidence-based" legitimacy and social control. The politics of mutual accountability describes the norms of multilateralism fostered by the OECD, which bring "a sense of sharing and participation, inviting each country (and each citizen) to a perpetual comparison to the other." However, mutual accountability also generates a vertical "system of classification of schools according to standards that are accepted without critical discussion" (427). In other words, the political norms, technical infrastructure, methodological tools, and conceptual frameworks that enable comparison can steer perceptions in ways that are not often made explicit, helping to shape the spectacle that has become widely referred to as a "global education race," echoing last century's "space race," which also had implications for education policy—think of the Sputnik effect on USA schooling policy. This concept of global "mutual accountability" and what we term global panopticism underpins the analyses provided across the chapters of this book.

The introduction of PISA in 2000 coincided with, and in many respects arose from, the emergence of a global politics of mutual accountability since the Second World War and more recent trends toward governing by numbers (Rose, 1999; Ozga, 2009; Lingard, 2011). Under these conditions, PISA was able to have the significant effect that it did in 2001. The initial impact of PISA served to demonstrate the power of the assessment, strengthening its claim to offer the most policy-relevant assessment of education systems and enhancing the OECD's influence on education policy making globally. PISA's capacity to generate shocks can be understood, in terms of a performative use of language, to bring about what Deleuze and Guattari (1987) describe as an "incorporeal transformation": an almost instantaneous transformation of perception effected by particular signs (what Deleuze and Guattari call "order-words") in a particular context.

> The incorporeal transformation is recognizable by its instantaneousness, its immediacy, by the simultaneity of the statement expressing the transformation and the effect the transformation produces; that is why order-words are precisely dated, to the hour, minute, and second, and take effect the moment they are dated.
>
> (Deleuze & Guattari, 1987: 81)

The quintessential example of an incorporeal transformation is a judge's pronouncement of guilt, which changes the accused into the convicted. The word "guilty" only effects this transformation, however, when pronounced in a courtroom, by a person invested with authority, and in the broader context of a system of law. Likewise, the ranking of German performance in PISA 2000 changed the landscape of the German federal education system, but it required particular conditions—a globalized system of educational accountability—for this transformation to occur.

Our argument, then, is that the incorporeal transformation that occurred on December 4, 2001, established the efficacy of the PISA approach and ushered in a new era of regular, high-impact, large-scale international assessments in education. This is not to suggest that PISA has not had the same degree of impact since this time; indeed, we argue that PISA has become increasingly influential since. Nor are we suggesting that global educational accountability is limited to PISA and the education work of the OECD. We argue that PISA catalyzed a new era of global educational accountability through mobilizing a form of panoptic power, and now provides the template for others seeking to have a global impact on education policy, including the initiatives of private education companies that we will consider later in the book (for example Pearson's *The Learning Curve*). In a later chapter of this book, we analyze what we call "catalyst data" (Lingard & Sellar, 2013a), that is, data that have effects on educational systems, both in policy and practice terms.

This chapter aims to describe the conditions in which PISA emerged and had its initial impact and the conditions that have developed as the OECD expands PISA and other related dimensions of its education work. The empirical basis for the chapter includes data collected through more than fifty interviews conducted with policy actors located at the OECD, the IEA, and in national education systems (Australia and England), as well as analysis of OECD documents, media reporting, press releases, and research reports. In the following section of the chapter we provide a brief introduction to and history of the OECD (see also Papadopoulos, 1994; Henry, Lingard, Rizvi, & Taylor, 2001). We then discuss the changing role and significance of PISA within the OECD's Directorate for Education and Skills, before turning to an examination of how the education work of the OECD, and specifically PISA, is helping to constitute a global education policy field through the creation of the globe as a commensurate space of measurement and a global community of policy makers who share similar values and dispositions (see Lingard, Sellar, & Baroutsis, 2015). Finally, we theorize the education work of the OECD using the concepts of *epistemological* and *infrastructural* governance. These modes of governance help to create conditions in which data can be generated to change perceptions and effect the transformations through which PISA "counts" as a primary technology of globalized educational accountability.

A Brief Introduction to the OECD

The OECD's education work must be situated in relation to the broader mission and structure of the Organisation. The Organisation was established in 1961 to supersede the Organisation for European Economic Cooperation, which was established in 1948 to facilitate the reconstruction of Europe under the USA Marshall Plan. The OECD initially had 20 member countries, all of which were European except for the USA. Japan acceded in 1964 and, since then, the USA and Japan have provided a significant percentage of the core funding and exerted commensurate influence over its agenda. From the beginning, the OECD was seen as an international organization focused on economic policy and networked governance, bringing together a group of like-minded rich countries and providing a bulwark against Soviet communism during the Cold War era. The Constitution of the OECD sets out its chief aims as enhancing economic growth, international trade, and economic development, and these aims frame its work across all policy areas. Given its focus on economic growth and productivity in capitalist economies, the Organisation was regarded as an "economic NATO." Membership requires commitment to three broad values: a market economy, liberal democracy, and human rights. Many more nations have thus become eligible for membership in the post–Cold War era of neoliberal globalization and nine nations have acceded in this time, including former members of the Soviet Union.

It is interesting in that context that China has not pursued membership of the OECD, but the Organisation, particularly in respect of PISA, has worked assiduously to get various schooling systems in China to participate in the test. The OECD has also strengthened its relationships with so-called nonmember economies, including the BRICs and other developing nations.

The OECD has been variously described as "a geographical entity, an organisational structure, a policy-making forum, a network of policy makers, researchers and consultants, and a sphere of influence" (Henry et al., 2001: 7). We can see the OECD as an important node in a network of relationships, including member and nonmember countries and relationships with other international organizations. Indeed, Carroll and Kellow (2011) characterize the OECD as an institution adept at adaptation, changing in the face of shifting contexts and pressures, and draw attention to the Organisation's committee structure through which member nations influence its work program. This elaborate organizational structure is overseen at the apex by the OECD Council, chaired by the Secretary-General and comprising representatives from all member nations. It is important to reiterate that while the Organisation puts forward coherent policy positions, these are arrived at through the machinations of this committee structure, which involves various policy actors from member nations, as well as the contributions of an influential secretariat. The multiple voices, stances, and, of course, political orientations of the member nations and OECD staff have given rise to considerable organizational complexity, and the ensuing necessity to walk a fine policy line to manage these competing orientations. Woodward (2009) also emphasizes the adaptive character of the OECD and its adeptness at "carving out niches" for itself across the policy domains covered across its various directorates. Here we will trace the OECD's recent evolution in response to important global political and economic events that have bearing on the emergence of global educational accountabilities.

The end of the Cold War precipitated a minor crisis of purpose for the OECD and it recognized the need to reinvent itself. At this time the OECD also refashioned itself as an important global center for the production of statistics for policy making, particularly international comparative data. The OECD was ahead of other international organizations in this respect (Carroll & Kellow, 2011), developing its statistical capacities and data infrastructure to strengthen this dimension of its work. The OECD's statistical work has grown substantially since the mid-1990s, including in education with the creation of the *Education at a Glance* indicators, a compendium of data from member countries that is now published annually, and the move to develop PISA in the late 1990s. The OECD has been an important bearer of, but also a response to, neoliberal globalization, and has used the term globalization to describe a commitment to neoliberal market economics. This is what Bourdieu (2003) called a performative usage of globalization, and the OECD for a time "ontologized" this construction of globalization in its policy recommendations (Rizvi & Lingard, 2010).

In 2008, the financial crises in Europe and globally presented a new challenge to the Organisation's proselytizing of a neoliberal version of market economics. With government bailouts for banks and austerity policies being put in place in various nations of Europe, the OECD began once again, though perhaps somewhat tentatively, to rethink its economic policy position. The Organisation has responded to this context through its New Approaches to Economic Challenges (NAEC) initiative. In this context, education has become more important inside the Organisation, linked to the launch of a cross-committee OECD Skills Strategy (2012), which is an attempt to create and ensure policy coherence across the work of the OECD's various directorates, and to a rebalancing of its economic message to focus on social well-being as the purpose for economic development and growth. The virtues of education can be easily argued in terms of improving both social and economic outcomes and, particularly in the context of financial crises and pressures on the European Union, education is a policy area that allows for a greater convergence of views than some others.

As Woodward (2009) argues, the OECD has become an influential international organization because of its capacity to "sow the seeds of international consensus and cooperation" (5). Woodward argues that the OECD's contribution to global governance occurs through four modes: cognitive, normative, legal, and palliative governance. Cognitive governance functions through the alignment of values across member nations. Normative governance "is the vaguest dimension of the OECD's policy work but it is arguably through challenging and changing mindsets of the people involved that the Organisation achieves its greatest influence" (Woodward, 2009: 8). Here we can see the importance of PISA as a policy technology that alters perceptions. Cognitive and normative governance, which we might see as *epistemological* forms of governance aligned to the creation of epistemic communities (Kallo, 2009) in nations across the globe, together constitute the soft power of the OECD in policy making globally. This form of networked governance also functions through the aligned habitus of policy makers and professionals at the OECD and those in senior positions within national schooling systems (Lingard et al., 2015). However, one must not forget that the materialization of such "soft power" that is enacted through the mobilization of panoptic regulatory processes is facilitative of a form of networked governance that is invested in the instantiation of a culture of performativity. It is in this sense that palliative governance refers to the OECD's function in lubricating "the wheels of global governance." For example, the OECD can provide a forum for discussing policy matters that do not fit easily within the mandates of other international forums and it supports the work of the World Trade Organization and the Group of Eight (G8), Group of Seven (G7), and Group of Twenty (G20) nations. As we will argue, this palliative role extends to the development of infrastructure, such as PISA, for generating data that are used by the OECD, member nations, and other international organizations. Palliative governance can thus be seen as a form of *infrastructural* governance. As mentioned earlier, legally binding agreements are not a common instrument in the work of the OECD, particularly in education, and we do not deal with these any further. However, we extend the other elements of Woodward's framework in our concluding discussion of the role of the OECD's education work in global educational governance. We note here as well how Sassen (2007) has written of globalization as the creation of a global infrastructure that allow and enable various flows of ideas, people, finance, capital, policy discourses, and so on around the globe. The data infrastructure that supports PISA can be seen in this light and, indeed, Spivak (2012: 1) has suggested that "globalization takes place only in capital and data."

Education at the OECD and the Growth of Comparative Data

In the early years, education had an "inferred role" in the OECD's work (Papadopoulos, 1994: 11), and it was framed in terms of the need to strengthen science and mathematics performance to support the production of knowledge workers for advanced economies. Accordingly, it was located within the Office for Scientific and Technical Personnel. Much of the Office's work involved documenting the technological gap between Europe and the USA in the Cold War context of the post-Sputnik period (Istance, 1996: 1). In 1968, the Centre for Research and Innovation (CERI) was established and this gave education a firmer organizational location. The Education Committee was created in 1971, with a new focus on the contribution of education to quality of life issues. The Committee was supported by the Directorate for Scientific Affairs, and this is where CERI was located, but in 1975 education became part of the new Directorate for Social Affairs, Manpower and Education. In 1991, this Directorate was renamed the Directorate for Education, Employment, Labour and Social Affairs (DEELSA) and this remained education's organizational location until the Directorate for Education was established in 2002, in the wake of PISA's initial success.

Papadopoulos (1994) suggests that the move from the Directorate for Scientific Affairs in the 1970s broadened the conception of education underpinning the Organisation's work, while others argue that this relocation linked education inextricably to labor markets and employment trends (Istance, 1996). Papadopoulos (1994) notes that through the 1970s, education was framed by progressive concerns about schooling and inequalities derived from the sociology of education, but we also need to acknowledge the influence exerted on this work by the economic rationale of the OECD and a particular version of human capital theory. Changing conceptions of human capital theory have been a deep structural underpinning of the OECD's education work from 1961 through until the present and education has thus always been framed by economic concerns. However, at the same time, equity concerns have always featured in this work to varying extents.

The position of education within the OECD was consolidated with the creation of the Directorate for Education in 2002, but we would suggest it has been strengthened further with its renaming as the Directorate for Education and Skills Directorate in 2012 and the associated launch of the OECD's Skills Strategy. The OECD (2012) argues that, "Skills have become the global currency of 21st-century economies" and that "the OECD Skills Strategy provides an integrated, cross-government strategic framework to help countries understand more about how to invest in skills in a way that will transform lives and drive economies" (3). We would argue that the Skills Strategy reflects an intensification of human capital framing of education. This Strategy has enhanced the position of the OECD's education work, with PISA data and other education data now being included, for example, in the Organisation's *Going for Growth* reports.

It is important to understand the funding arrangements for the OECD's education work. There are two elements to the OECD budget: Part I comes from member nations' contributions, while Part II is funded by participants in specific projects. For example, nations pay to participate in PISA, which is funded out of Part II of the budget. Education relies heavily on Part II budget contributions, which some suggest has led to more efficiency and effectiveness in securing support for and the delivery of specific projects such as PISA. CERI receives Part I budget support, as well as project-based funding.

Paralleling the changing place of education within the OECD was the changing place of statistics in the Organisation's education work. From the 1990s, and linked to the post–Cold War context, there was considerable pressure inside the OECD from member nations and other international organizations for the development of comparative educational statistics. The OECD has always had an interest in educational statistics, particularly during the 1960s in respect of educational planning. However, the OECD's work in relation to the educational performance of member nations during its early phases was largely through reviews of national systems conducted at the request of member nations. Regarding the growing focus on educational statistics, Papadopoulos (1994) comments on a European Ministers of Education meeting in London in 1964, where it was recommended that the OECD,

> whose work in this field is greatly appreciated, be invited to formulate clearly in a model handbook the various factors involved in effective educational investment planning, so that countries may have basis for the compilation of comparable statistics.
>
> (50)

This recommendation was subsequently endorsed by the OECD Council and served as an impetus for the expansion of statistical work, extended further in the 1970s through advanced mathematical modelling and increasing computational capacities. In the early 1970s, the OECD began serious work on educational indicators, which initially involved attempts at collaboration with UNESCO. From the late 1990s, there was a focus on more thematic reviews and international comparisons. Statistical data became increasingly significant in relation to this work, but it also drew on qualitative data.

Henry et al. (2001) have documented a granular narrative of the increasing significance of quantitative data in the OECD's education work, especially into the 1990s with strong encouragement from the USA. The initial *Education at a Glance* indicators were released in draft form in September 1991, and along with accompanying analyses, have become a more significant part of the OECD's work since that time. Henry et al. (2001) summarize this shift in the OECD's stance on educational indicators and their enhanced role:

> In short, the 1990s saw some remarkable shifts in the development of educational indicators within the OECD: from philosophical doubt to statistical confidence; from covering some countries to covering most of the world; from a focus on inputs to a focus on outputs; and from occupying an experimental status to being a central part of the Organisation's work.
> (90)

These developments were, of course, set against the backdrop of globalization, the restructuring of the bureaucratic state within nations under new public management (OECD, 1995), the growing focus on educational outcomes as opposed to policy inputs, and the enhancement of computational capacities. They were also set against what has been referred to more recently as the rise of policy as numbers that accompanied the new managerialist state (Rose, 1999; Ozga, 2009; Lingard, 2011). These developments were part of the "audit explosion" (Power, 2007: 326)—"the growth of audit and related monitoring practices associated with public management reform processes"—and are linked to the emergence of new modes of neoliberal accountability, as we explicate further with regards to the Canadian and USA cases in Chapters 5 and 6 (Ranson, 2003). Indeed, as Ranson argues, "Since the late 1970s such regimes of public accountability have been strengthened systematically so that accountability is no longer merely an important instrument or component within the system, but constitutes the system itself" (459). The OECD's statistical capacities positioned it as a powerful node within this system of global accountability in education.

International comparative performance data became central to assisting nations in monitoring their potential economic competitiveness globally; in effect data on human capital became surrogate measures of the future competitiveness of a nation's economy (Brown, Halsey, Lauder, & Stuart Wells, 1997). It was in this context that the OECD launched, in 1997, what was to become PISA (see OECD, 1999). The USA was important in the pressuring for this development of an international comparative measure of national schooling system performance, as they had been with the earlier Indicators of Education Systems (INES) work. This pressure was fuelled by internal concerns about educational standards in the USA, driven by earlier reports such as *A Nation at Risk* and linked to the view of economists that more sophisticated measures of educational outputs were required, rather than using years of education as a proxy for achievement.

Education at the OECD is becoming increasingly central to the Organisation's overall work and Andreas Schleicher, head of PISA and now Director of Education and Skills, has become a very powerful policy player, both within the Organisation and in education globally. Here we are in agreement with Woodward's (2009) assessment that the OECD's education policy work has become increasingly important and that the OECD has overtaken UNESCO as the major international organization for education. Its production of statistics that enable international comparisons of educational performance and thus comparison as a mode of governance has been central to this shift. We thus acknowledge Eccleston's (2011: 248) point that an "international organisation's political authority is at its zenith when its rational/technical agenda aligns with prevailing social values and sentiments" and we suggest that this is the case with the OECD's education work today. National schooling systems across the globe have bought into this global system of mutual accountability. This applies to both OECD member countries and others.

International Large-Scale Assessments and the Rise of PISA

As mentioned earlier, international large-scale assessments have a history that goes back to the 1950s, when UNESCO hosted a meeting that led to the establishment of the International Association for the Evaluation of Educational Achievement (IEA) (Kirsch, Lennon, von Davier, Gonzalez, & Yamamoto, 2013). In 1960 the IEA conducted the Pilot Twelve-Country Study, the first of its international assessments that were to become more regular from the late 1970s. Important technical developments occurred with the implementation of the US National Assessment of Educational Progress (NAEP) in the late 1960s and these influenced the methodology of international assessments. Similarly to the OECD's work, important developments in the IEA's work occurred during the 1990s and into the first decade of this century. The IEA began regular assessment cycles for its Trends in International Mathematics and Science Study (TIMSS) in 1995 and its Progress in International Reading Literacy Study (PIRLS) in 2001. The IEA was an important pioneer of international large-scale assessments.

The development of PISA began in the late 1990s and the tests were first administered in 2000. PISA has been conducted every three years (2000, 2003, 2006, 2009, 2012, and 2015) with an increasing number of participating nations and subnational systems such as Shanghai, China. The assessment measures reading, mathematical and scientific literacy, and putatively tests the knowledge that 15-year-olds are able to apply in real-world situations, although we note that the test is of the classic paper and pencil variety. Indeed, one criticism levelled at PISA, and any similar large-scale quantitative assessment, is that "PISA assesses how well students are able to exercise knowledge and skills within the PISA focus areas in precisely one 'real life setting', namely a test situation" (Dohn, 2007: 10). Further, PISA is not based in national curricula, which distinguishes it from the IEA's TIMSS and PIRLS surveys and is used to promote its potential for policy learning across contexts. However, at a deep structural level the test assumes an isomorphism across the curricula of different national schooling systems, somewhat akin to the assumptions of the world polity theorists such as Meyer and colleagues (1997). This assumption of isomorphism and commensurative work underpin what psychometricians refer to as "differential item functioning" (Zumbo, 2007) and the exclusion from analyses of PISA of test items for which there is too much variance across different cultural contexts.

We argue that PISA is helping to create a global educational policy field through its work in constituting the globe as a commensurate space of measurement and that this has been facilitated through its capacity to mobilize a form of panoptic power that functions in a regulatory steering capacity at the national level in terms of instantiating a global culture of comparative neoliberal performativity (Lingard & Rawolle, 2011; Sobe, 2015). It is in this sense that this field functions as a global mode of mutual accountability for national schooling systems, and is part of a global move towards standardization, as we explicate in Chapters 5 and 6 with specific reference to the Canadian and USA cases. It has been argued that authority for this move has been "increasingly lodged in the global-level organisations" (Loya & Boli, 1999: 176). We might see this occurring at the OECD through PISA, other tests, and educational statistics, with alignments between statistical categories being achieved across nations and international organizations. We see here numbers as a governance technology that works across distance (Porter, 1995). We note, as well, the voluntarism in these developments and the nature of the processes involved in extending what has come to be seen as "universal, consensually derived standards of unimpeachable technical merit" (Loya & Boli, 1999: 181). This voluntarism is why we return to a critical consideration of global panopticism in the final chapter of the book. PISA helps to make educational systems across the globe commensurable and comparable, thus making them legible for governing in new ways (Scott, 1998).

National schooling system performance on PISA is ranked according to quality (scores on the tests) and equity (the spread of the scores and strength of the effect of socioeconomic background on performance). PISA has had differing impacts on national schooling systems and their policy frames (Carvalho & Costa, 2014; Simons, 2014), with many nations using it in conjunction with, or developing new, complementary national testing regimes, in acceptance of the axiom that one can only improve what one can measure. The latter is an important aphorism underpinning all of the OECD's work. We must see the relationships between the OECD and nations as reciprocal, involving the "circulation of PISA as part of multidirectional processes that involve reinterpretation, de-contextualisation, and re-contextualisation, and where national, local, regional and international agencies intertwine" (Carvalho & Costa, 2014: 3).

The analyses of equity enabled by PISA are important and show the growing impact of socioeconomic background on school performance across OECD countries since the first tests were conducted. But PISA has also helped to rearticulate notions of social justice in schooling as equity within a meritocratic system based on test performance, a point that we expand on in Chapters 5 and 6 with regard to the phenomena of deracination and the politics of "failing boys" (Lingard, Sellar, & Savage, 2014). Here equity becomes rearticulated as simply improving the test performance of students from disadvantaged backgrounds. At the same time, the OECD's media strategy and national media pressure for PISA league tables gives overriding emphasis to quality of national mean performance and not to equity (Wiseman, 2013), even though the OECD's PISA reports, especially secondary analyses, emphasize both issues and stress that quality demands equity. We also note that OECD analyses of PISA tend to overplay the significance of policy in the aetiology of systemic performance and downplay the impact of societal inequalities that need to be understood more in terms of intersectional and epistemological frameworks that address interweaving and interlocking systems of oppression (Anthias, 2012; Condron, 2011; Hill Collins, 1990; Meyer & Schiller, 2013).

Driven by the success of PISA, the OECD's education policy work is currently expanding along three interrelated fronts: the scope of its educational assessment programs is widening to generate data about a broader set of skills; the scale of these assessments is expanding to include a larger number of participants; and efforts are being made to increase the explanatory power of these assessments by linking different data sets and by providing data in formats that are likely to change the perceptions of policy makers. This expansion involves growing the infrastructure through which the OECD produces, analyzes, and disseminates education data, including the ongoing development of well-established programs such as PISA and the introduction of a suite of new programs. The strategy of building on the PISA brand is reflected in the description of new programs as "PISA for adults" (Programme for International Assessment of Adult Competencies [PIAAC]) or "PISA for schools." The expansion of the OECD's education data infrastructure is helping to cement the place of PISA as the best known and most widely influential international large-scale assessment, at least in terms of its media and policy impact.

The expanding *scope* of the OECD's educational assessments reflects its ability to keep pace with developments, and even set trends, in the fields of psychometrics and the economics of education. With each PISA assessment the OECD has sought to extend and experiment with the skills that are assessed beyond the core areas of reading, mathematical, and scientific literacy. More than a decade ago the OECD identified the need to widen the concept of human capital that informs its educational assessments and to measure the diverse set of dispositions that contribute to the value of human capital. In 2002, the OECD argued that "there is more to human capital than the readily measurable—and very important—literacy, numeracy and workplace skills" (OECD, 2002: 124). The OECD has argued that education policy analyses require wider conceptions of human capital that include both cognitive and *noncognitive* skills (OECD, 2002).

The past decade has witnessed a growing interest in noncognitive skills among economists and psychometricians, including attention to meta-cognition, motivation, and personality traits such as grit, and work is being done to incorporate the measurement of these skills into large-scale assessments (Levin, 2013). PISA has been collecting student self-reports relating to motivation, self-belief, and engagement with learning since the first round in 2000, and in each assessment one volume of the PISA report is dedicated to the analysis of motivation and engagement with learning (for example OECD, 2013d). The OECD holds the view that "a range of non-cognitive skills, such as the capacity to work collaboratively or as a member of a team, communication skills, and entrepreneurship, is also of importance in the modern workplace, and there is considerable interest in comparative information on both the supply of and demand for such skills" (OECD, 2013c: 41).

The expanding scope of the OECD's educational assessments, including plans to measure "21st century skills" in 2018, constitute an expansion of what counts and what is counted as a "skill." As an aside, we note here that the OECD has commissioned the global edu-business, Pearson, to develop these 21st-century skills. This agenda is drawing more aspects of individual learning, personality, and social life into human capital models and is facilitating the quantification and comparison of these domains. In turn, this broader scope of what is assessed increase the potential for PISA to change perceptions and open up possibilities for new kinds of policy interventions. Beyond a concern with noncognitive skills, we might also see the expanding scope of OECD education assessments reflected in moves to conduct PISA online in OECD member countries in 2015, which will generate a range of new meta-data relating to young people's interaction with the computers used to complete the test.

The expanding *scale* of the OECD's education assessment work is being driven by the growth of the PISA program and the development of related programs such as PISA for Development, which is extending PISA-comparable assessments into developing countries. PISA for schools is also important here as it offers the OECD the opportunity to work directly with schools and subnational schooling systems. For example, in the USA, Fairfax County in Virginia is heavily involved in

PISA Tests for Schools. The edu-business CTB/McGraw-Hill has been awarded the initial contract for managing PISA in the USA. PISA is one of the OECD's most successful policy "products" and the changing scale of PISA and related programs reflect the capacity of the OECD to interest a range of new users in the data it can provide: non-OECD countries, subnational education systems, and individual schools (Rutkowski, 2014; Engels & Frizzell, 2015). This is increasing the global coverage of the OECD's education work.

Participation in PISA has grown substantially. There were initially 32 participants in PISA 2000, including 28 member countries and 4 nonmembers, with a further 11 nonmember countries later participated in this first assessment. The 65 participants in the 2012 round reflects a doubling of the program's size and includes all 34 member countries and 31 nonmembers. Efforts to bring China into the assessment, with Shanghai, Hong Kong, and Macau participating in the publication of results so far, have been important to expanding this coverage and building relations with a major nonmember economy at the outset of the so-called Asian century. Assessments have also been conducted in other Chinese provinces, although the OECD has agreed with China not to release these results publicly, and Beijing, Guangdong, and Jiangsu will participate publicly in PISA 2015. With the inclusion of a range of other nonmember countries the OECD now promotes PISA as representing 80 percent of the world economy (OECD, 2013a).

The expanding scale of PISA must be understood in relation to the post–Cold War reworking of the Organisation's role, the expansion of membership, and efforts to engage with nonmember economies. In 2007, the OECD launched its Enhanced Engagement program to develop the Organisation's relationship with five major nonmember nations—Brazil, China, India, Indonesia, and South Africa—including by integrating these countries into the OECD's statistical collection and reporting. To date, South Africa is the only "key partner" that has not participated in PISA. The OECD is also currently piloting PISA for Development in the context of the expiry of the UN Millennium Development goals in 2015 and the establishment of a new post-2015 Development Agenda. PISA for Development promises to offer a more relevant instrument to developing countries, while enabling them to collect baseline data that can be used to assess development in education and to compare education performance with countries and systems participating in main PISA.

A particularly interesting development with respect to the expanding scale of PISA has been the recent introduction of PISA Tests for Schools. This program is currently being implemented in the USA and England, with moves toward implementation in Spain. PISA Tests for Schools are based on PISA items and allow schools to benchmark their performance against others schools, nationally and globally, and against other participants in PISA (nations and subnational systems). The program marks an innovation in the OECD's assessment work insofar as it is not funded by member nations, but is made available directly to schools, which must pay an accredited private supplier to conduct the analysis and reporting of results (currently CTB/McGraw-Hill in the USA). The program involves new contractual relationships with education companies who are accredited as national suppliers and thus provide one example of the development of new modes of network governance in education (Ball & Junemann, 2012) and the heavy involvement now of edu-businesses in education (Ball, 2012; Au & Ferrare, 2015; Hogan, Sellar, & Lingard, 2015). The program also enables the reporting of OECD data at a level that increases the relevance and usefulness of these data for polities and institutions for which PISA has not previously been useful. For example, by providing school-level assessments in the USA, the OECD is able to bypass the national level at which PISA data are currently collected (although the states of Florida, Connecticut, and Massachusetts participated individually in 2012), in order to provide data directly to schools and systems, which can then mobilize these data as evidence of performance and to support claims on funding within the current accountability relations through which USA schooling is governed federally (see Rutkowski, 2014; Engels & Frizzell, 2015).

The OECD is also seeking to enhance the *explanatory power* of its educational assessments and data collections, and this includes efforts to improve the claims about educational performance that can be sustained on the basis of OECD data. For example, the OECD is currently developing methods to match student and teacher data gathered through different assessment programs. The Teaching and Learning International Survey (TALIS) was introduced in 2008 and was conducted again in 2013 with 34 countries. The OECD is linking PISA data with TALIS data to enable student performance to be understood in relation to teaching environments (Kaplan & Turner, 2012). There has been resistance to this initiative from teacher unions that hold reservations about the potential for, and problems with, linking student performance on PISA to assessments of teaching. Such efforts to enhance explanatory power by linking up PISA and TALIS is part of a broader trend "to create standardized, interoperable and dynamic databases to support evidence-based policy, enable individually tailored and targeted services, reduce costs, and provide robust population statistics for analysis and research" (Ruppert, 2012: 118–119).

The Directorate for Education and Skills also publishes regular notes, such as *PISA in Focus*, that present data with policy-relevant analysis and commentary. This is another example of efforts to enhance explanatory power. These notes often receive high-profile media coverage and reflect the Education Directorate's savvy in relation to the impact it has been able to generate from PISA and related products. Indeed, PISA is the largest media event for the Organisation and now attracts substantial media coverage globally. As discussed above, media coverage of national performance has played an important role in PISA's capacity to shift perceptions, although this has varied from nation to nation (Martens & Niemann,

2013). Efforts to sustain and increase explanatory power are also reflected in the ongoing psychometric and statistical work, often in partnership with private contractors and national research organizations, to sustain the comparability of PISA items across countries and cultures and to ensure the viability of trend analyses across each triennial round of PISA.

The expansion of scope, scale, and explanatory power is clearly interrelated. Increasing the scope of the assessment enables analysis of a wider set of skills and thus potentially increases the explanatory power of the OECD's data for understanding economic growth. Increasing the scale of the assessment potentially increases the explanatory power of the comparisons that can be made between educational performance across different countries and subnational units of assessment. Efforts to increase explanatory power generally involve expanding the scope and scale of the OECD's data infrastructure. PISA and related programs have clearly been very successful over the past 15 years in terms of changing perceptions by producing data and enabling comparisons. The OECD is building on this influence by expanding its measurement work and its influence in education policy thinking globally.

Educational Accountabilities and the OECD's Role in Global Governance

The OECD's role in globalizing educational accountabilities is linked to its global governance role in in relation to education. Weiss (2013: 2) defines global governance as "the sum of the informal and formal values, norms, procedures, and institutions that help all actors—states, intergovernmental organizations, civil society, transnational corporations, and individuals—to identify, understand and address trans-boundary problems." We find this definition useful because of its emphasis it on the shaping of values, norms, procedures, and perceptions; that is, the operation of soft power in its capacity to mobilize panoptic regulatory processes in formulating policy problems and solutions as part of a broader global policy field of networked governance. Jakobi and Martens (2010), for example, observe that, "[g]overnance by international organizations . . . changes over time, and the recent development of internationalization processes might be a result of changed mechanisms of governance" (176). In relation to the OECD, they argue that "[t]he OECD today not only defines the problem, but also offers the solution. . . . With the new generation of indicators, the Organization has therefore gained an important status in several stages of national policy-making, ranging from agenda setting to policy formulation and implementation" (176). The technical work of the OECD is helping to shape the definition of educational problems and approaches to educational assessments and education research more broadly. This is manifested in policy developments in many national schooling systems around the globe, as further explicated in Chapters 5 and 6 with specific reference to the North American context.

Reviewing the 50-year history of the OECD, Carroll and Kellow (2011) conclude that the soft power exerted by the Organisation has been the key to its success and that its substantial influence has been "epistemic in nature" (264). Carroll and Kellow (2011) argue that "the largely voluntary nature of the measures that are the products of the OECD can be seen to be more effective [than binding obligations] because they can embody clarity and higher quality that give rise to fewer concerns by members, precisely because they rarely threaten members' key interests" (264); this is perhaps an example of "the unimpeachable technical merit" (Loya & Boli, 1999) of the OECD's metrics. We agree that the OECD's global governance role must be understood in terms of this epistemic influence and we see this as linked to the development of the Organisation's data infrastructure, or the range of practices, instruments, and technological capacities it has developed for undertaking statistical work.

Woodward (2009) reminds us that the OECD is "devoid of the sticks and carrots available to other global institutions" and points to its success in establishing rapprochement between members and nonmembers. As noted earlier in this chapter, the OECD's soft power works through four dimensions of governance that rely to some degree on a capacity to mobilize forms of regulatory and panoptic power: cognitive, normative, palliative, and legal. The three main modes of governance (cognitive, normative, palliative) provide a useful framework for understanding the OECD influence, and we see them as facets of two interrelated overarching governance mechanisms: *epistemological* governance (cognitive and normative); and *infrastructural* governance (palliative), in the sense that the development of infrastructure can help to identify and enable engagement with transboundary problems. We argue that infrastructural governance also involves a type of logistical power that is significant in the OECD's governance mechanisms.

Mukerji (2010) makes a distinction between strategic and logistical forms of power, and argues that "[s]trategic power works because people respond to favors and threats (and by extension surveillance), aligning their behaviours to regimes" (402), whereas logistical power operates through

> A politically infused culture that shapes cognition as well as action. The culture consists not only of a constellation of ideas, but also physical forms systematically infused with meaning. It is a physical arrangement of the material environment that intentionally ratifies cultural conceptions of reality.
>
> (406–407)

As mentioned previously, the OECD produces few legally binding instruments and seldom exercises strategic power in this way, as do other international organizations and national governments. However, it does exercise strategic power through peer pressure and surveillance, or the "politics of mutual accountability" required by membership understood in terms of its capacity to mobilize both regulatory forms of power and panoptic surveillance as central to the form of networked governance and building of OECD as an administrative apparatus in which PISA and other assessment instruments it develops function as specific technologies in the Foucauldian sense of the term. This strategic power is combined with the logistical activity through which the Organisation "shapes social life differently, affecting the environment (context, situation, location) in which human action and cognition take place" (Mukerji, 2010: 402; see also Holland, Lachicotte, Skinner, & Cain, 1998). This is the same point made by Novoa and Yariv-Mashal, who point to the position of standardization and classification imposed by a more vertical functioning of power within relations of mutual accountability. But it is important to note that such vertical and horizontal forms of power are implicated in the workings of panoptic power in terms of their material effects and operations.

The OECD's development of data or information infrastructure (Bowker, Baker, Millerand, & Ribes, 2010; Star & Ruhleder, 1996; Sellar, 2014) is important in the globalization of education policy, framing global education policy discourses, and creating a global field of mutual accountability in education. This infrastructure involves modifications of the environment in which politics and policy making take place and thus creates the conditions for cognitive/normative governance. The epistemological governance role of the OECD must therefore be understood as linked to the infrastructure that has developed and become embedded to support its data generation and analyses, and which enables a particular combination of logistical and strategic power, which Anagnostopolous, Rutledge, and Jacobsen (2013) term "informatic" power. Moreover, shared values regarding the need for data to inform governance and policy create an ongoing demand for the expansion of data infrastructure and testing, including testing of a greater range of skills and capacities.

The implementation of PISA required the establishment of a data infrastructure that includes a multiplicity of elements that are central to the materialization of its operations as an administrative apparatus (Miller & Rose, 2008): the physical paper and pencil tests (online tests from 2015 for member nations) and the technical work of development embedded within them, the technological capacities of organizations that manage the testing inside nations, the proliferation of particular testing methodologies and standards, the alignment of the categories of measurement, and so on. This infrastructure supports the OECD's work in relation to national governments and other international organizations, contributing to its palliative governance function. It also involves restructuring of the professional and technical environments of education research and education policy making globally, which creates conditions in which the OECD can encourage an alignment of values (for example the need for education performance data as a tool for governing systems; the usage of particular psychometric techniques) and can draw on "evidence" to shift perceptions (for example creating "shocks" when performance data can be used to argue the need for reform). We thus see the expansion of PISA and related programs as an infrastructural expansion, but one that is closely linked to the OECD's capacities to promote, as an administrative apparatus for materializing technologies of networked governance (Miller & Rose, 2008), both a cohesive set of norms and values (cognitive) and to generate research and knowledge that shifts perceptions and supports particular policy agendas (normative).

Ranson (2003) defines accountability as "a *social practice* pursuing particular purposes, defined by distinctive relationships and evaluative procedures. Participating in communities of practice shapes the dispositions of its members, their taken for granted ways of perceiving, judging, imagining, and acting" (462). Infrastructural and epistemological governance are closely linked and mutually reinforcing and we see these governance mechanisms contributing to global accountabilities through the creation of global epistemic communities engaged in comparable technical work guided by a shared set of norms and values. This is facilitated by the alignment of the habitus of psychometricians and other professionals across the OECD and national schooling systems (Lingard et al., 2015), what we might see as the alignment globally of epistemic communities.

Increasing the scope, scale, and explanatory power of PISA and related programs enhances the usefulness of the data generated for a range of international organizations and national governments and helps to shape values and norms, as well as education research practices, political debate, policy making, and, ultimately, practices in schools and other educational institutions, as we explicate in Chapters 5 and 6 with regards to addressing specific questions of race and gender equity. Power (2000) has argued that "audit processes are not neutral acts of verification" (114). Audit and accountability have impacts on "local cultures of first order practice" (Power, 2000: 115), such as professional teaching communities, with the potential to damage them in the process. Power (1997: 114) also suggests that external accountability begins to reshape internal practices of audit, so that they begin to fit together. This data work now extends to a new array of economic indicators relating to well-being, citizenship, and so on, and efforts are being made to draw new sets of actors into the global epistemic communities supported by the OECD, with the potential further to shape the way we think about and view education today.

Conclusion

In this chapter, we have traced the conditions that have enabled, and followed from, the success of the OECD's PISA and its related education work. The OECD has adapted successfully to changing global changes and pressures, and set against those changes, we have provided a cartography of the developing place of education inside the Organisation and the place of the OECD's education work in new global geographies of governance and the global politics of mutual accountability. While statistical analyses have been important to education from the establishment of the OECD, this work has taken on greater salience, particularly from the 1990s with the creation of INES, the publication of *Education at Glance*, and, more influentially, with the rise of PISA and subsequent PISA-related developments. The post–Cold War reworking of the Organisation's role to strengthen its position as a global "centre of calculation" (Latour, 1987) provides an important entry point into analyzing its current governance mechanisms and its place in the emergent global education policy field and global mode of educational accountability.

In the 21st century, the OECD, as an administrative apparatus for mobilizing powerful forms of networked governance, has become the major international organization in respect of education policy and is helping to constitute the global educational policy field through its exercise of soft and panoptic modes of power to shape the perceptions of politicians, policy makers, and a variety of different publics concerned with education. These ultimately impact on schooling within nations with potential flow-on to schools and teacher practices, especially when PISA is augmented by national testing. The establishment and expansion of the OECD's data infrastructure has been very important in making the globe legible for governing and this infrastructural governance is linked to its constitution of global epistemic communities. Through its data infrastructure and these communities the Organisation exerts a form of global epistemological governance in education. The OECD's nimble capacities to adapt to changing contexts and to grasp the policy and technical zeitgeist have also contributed to the enhanced significance of its education work in global educational governance. We see it as potentially also crowding out the testing work of the IEA. In the following chapter we turn to a specific case of global "PISA shock," in which the OECD's education work has helped to refashion the global politics of mutual accountability in education.

3
POLITICS OF MUTUAL ACCOUNTABILITY

Introduction

In this chapter we examine the impact of Shanghai's strong performance on the Organisation for Economic Co-operation and Development's (OECD) Programme for International Student Assessment (PISA) in 2009. Our aim is to understand the role that international assessments and comparisons of student performance play in the globalization of educational accountabilities. The main focus of the chapter is on the effects that Shanghai's performance had within the emerging global education policy field (Lingard & Rawolle, 2011) and, specifically, the political responses to this performance in three nations: the USA, England, and Australia. We argue that each of these nations is now "looking East" to compare their educational performance and is using these global comparisons to legitimize certain policy directions (Sellar & Lingard, 2013a).

National and international large-scale assessments such as PISA have become surrogate measures of the putative global competitiveness of national economies (Brown & Scase, 1997). The proliferation of both national and international assessments is helping to constitute an emergent global infrastructure in education (Anagnostopoulos, Rutledge, & Jacobsen, 2013). This infrastructure is helping to produce a commensurate global space of measurement and provides a significant policy lever that helps to lubricate education policy making within and across nations. Building on the arguments of Chapter 2, our analysis illustrates the enhanced significance of PISA, and of education policy more broadly, in efforts to measure and improve human capital production and productivity, both in the work of the OECD and within nations. We argue that the emergent global education policy field has contributed to the reconstitution of "reference societies" (Schriewer & Martinez, 2004) for national schooling systems, partly through the trend toward international comparisons and associated reform initiatives and accountability imperatives. This reconstitution thus involves a shift from historical bases of reference to assessment-based reference societies, while at the same time extending the spatialities of reference to include subnational units of comparison as reference "systems" (for example Shanghai).

While Finland was the PISA "poster child" from 2000 until 2006 (Sahlberg, 2011), Shanghai's outstanding performance in 2009 provoked a "PISA shock" around the globe, but especially in the US, England, and Australia. Interestingly, Asian nations that participate in PISA, such as Japan, Singapore, and South Korea, did not experience the same "shock," and for these systems Finland remains a significant reference society (Takayama, 2008). Apart from Finland, the top performing nations and systems in PISA 2009 were all in Asia: Shanghai, Hong Kong, South Korea, Singapore, and Japan. This result must be understood in the context of talk about the "Asian century," which Wolf, in a *Financial Times* article on September 22, 2003, encapsulated in the following statement: "Europe was the past, the US is the present and a China-dominated Asia the future of the global economy." This epochal political and economic shift has raised policy concerns around the globe, including in education, where we have seen the economization of education policy and its rearticulation as a central policy tool for nations pursuing the promises of the knowledge economy.

Our analysis in this chapter focuses on political and media responses to Shanghai's performance in the USA, England, and Australia. These responses were prompted by the dominance of Asian nations at the top of the PISA 2009 performance rankings and have vernacular features that reflect national political structures, policy histories, and different positioning within the global education policy field.

PISA has had diverse effects in national policy contexts (Grek, 2009; Carvalho & Costa, 2014), including producing the now well-documented phenomenon of "PISA shock". For example, Ertl (2006) describes the shock that occurred in Germany after PISA 2000, when Germany's poor comparative performance came as a surprise to a nation that had considered its education system to be a world leader. As suggested in the opening to Chapter 2, this was a definitive moment in the history of PISA and demonstrated the impact that the assessment could have on public debate and policy reform. Japan experienced similar shocks following the release of results from PISA 2003 and 2006 (Takayama, 2008). Wiseman (2013) describes the phenomenon of PISA shock as follows:

> When there is evidence that nation's educational system and performance is not (or, more specifically, is below) what has been assumed, expected or taken for granted, there is some "shock" that occurs. And when this evidence

is displayed publically, internationally, and in comparison with other nation's educational systems and performance, the shock is exacerbated.

(306–307)

Importantly, as Wiseman (2013: 305) notes, initial media reporting of PISA results plays an important role in producing shocks and these reports "tend to rely on initial descriptive results" and crude rankings of performance, rather than nuanced analyses of the data. Indeed, the release of PISA is the OECD's largest media event and is carefully coordinated to have an impact on public perceptions in participating nations. But shifting perceptions of performance are not sufficient. Martens and Niemann (2013: 2) argue that in order for PISA shock to occur, the following two conditions must be met: "a substantial gap between national self-perception *and* the empirical results ('perception') can be observed, and the evaluated topic is framed as crucial for state purposes ('framing')." In the USA, as Martens and Niemans note, PISA performance has generally been poor, but it was not until China entered the assessment and performed well that this performance became framed as a policy problem of national importance.

In this chapter we argue that the top performance of Shanghai and other East Asian nations in 2009 produced what we might see as a "global" PISA shock. In this case, the shock was prompted by the unexpectedly strong performance of a foreign "competitor," rather than unexpectedly poor domestic performance. Following Martens and Niemann, we argue that this shock was felt in the USA, England, and Australia following PISA 2009, because performance in those nations was *framed* in terms of being outperformed educationally by an ascendant China. Debate about education performance was prompted by the perceived threat of being left behind by a newly threatening economic competitor and an imposing global political presence. Each of these nations turned to China (Shanghai) and other Asian schooling systems (for example Singapore, South Korea) for external rationalization of the need for national reforms in schooling.

The next section of the chapter proffers a framework for our analysis, which focuses on the growing significance of the OECD's PISA in the emergent global education policy field. This builds on our analysis in Chapter 2. We then document the performance of Shanghai on PISA 2009 and contextualize this performance in relation to historical and cultural influences on education in China, the position of education within the current Chinese approach to economic reform, and specific system level reforms and approaches to education in Shanghai. This is followed by three case studies of the impact of Shanghai's performance on political and policy discourses in education in the USA, England, and Australia. We conclude by drawing out significant features of our analysis in relation to what we characterize, following Novoa and Yariv-Mashal (2003), as a new global "politics of mutual accountability" in education. We draw on two sources of data for our analysis: (1) interviews with key policy actors from national education systems in England and Australia and from two international organizations (OECD and IEA); and (2) relevant speeches, policy documents, commissioned research reports, and media coverage from England, Australia, and the USA.

Reference Societies and Externalization

There is an established literature examining the significance of statistics in the "construction of the state, with its unification and administration" (Desrosieres, 1998: 8; see also Hacking, 1986, 1990; Porter, 1995). More recently, we have seen a proliferation of studies examining policy as numbers in education (for example Grek, 2009; Grek et al., 2009a, 2009b; Ozga, 2009; Lingard, 2011; Ozga, Dahler-Larsen, Segerholm, & Simola, 2011), in the context of a widespread turn to so-called evidence-based policy (Head, 2008; Wiseman, 2010). We draw on both literatures here to argue that we are currently witnessing the emergence of a global education policy field in which numbers and statistics play a central role. Further, we argue that the OECD's PISA and other OECD statistical programs, such as their Indicators of Education Systems (INES), along with the IEA's Trends in International Mathematics and Science Studies (TIMSS) and Progress in International Reading Literacy Studies (PIRLS), are central to the constitution of this global policy space. Indeed, this space is constructed through what Torrance (2006) describes as a "globalizing empiricism."

The histories of statistics and their imbrication in the development of nation-states demonstrate how nations were established as commensurate spaces of measurement. Indeed, the etymology of the word "statistics"—state numbers—reflects the role of these numbers in making societies legible for governing. As Porter (1995: 37) argues, "the concept of society was itself in part a statistical construct," and Rose (1999: 198) similarly observes that numbers are "inscription devices" that actually help to "constitute the domains they appear to represent." Providing a contemporary example, he suggests that Europe is being created primarily through the "language of quantification" rather than through a common spoken language. For example, the application of statistical categories across the geographical space of Europe, and their alignment with OECD categories and those of UNESCO, is helping to create a "magistrature of influence" (Lawn & Lingard, 2002) that operates across a "space of equivalence," a commensurate space of measurement. Lawn and Grek (2012) have shown how similar processes are at work in the constitution of a European education policy space.

Extending beyond nations and supranational regions such as Europe, statistical categories are now applied globally, as is the case with the OECD's PISA, contributing to the creation of a global space of equivalence in education. Commensuration is thus helping to render the globe legible for new modes of governance and is contributing to the constitution of a global education policy field. This is one important aspect of the rescaling of governance that has accompanied globalization. We argue that comparative measures of the performance of national schooling systems can be seen as part of a global infrastructure (Sassen, 2007) that enables flows of data that are central to globalization (Spivak, 2012). Wiseman (2010: 18) argues that "what widely available international data on education has done is create an intellectual space where educational policy making is not geographically or politically bounded but is instead bounded by the extent of the legitimated evidence used to support one decision or policy versus another." Elsewhere, we have argued that in this global intellectual space we may be seeing the emergence of a new policy disposition or habitus among policy actors within nations and international organizations (Lingard, Sellar, & Baroutsis, 2015). This disposition is promulgated through global policy networks (Ball & Junemann, 2012) and epistemic communities (Kallo, 2009) that are characterized by belief in the possibility of, and the need for, a global space of measurement. This is a manifestation of what Novoa and Yariv-Mashal (2003: 427) describe as a central element in a new global "politics of mutual accountability": an "expert-discourse [that] plays an important role through the production of concepts, methodologies and tools used to compare educational systems." The spread of such dispositions and discourses is a key process of globalization, understood in Strathern's (1995) terms as "the infinitely recurring *possibility* of measurement—not the scales *but the capacity to imagine them*" (179). This disposition is important in the commensurative work that underpins the creation of LSAs that constitute the globe as an equivalent space of measurement and comparison.

The rise of policy as numbers both nationally and globally is linked to the influence of neoliberalism and the turn from government to governance (Rhodes, 1997). As Ozga (2009) persuasively argues, "Data production and management were and are essential to the new governance turn; constant comparison is its symbolic feature, as well as a distinctive mode of operation" (150). The enhanced significance of numbers in policy today is associated with the restructured state's new managerialism, the subsequent move to network governance, and steering at a distance *modus operandi*: "Data support and create new kinds of policy instrument that organise political relations through communication/information" (Ozga, 2009: 150).

Comparison is an important feature of this governance turn (Novoa & Yariv-Mashal, 2003; Torrance, 2006; Ozga, 2009). Central for our argument here is Novoa and Yariv-Mashal's (2003) observation that, in contemporary policy contexts, "Comparative research [has become] important regardless of its conclusions or even its recommendations. It is important as *a mode of governance*, one of the most powerful being administered not only in Europe but also worldwide" (429). Comparison as a mode of governance involves what Novoa and Yariv-Mashal (2003) describe as a "politics of mutual accountability," which brings a sense of sharing and participation, inviting each country (and each citizen) to a perpetual comparison to the other. In fact, much more than a horizontality of exchanges, this process brings a kind of verticality, that is a system of classification of schools according to standards that are accepted without critical discussion.

(427)

This politics of mutual accountability is linked to what Novoa and Yariv-Mashal (2003) call "the society of the international spectacle," referencing the work of Guy Debord and pointing to a regime in which, "Surveillance is exercised through an exposure to public opinion, a spectacular display of indicators, ultimately serving to control individuals and performances" (427). The concept of an international society of the spectacle points to a similar set of developments to those we have described in terms of the global panopticon. The international comparative measures offered by the OECD and the IEA are part of what Novoa and Yariv-Mashal characterize as the "global eye" of comparison that functions in conjunction with a "national" eye. The latter operates, for example, through national testing programs that have become increasingly prevalent and that are now complemented by international testing. Comparison is thus a central technology in the globalizing of educational accountabilities and it is important, therefore, to consider the place of comparative education in these developments.

The disciplinary field of comparative education emerged with the desire of educational leaders to learn and borrow from other systems, thus creating what have been called reference societies (Schriewer & Martinez, 2004). Historically, nations have looked to particular reference societies in order to learn from their schooling systems (Phillips & Ochs, 2004; Steiner-Khamsi, 2004). For example, during the 1980s, in the context of the *A Nation at Risk* (1983) report and a buoyant Japanese economy, the USA looked to Japan for educational lessons (Takayama, 2011). During the Blair era in the 1990s and early 2000s, England tended to look across the Atlantic to the USA, while Australia has tended to look to England, but also more recently to the USA.

Reference societies have been essential to processes of "externalization" in policy production (Schriewer, 1990). Externalization involves the use of policies in other systems to justify and legitimate the necessity of domestic reform. Schriewer (2000) argues that there is a "semantics of globalization" that pushes nations to look to others in terms of comparative global performance. Waldow (2012) describes such externalization as "a discursive formation that can become relevant in the context of borrowing, and lends itself easily to the purpose of producing legitimacy" for national reform agendas (418). We would suggest that this semantics of globalization is now part of the disposition (habitus) of influential policy makers within international organizations and national education systems and contributes to the prevalence of externalization.

Traditional constructions of reference societies are now being challenged by globalizing policy as numbers, comparison as a mode of governance, the emergence of a global education policy field, and the different positioning of agents and nations within this field. PISA is helping to constitute new reference societies by positioning national and subnational schooling systems within a global space of measurement and comparison of educational performance. Finland has so far been the most prominent new reference society produced by this process, but we argue that, in the so-called Asian century and the context of post–Cold War neoliberal globalization, the performance of Shanghai and other East Asian systems is encouraging certain "Western" nations to "look East." This is changing how externalization now functions in national education policy production in these nations.

A Class Above: Shanghai's Performance in PISA 2009

Shanghai is one of China's largest cities, a province-level municipality with a population of more than 24 million people. Shanghai is rapidly becoming part of what Sassen (2001) describes as a transnational network of "global cities." This network is emerging with the "rescaling of the strategic territories that articulate the new system" of economic globalization and has seen a rise in the importance of spatial units at the subnational level (for example Shanghai) and the supranational level (for example the OECD) (Sassen, 2009: 3). Shanghai has experienced a renaissance since the early 1990s, resulting in dramatic socioeconomic and spatial transformation (Chen, 2009). The city has become a popular location for multinational corporate headquarters in China (including for research and development facilities) and is now a major financial center in Asia (Sassen, 2009). The economic success of Shanghai and its status as an emergent global city has made it an important site of comparison for other nations and cities (Chen, 2009), reflecting the rise of global comparisons across multiple spaces.

Shanghai's education system is a top performer within China and it is the only region of mainland China that participated in PISA 2009 *and* had its results published as part of the international data set. A number of other provinces in China have been involved in PISA on the basis that they are exempted from making their results public (Chan & Seddon, 2014). China first began discussing its involvement in PISA with the OECD in 2001 and Shanghai has participated fully from 2009. A research interviewee explained that China is "using PISA as a lever for improvement in other provinces, for the western provinces for example" and "[t]hey are going to ensure that they get things right before going fully into it. I think the plan is that more and more Chinese provinces come in as and when the infrastructure is there." Shanghai's involvement has provided China with a comparison of its top-performing system against other systems internationally and has provided a benchmark for educational developments internally. A further three cities—Beijing, Jiangsu, and Guangdong—will have their PISA 2015 results included in the international data set.

Shanghai's PISA 2009 results followed the earlier strong performances of other Asian education systems like South Korea, Japan, and Hong Kong, which have consistently performed well on PISA and, along with Singapore and Taiwan, have also been strong performers on TIMSS. This trend has continued in PISA 2012. However, Shanghai's outstanding performance in PISA 2009 across reading, mathematics, and science drew new levels of attention to education systems in Asia. Notably, many of these education systems are in countries that are not OECD members.

Shanghai substantially outperformed all other OECD countries, partner countries, and economies in 2009 and repeated this performance in 2012. However, our focus in this chapter is on the shock created by its initial results, when Shanghai scored 556 in the reading assessment (Finland 536, Australia 515, USA 500, England 495, Average 493), 600 in mathematics (Finland 541, Australia 514, Average 496, England 493, USA 487), and 575 in science (Finland 554, Australia 527, England 515, USA 502, Average 501). One of our interviewees observed that "people who know Shanghai were not surprised by those outcomes, but for people who don't know Shanghai's education system it was sort of a wakeup call."

As Wiseman (2013) observes, nations attend to PISA performance in terms of both academic excellence and equity, and Shanghai's results were also strong in respect of the latter: 12.3 percent of variation in reading performance in Shanghai can be explained by socioeconomic background, compared with 12.7 percent in Australia, 14 percent in England, and 16.8 percent in the USA. This suggests that, based on PISA data, not only were Shanghai's students the top performers on the reading assessment, but Shanghai's schools are also comparatively successful at helping students to overcome disadvantageous socioeconomic backgrounds. We note that the width of the Shanghai sample might explain this equity measure, with very disadvantaged internal migrant young people excluded from the sample.

There has been much debate about the causes of Shanghai's results. In the OECD's *Strong Performers and Successful Reformers: Lessons from PISA for the United States* report, Cheng (2011) acknowledges the cultural and historical context for Shanghai's performance, including China's long history of examination-driven education, which extends back to the civil service exams of the 7th century, as well as the view "that students in China learn by rote and that much in schools is about memorization and cramming for examinations" (Cheng, 2011: 21). As Simola (2005) has argued, specifically in relation to Finland, idiosyncratic historical and cultural factors of this kind must be taken into account when seeking to explain performance on international comparative assessments such as PISA. Context cannot be transferred!

There are certainly cultural factors that likely contribute to the strong performance of East Asian education systems on PISA and these include dispositions and practices associated with Confucian values, such as disciplined study habits (including private tuition), educational commitment, competitiveness, and ambition (Tan, 2012). For example, Tan (2013) notes how *gaokao*, the exam at the end of secondary schooling that determines university entrance, still drives a deeply embedded "cultural script" for Shanghai parents that creates pressure for academic achievement and high grades. Tan draws attention to the "Tiger Mother" phenomenon, popularized by the best-selling US book, *Battle Hymn of the Tiger Mother* (Chua, 2011), and notes how this dominant cultural script reflects a "mark-obsessed exam culture in China" (53) that has a long and illustrious history. The one child policy and competitive culture of Shanghai for top university places and jobs reinforce this cultural script. For example, in Shanghai there is parental pressure for children to attend good pre-, primary and secondary schools, as a precursor to enrolment in prestigious universities. These school choice elements are manifest in the number of unofficial rankings of Shanghai schools that have appeared on the web. Young people are affected by these various pressures to succeed academically, and Tan (2013: 62) emphasizes that "Shanghai students are . . . competitive, highly motivated, hardworking and pragmatic." Tan's research suggests that pressures to succeed educationally are exerted within low socioeconomic status families as well as in professional ones, though we note the impact of the *hukuo* household registration system (see Jacques, 2012: 197–198) on the reduced educational prospects of internal migrant students in Shanghai, who attend poor-quality private schools (see Wang & Holland, 2011). There has been much debate about the effect of this system on Shanghai's PISA results, for example because students attending these schools may leave early or return to rural areas for secondary education (for this debate, see Loveless, 2013a, 2013b, 2014). These complexities are important to keep in mind when evaluating Shanghai's performance both in terms of academic excellence and equity.

There is thus a strong argument for the contribution of cultural factors to Shanghai's PISA 2009 performance, although clearly education policy and curriculum must also be taken into account. Tan (2012) argues that curriculum reform in China and Shanghai has contributed to Shanghai's top results and distinguishes between two broad periods of reform since the Cultural Revolution. The "First Curriculum Reform" occurred from 1988 to 1997 and was initiated by Deng Xio Peng as part of broader economic reforms. The "Second Curriculum Reform" has been underway since 1998 and has seen schools in Shanghai move away from transmission pedagogies and a strong focus on exams. Echoing the focus of PISA, there is now a move toward curriculum that focuses on "real-world" problems. These reforms have also increased autonomy for schools and compulsory English language learning, as well as shifting the balance between summative and formative assessments.

These developments reflect the tendency to look outwards during the second phase of curriculum reform and the response to concerns that Chinese students were overly pressured and too focused on rote learning and exams (for example Wong in an *International Herald Tribune* article on July 2, 2012), at the expense of developing the creative and innovative skills and dispositions promoted as necessary for economic competitiveness in the era of knowledge capitalism. Tan (2012: 159) observes that "the Shanghai authority justifies the 'Second Curriculum Reform' using the global imperative to reform education to meet the challenges of globalization," and that references "to education reforms in developed countries such as the USA, the UK and Japan testify to Shanghai policymakers' desire not to lose out in the [global education/economic] race by borrowing similar policies and practices for the city." This concern to look outside of Asia is also shared by other nations such as South Korea and Japan. However, while looking outwards for policy ideas, it is important to recognize that in China the borrowing of policy from other contexts has been significantly influenced by sociocultural factors, giving rise to globalized "education policy with 'Chinese characteristics'" (Tan, 2012: 165). Shanghai's performance is thus most likely attributable to a complex conjunction of cultural and policy factors, including the conditions in which students come to the test.

Testing literacy is an important factor to consider when seeking to explain PISA performance. Tan (2012) observes that while PISA tests for the application of knowledge to real-world problems, and not simply the memorization of facts, this application is framed by the test-taking situation. While the OECD promotes PISA as a test of students' capacities to apply knowledge in order to solve real-life problems, Dohn (2007) argues that "PISA assesses how well students are able to exercise knowledge and skills within the PISA focus areas in precisely one 'real life setting', namely a test situation" (10). In other words, PISA tests how well students are able to sit tests like PISA. In this case, exam-oriented educational systems are likely to prepare students to perform well in these situations. Ironically then, long-standing Chinese educational approaches may be contributing to the PISA success of Shanghai's students at a time when contemporary curriculum reformers are looking outward in efforts to move the system away from these approaches.

The contribution of contextual and cultural factors to PISA performance is often played down by the OECD (2011a, 2011b) and other analysts (for example Jensen, Hunter, Sonneman, & Burns, 2012; Tucker, 2011), who have tended to emphasize the influence of policy settings and education reforms. Cheng (2011: 40–45) argues that a number of policies have contributed to Shanghai's performance, including: clear and ambitious system-wide goal setting for comprehensive reforms, drawing on the reform-oriented culture in Shanghai and embedded in a wider agenda to position the city as a global leader; a focus on learning and instruction, informed by the structuring of teachers' work to prioritize research and professional learning; and a strong accountability and transparency agenda. The OECD has also emphasized Shanghai's strategies for improving "weak" schools by pairing rural schools with urban partners in professional learning communities, including transferring teachers between schools, and the "empowered" administration approach in which poor performing schools are taken over by experienced leaders and teachers in strong performing schools (Cheng, 2011; see also www.pearsonfoundation.org/oecd/china.html). The capacity of PISA to influence the politics of mutual accountability promoted by international comparisons of educational performance depends on this performance being attributable to such policy factors, at least to a significant extent. Cultural factors influencing performance are unlikely to be transferable or easily reformed, whereas policy factors can provide the basis for policy learning and reform in other contexts. We argue that policy issues cannot be separated from the contextual and cultural factors with which they combine to influence performance on tests such as PISA. However, as we illustrate in the following sections, the response to Shanghai's performance in the USA, England, and Australia has focused on the policy side of this equation.

This Generation's Sputnik Moment: The USA Case

There have been a number of reference societies, including Canada, towards which the USA has looked to learn and from which they have sought to borrow policy ideas at various points in its educational and broader history. The USA has also had changing patterns of looking outwards and inwards for ideas about reforming their schooling systems, which are largely a state responsibility rather than a federal one. For example, Horace Mann, in the early decades of the 19th century, looked outwards to Prussia for a model of and justification for the creation of a mass, secular public schooling system in Massachusetts. This system formed the prototype for subsequent comparable state legislation on schooling in other US states. In the early years of the 20th century, the USA sought to "benchmark" itself against schooling systems in Germany and Scotland (Tucker, 2011: 169). However, in the post–World War II era, as it became the major global economic and military power, the USA turned inwards in its attention to educational ideas. During the postwar boom, the USA led the world in terms of full secondary school participation and the percentage of age cohort participation in, and graduation from, university. During this time, schooling remained largely governed at state and school board levels, apart from some federal interventions in relation to social justice matters. During the 1980s, Japan became an important reference society for the USA, in the wake of the *A Nation at Risk* report in 1983 and with the commissioning of the *Japanese Education Today* report in 1987 (Takayama, 2007, 2011), and the concerned rhetoric of that time was echoed in response to Shanghai's PISA 2009 performance.

Since the 1990s, following the end of the Cold War, growing economic globalization, and the emergence of a global education policy field, the USA has again begun to look outwards. In the context of globally competitive labor markets and a "global war for talent" (Brown & Tannock, 2009), along with the growth of the "knowledge-based economy" (OECD, 1996), educational systems have become important as a means for nations to create human capital and increase productivity. International large-scale assessments such as PISA have become a surrogate measure of national economic competitiveness (Brown & Scase, 1997) and this has challenged the traditional reference societies for most nations, including the USA, where comparative PISA performance has focused attention on China's rise in the "Asian century," offering a challenge to the one superpower scenario since the collapse of the Soviet Union.

Until the release of PISA 2009 in December 2010, the impact of PISA in the USA was minimal (Breakspear, 2012), with no shocks akin to that experienced in Germany following PISA 2000, even despite the USA's low academic and low equity performance (Condron, 2011). One explanation for this lack of impact is that from 2006 to 2009 PISA samples in the USA did not enable disaggregation of performance at the state level, where responsibility for education resides (Rutkowski, 2014). It should be noted, however, that the USA had a powerful political and financial influence on the development of the OECD's INES program, resulting in the annual publication of comparative international educational statistics in *Education at a Glance*, as well as the establishment of PISA (Henry, Lingard, Rizvi, & Taylor, 2001). This influence reflected growing concerns in the USA about educational standards, expressed as far back as the *A Nation at Risk* (1983) report during the Reagan Presidency, which catalyzed the failing schools discourse in the USA.

During the 2000s there have been substantial school reforms across the USA. The central features of these reforms, as summarized by Darling-Hammond (2011: ix), have been: the introduction of frequent high-stakes testing; the expansion of entrepreneurial charter schools; the provision of alternative routes into teaching and efforts to improve teaching by abolishing teacher tenure; and the introduction of teacher merit pay and sanctions for teachers whose students perform poorly on tests. Sahlberg (2011) has described this USA reform pattern as a manifestation of what he calls "GERM," the Global Education Reform Movement, which is exemplified by standardized testing and teaching, a focus on literacy and numeracy, prescribed curriculum, market-oriented reforms, and test-based accountability. Recent USA reforms can thus be seen as a vernacular expression of the neoliberal education policy agenda (Ball, 2008), and both Sahlberg (2011) and Darling-Hammond (2011) observe that these reforms are the antithesis of those instigated by the most successful schooling systems as measured by PISA.

Since 2009, the Obama Presidency has strengthened the federal presence in USA schooling. For example, Obama was very supportive of the Common Core State Standards initiative. He has also been an activist education president, replacing Bush's No Child Left Behind program with his Race to the Top program and linking federal school funding to teacher performance. Competition between the states for extra federal school funding through Race to the Top was intended "to push the US ahead in the nation-versus-nation competition for jobs" (Collin, 2012: 163) in the global economy.

While the USA has never performed particularly well on PISA, at least in comparative terms, the release of the 2009 PISA results in December 2010 produced a form of PISA shock and the response was immediate. Before looking at this response, however, we note that there were inklings of the disparity between the top PISA performers and the USA in earlier policy developments. For example, in March 2009 Andreas Schleicher, who oversees PISA at the OECD, spoke to the US Senate Education Committee (see *New York Times*, March 9, 2010) and warned that the USA was falling behind many other nations on high school completion rates and in the PISA results. Schleicher observed, "In one way, international educational benchmarks make disappointing reading for the US" (*New York Times*, March 9, 2010).

Following the release of the PISA 2009 results and documentation of the outstanding performance of Shanghai students, the media coverage in the USA was, to say the least, extensive. The headline in the *New York Times* (December 7, 2010) read, "Top Test Scores from Shanghai Stun Educators." In this article, former assistant secretary of education under President Reagan, Chester E. Finn Jr., was quoted as saying, "Wow, I'm kind of stunned, I'm thinking of Sputnik." He continued, "I've seen how relentless the Chinese are at accomplishing goals, and if they can do this in Shanghai in 2009, they can do it in 10 cities in 2019, and 50 cities by 2029." The article also quoted an earlier speech by President Obama, in which he noted how the USSR launch of Sputnik in 1957, taken as a symbol of the Soviet's progress ahead of the USA during the "space race," led to increased investment in and focus on mathematics and science education. Investment of federal monies in science, technology, engineering, and mathematics (STEM) teaching and research in schools and universities has also been a focus for President Obama. Indeed, in his State of the Union address on January 25, 2011, he stressed the importance of the quality of mathematics and science education to the USA's competitive future in the new global economy: "We know what it takes to compete for the jobs and industries of our time. We need to out-innovate, out-educate, and out-build the rest of the world." The *New York Times* story continued to quote President Obama: "Fifty years later, our generation's Sputnik moment is back. With billions of people in India and China suddenly plunged into the world economy, nations with the most educated workers will prevail." He continued, "As it stands right now America is in danger of falling behind." This generation's "Sputnik moment" for the US has been the basis of the new "looking East" in this policy context.

Interestingly, the *New York Times* article also quoted Mark Schneider, a Commissioner of Research in the Department of Education during the George W. Bush presidency, who noted that, "Shanghai students apparently were told the test was important for China's image and thus were motivated to do well." Schneider continued, "Can you imagine the reaction if we told the students of Chicago that the PISA was an important international test and that America's reputation depended on them performing well?" Indeed, the impact of different approaches to test preparation for students in the PISA sample in different countries is an issue that would benefit from further research and debate. This observation is an example of rumors about factors influencing Shanghai's performance, including questions about sampling and test preparation, which circulated in the wake of results being released.

Arne Duncan, then US secretary of education, was also quoted in the *New York Times* article. He suggested that, for the USA, "We have to see this as a wake-up call." He added, "The United States came in 23rd or 24th in most subjects. We can quibble, or we can face the brutal truth that we're being out-educated." In a press release of December 7, 2010, Duncan quoted the president as saying that the nation that "out-educates us today will out-compete us tomorrow." Duncan observed further, "So, the big picture from PISA is one of educational stagnation, at a time of fast-rising demand for highly-educated workers. The mediocre performance of America's students is a problem we cannot afford to ignore." Duncan proposed that the USA must adapt and look outwards in order to learn policy lessons from other nations and systems. He commented, "The US currently has many of the world's top universities. But a century ago we adopted the concept of the research university from Germany. Vocational and technical education in the US has its roots in Scotland's mechanical institutes, which were then on the cutting edge of technology training. Our leading prep schools are modeled after England's. Today, America has to study and learn from other nations once again."

This raises a question posed by Luke (2011): "Could it be that American education is on the cusp of 'outside-in' reform—that the historical flows of expertise, innovation, educational science, and policy from the United States have been reversed?" (368). As suggested earlier, we would argue that the USA has now made such a shift. For example, in response to the PISA 2009 results Arne Duncan commissioned an OECD/National Centre on Education and the Economy (NCEE) report on the best-performing school systems and what lessons could be learnt from them. The findings of this report are collected in a popular book, *Surpassing Shanghai: An Agenda for American Education Built on the World's Leading Systems*, edited by Marc Tucker (2011) from the NCEE. The publication of this report and edited book, in conjunction with related conferences that Duncan organized on the topic, support an affirmative answer to Luke's question.

The argument that the USA is now looking outwards for reform ideas is also supported by Collin's (2012) critical discourse analysis of President Obama's 2011 State of the Union address. Collin illustrates how the president's speech functions around two binary and contrasting worlds: the old local, manufacturing, low-skilled economy and the new high-tech, high-skilled global economy, where education levels and comparative educational performance will determine a nation's future.

The president represents the future as a global economic competition paralleled by international competition in educational performance in which there are new competitors; the president mentions China and India, which, in his words, could beat the USA in this global competition by "educating their children earlier and longer, with great emphasis on math and science." In recognition of the federal political structure in the USA and the location of the control of schooling at state and local levels, Collin (2012) argues that President Obama accepts that the federal government "must operate less as a central command structure and more as a provider of incentives and an issuer of challenges" (159). This steering at a distance mode of governance is evident in the *Race to the Top* legislation.

One final point should be made here regarding the USA's PISA performance and its position within the global field of comparative school performance. Darling-Hammond (2010, 2011) and Condron (2011) have both demonstrated how the inequitable funding of schooling in the USA and the extent of poverty are very significant factors in the poor comparative performance of USA schools on international tests in both equity and academic terms (see also Chapters 5 and 6). Condron (2011) shows how deep structural inequality is neglected in discussions of USA schooling performance and demonstrates that if the Gini coefficient of inequality in the USA were the same as Finland—that is, if there were less poverty and a more equal distribution of income and wealth—then USA PISA performance would be 25 points better on mathematics. Thus, Condron (2011) raises the significant issue of the impact of inequality and highlights the need for broader policies to address the influence of inequality on educational performance (see Anyon, 2005). Darling-Hammond also argues that confronting this set of equity issues will be central to the future of the USA. Education alone cannot compensate for society and this is particularly so in the contemporary USA of competitive neoliberal market capitalism, where inequality is growing (Piketty, 2014). While OECD representations of PISA outcomes stress the significance of policy factors and tend to play down cultural explanations of different national performances, we would also suggest that they also do not sufficiently emphasize the effects of structural inequality. Indeed, even though PISA results are reported in relation to academic performance and equity, the construction of equity in the OECD's work focuses on ensuring fair opportunities for success at school for students from different backgrounds, rather than directly addressing the relationship between inequality and performance.

Looking East Like Never Before: The England Case

Historically, Britain has exported its educational structures, policies, and practices from the center of its empire to its colonies (for example Seth, 2007). Like the USA, England has tended not to look outwards for education policy ideas (Knodel & Walkenhurst, 2010) or has looked across the Atlantic to the USA as a key reference society. Many recent reforms to the English education system have been at the forefront of global education policy trends, particularly those associated with neoliberal education policy agendas (Ball, 2008). English policy makers have also had confidence in the quality of national education data collections and have thus tended to be skeptical about the value of international data and comparisons (Grek, 2009; Knodel & Walkenhorst, 2010). For example, one of our interviewees explained that "up until now [England has] been very focused on our national data, we are probably ahead of other countries in terms of data" and "for the actual conduct of the [PISA] studies I don't think we get anything new because we are so far ahead in terms of data collection than most countries." However, as this case demonstrates, attention to PISA results in English politics and policy making has increased substantially since the initial rounds of the assessment and particularly following the change of government in 2010. Since this time, international data has taken on a much more significant role in English education and policy makers have begun to "look East" to new reference societies in Asia.

The United Kingdom is the unit of analysis and comparison for PISA, however the UK oversamples schools in England, Scotland, Wales, and Northern Ireland. Oversampling enables the disaggregation of results for, and comparisons between, in each of these education systems. In this case we focus specifically on England, although some of the media coverage and comment that we analyze here inevitably extends to the broader UK context. In England, Wales, and Northern Ireland PISA is overseen by the UK Department for Education, which has a representative on the PISA Governing Board (PGB), while Scotland has its own seat on the PGB. In contrast to England, Scotland has placed greater emphasis on PISA performance and results have been used to support a nationalist agenda in the media and politically (Lingard & Sellar, 2014). For example, Scotland has used its strong performance compared with England in order to emphasize systemic differences and to align itself with top-performing European nations (Grek et al., 2009a; Lingard & Rawolle, 2009; Pons, 2011). Scotland's strategy here has also been linked with the Scottish nationalist project (Lingard & Sellar, 2014).

Following the first two rounds of PISA in 2000 and 2003, the response in England was ambivalent. Following PISA 2000, the government celebrated a relatively strong performance, but the 2003 results showed declining performance and these were suppressed on the basis that there was a low response rate. Interestingly, this response rate was only marginally lower than in 2000 (Knodel & Walkenhorst, 2010). England saw a further decline in performance in PISA 2006 and these results received extensive, negative media coverage (Grek, 2009). This intensified coverage reflected the growing influence of PISA globally and the increasingly politicized nature of this coverage since 2006 (Pons, 2011). As discussed above, media coverage of PISA generally focuses on rankings and simplistic narratives of success or failure, rather than contextual detail and careful secondary analyses of the data. As one of our interviewees commented, "what tends to happen, it is the rankings that are used by the politicians and the media rather than underlying interest in data."

The coalition government, elected in 2010, used the decline in English PISA performance between the 2000 and 2006, and England's comparative rankings in 2006, to criticize the record and achievements of the Blair and Brown New Labour governments in relation to education. This strategy can be seen as contributing to a new framing of comparative international performance and thus as setting the scene for a shock in response to PISA 2009 results (Martens & Niemann, 2013). PISA results have been used by the coalition government to support a narrative of declining standards and to push for reform. The new attention to international data and comparisons differentiates the coalition government's approach to education from both New Labour and previous Conservative governments. For example, the Coalition's 2010 white paper, *The Importance of Teaching*, begins by emphasizing the importance of international comparisons: "what really matters is how we are doing compared with our international competitors.... The truth is, at the moment we are standing still while others race past" (DfE, 2010: 1). England's performance in PISA 2006 is then used to frame the policy positions set out in the white paper, with the "Far East" and Scandinavia identified as having top-performing systems from which England must learn. Here we can see evidence of an outward-looking gaze in relation to educational ideas and the construction of successful PISA performers as new reference societies for England.

An interviewee from the English Department for Education explained that when the Conservative-led coalition government was elected, "the focus on international evidence sharpened hugely. When they had been in opposition they were consistently and constantly quoting PISA and also high performing jurisdictions like Singapore, Alberta etcetera, and that has continued now they are in government." While PISA had minimal impact on education policy under the previous government, this interviewee explained, "[t]hat has all changed. Ministers are absolutely clear that every policy that is developed they want to see underlying evidence not just from the national side, also the international level." This shift has not only occurred in terms of the political representation of PISA results, but has also been reflected in the internal systemic use of PISA data: "It is only with PISA 2006 that we've started to think very carefully about what we could be doing with this data."

This reframing of the importance of international comparative data for English education governance and policy is evident in speeches made by Michael Gove, the previous secretary for education. For example, speaking soon after the election of the coalition government in May 2010, and before the release of PISA 2009 results, Gove described the need to learn from other systems, specifically in countries such as Singapore, South Korea, Finland, Canada, and Sweden, as well as from the charter school movement in the USA (Gove, 2010a). Gove visited China in 2010 and penned a somewhat confused opinion piece in the *Telegraph*, where he observed that "[s]chools in the Far East are turning out students who are working at an altogether higher level than our own." Gove signaled the new English attention to East Asia by calling for a "Long March to reform our education system" and, displaying a lack of understanding of the history of Chinese education under Mao, "a cultural revolution just like the one they've had in China" (Gove, 2010b). While this visit preceded the official release of PISA 2009 results in December 2010, Gove would likely have been aware of Shanghai's performance. In later speeches, Gove regularly noted this strong performance and the need for England to learn from top-performing systems like Shanghai (Gove, 2011a, 2011b, 2012).

One speech in particular, delivered by Gove to the Education World Forum in 2011, stands out in terms of illustrating the new influence of PISA in England (Gove, 2011a). Here Gove identified Andreas Schleicher, now head of the Directorate for Education and Skills at the OECD, as vying for the title of "the most important man in world education" with Sir Michael Barber, author of the influential McKinsey reports on high-performing school systems (McKinsey & Co., 2007, 2010), former director of policy implementation for Prime Minister Blair, and now chief education advisor at Pearson plc. As one of our interviewees noted, Schleicher has been very active in promoting the value of PISA as an evidence base for national education policy making and reform: he "travels the world proselytizing PISA and has been very successful." The collective influence of both Schleicher and Barber is illustrated by the *Strong Performers and Successful Reformers in Education* initiative (www.pearsonfoundation.org/oecd/index.html), which showcases inter alia Shanghai. This initiative, including a series of videos, was sponsored by the Pearson Foundation, a now defunct philanthropic arm of the influential education publisher Pearson. As Ball (2012: 124) has demonstrated, the relationships between "nodal actors" in multinational companies and international organizations, such as Schleicher and Barber, now exert significant and "purposeful" influence on education policy within the emergent global education policy field. We turn to a consideration of the work of edu-businesses in global educational accountabilities in the final chapter of the book.

This case illustrates how, in response to the growing global influence of PISA, England is now looking outwards, particularly towards China, for educational ideas. This attention extends beyond high-level policy debate and in recent years there have been a number of exchange programs that have sponsored visits by bureaucrats, educators, and students between the two countries. Under previous Labour governments, the focus in education was very much on national data, which was used to support claims about the need to drive up standards and as the basis for school choice discourses and school effectiveness approaches. As we have shown here, the Coalition government and former Minister Gove turned the English policy gaze toward PISA data and high-performing systems in Asia. Indeed, in a 2012 speech Foreign Secretary William Hague declared that "[t]oday Britain is looking East as never before."

Keeping Up With the Neighbors: The Australian Case

Australia has a federal political structure, in which education is primarily the responsibility of states and territories, and there has been significant referencing and policy borrowing between these systems. In Chapter 4, we look at how educational accountability in respect of national testing has worked in Australia's federal political structure. Australia has also been relatively outward looking in relation to education policy and reform ideas, seeing the UK and other Commonwealth nations as relevant reference societies. Since the 1980s, Australia has been involved in reciprocal exchanges of policy ideas with the UK (Johnson & Tonkiss, 2002). More recently, Australia has also looked to top PISA performers such as Finland and has borrowed reform ideas from the USA, particularly the previous chancellor of the New York City Department of Education, Joel Klein, who now heads Amplify, an edu-business owned by Rupert Murdoch. The federal Labor governments that were in office from 2007 to 2013 implemented a set of national education reforms, under the banner of a so-called Education Revolution (Commonwealth of Australia, 2008), which introduced the National Assessment Program—Literacy and Numeracy (NAPLAN) and the My School website (www.myschool.edu.au). Together, NAPLAN and My School enable annual student testing and public comparisons of school performance, and in Australia PISA is considered to be part of the national assessment program. These reforms also tied federal money to a range of programs, including the introduction of performance pay for principals who improve test performance, following a similar logic to the Race to the Top program in the USA.

Australia has participated in PISA since 2000 and since this initial assessment, unlike in the USA and England, the results have influenced national policy debates. In part, this is due to Australia's close involvement with the education work of the OECD. Australia's geographical location and less-influential role in international affairs compared to the USA and the UK has encouraged a view that involvement in the OECD is an important forum for international engagement. PISA was developed and grew in prominence under the leadership of Professor Barry McGaw, an Australian head of education at the OECD from 1999 to 2005 and former executive director of the Australian Council for Educational Research (ACER), which led international consortia that managed PISA from 2000 to 2009. McGaw is an influential educational leader in Australia and the chair of the Australian Curriculum, Assessment and Reporting Authority (ACARA), a statutory authority that manages NAPLAN, national curriculum development, and the comparison and reporting of school performance via My School. PISA is oversampled in Australia to enable the disaggregation of results for each state and territory system. As a result, PISA data have been able to influence key loci of educational governance in Australia. These data have also been an important component of analyses undertaken by ACER for various Australian education systems including comparisons between systems that have spurred reform agendas, and have influenced the national narrative about education through their inclusion in a number of high-profile state and federal reports on education policy issues, such as the 2011 Review of Funding for Schooling. This context has contributed to the impact of PISA results in Australia and, together with its geographical location, has helped to frame the response to Shanghai's success in 2009.

Australia has generally performed well in PISA. However, it is one of only four nations that have seen a decline over time in both reading and mathematics (Nous Group, 2011). This has generated a narrative of decline and the risk of being outperformed by Asian neighbors in recent Australian policy debate. The most prominent manifestation of this narrative has been media reporting of then Prime Minister Julia Gillard's assertion that Australia needs to "win the education race" with other countries in the Asia-Pacific region (*The Australian*, January 24, 2012). This argument is based on comparisons between Australia and the performance on PISA 2009 of Shanghai, Singapore, Korea, and Japan. Gillard argued that "four of the top five performing school systems in the world are in our region and they are getting better and better," creating the risk that Australian students may become "workers in an economy where we are kind of the runt of the litter in our region and we've slipped behind the standards and the high-skill, high wage jobs are elsewhere in our region" (*The Australian*, January 24, 2012).

Reports published by the consultancy firm, Nous Group, and by an independent Australian think tank, the Grattan Institute, also made influential contributions to education policy debate in Australia following PISA 2009. These reports were linked to the preparation and public release in 2012 of the major national Review of School Funding. In 2011, the Nous Group produced *Schooling Challenges and Opportunities: A Report for the Review of Funding for Schooling Panel*. The report frames Australia's performance in relation to other strong performing systems globally and opens with an analysis of PISA results, drawing attention to Australia's decline in reading and mathematics performance and the risk of "falling behind" systems such as Shanghai, Korea, Hong Kong, and Japan (Nous Group, 2011: 7). This analysis was also taken up in the 2012 white paper on *Australia in the Asian Century*. Commissioned to help frame national policy settings in response to economic growth in the region, the white paper argues for school reform in response to Australia's declining PISA performance and the strong performance of its Asian neighbors.

In 2012, the Grattan Institute also published its report, *Catching Up: Learning from the Best School Systems in East Asia* report (Jensen et al., 2012), which asserts that, "Today's centre of high performance in school education is East Asia" (2). The influence of funding and cultural factors—"Confucianism, rote learning or Tiger Mothers" (Jensen et al., 2012: 2)—on this performance is downplayed in the report and the importance of reform agendas in countries such as Shanghai, Hong Kong, and Singapore is described in detail. The report had its basis in a

2011 roundtable titled *Learning from the Best*, which was attended by a number of participants, including the Australian prime minister and federal education minister, education academics from Shanghai, Singapore, Hong Kong, and Korea, and the OECD's Andreas Schleicher. The Shanghai system is a focus of analysis and comparison in the Grattan Institute report, which informed an opinion piece published by an author of the report in Australia's national newspaper, "Shanghai success a lesson in delivery" (*The Australian*, February 18, 2012). The report also generated other prominent and detailed articles in Australian papers, which suggested that: students in Shanghai are "A class above" (*Sydney Morning Herald*, February 17, 2012); Shanghai's performance was must constitute a "wake-up call for Australia" (*Sydney Morning Herald*, February 17, 2012); and "Lessons from Asia show the way forward for schools" (*The Australian*, February 17, 2012).

These research reports and associated media coverage influenced politicians, policy makers, and the public debate about education and marked a distinct shift of attention in Australian education policy, from a recent gaze toward the USA to a new "looking East" (or, more accurately, northwest). However, we are cautious not to overstate the case in respect of Australia's reference societies in education. There is a tension between those that continue to see Finland as an important reference society and the new attention to Shanghai and East Asia more broadly. This contestation over appropriate reference societies turns on the political persuasion of stakeholders, who tend to emphasize systems and policy settings that reflect their preferred reform agendas.

Conclusion

Shanghai's top performance in PISA 2009 provoked a global shock and provides a clear example of new global accountabilities created by international comparisons of educational performance. At the beginning of the so-called Asian century, Shanghai has become a new reference society for some nations, or more accurately a "reference system" given its subnational scale, in the context of an emergent global education policy field. We see here the new spatialities associated with globalization. Nations such as the USA, England, and Australia are using the performance of this reference society for "externalization" and to push internal reform agendas for their respective schooling systems. This new "looking East" is indicative of a postideological framing of education policy (at least in terms of old left and right constructions) and the prevalence of pragmatic policy incrementalism focused on identifying "what works." The functioning of numbers as governing technologies of distance (Porter, 1995) are central to this postideological moment in education policy and help to facilitate the travel of policy ideas around the globe. We note also that these ideas change as they travel.

Our analysis in this chapter has shown how reference societies are being reconstituted through a focus on educational comparison as a mode of governance that involves a "politics of mutual accountability" (Novoa & Yariv-Mashal, 2003), in conjunction with a new international regime of spectacle and surveillance, which we have described as global panopticism. Historically, reference societies have been chosen by particular nations based on factors such as colonial legacies, political alliances, or industrial benchmarking. Today, reference systems are being reconstituted within the global education policy field through comparative performance on international large-scale assessments, which are helping to create this field. This transition can be traced back to the pioneering work of the IEA and its development of international assessments such as TIMSS, but has accelerated considerably with the rise of PISA and its growing recognition and influence around the globe. Further, the OECD's focus on providing PISA as a "policy relevant" tool has helped to enhance the OECD's influence in education, including its relations with nonmember countries such as China. The rise of knowledge capitalism and the associated shift of education policy to a central position within economic policy have also contributed to the OECD's enhanced global reach in education through PISA and related programs. The priority given to policy explanations for PISA performance, as opposed to cultural factors and the effects of structural inequality, is a critical aspect of the OECD's strategy for promoting the explanatory power and usefulness of its educational assessments.

There are two final points that we wish to emphasize in conclusion to this chapter. First, the mutual accountabilities produced through international comparisons in education are facilitated by the creation of a community of global policy actors, nodal actors in global policy networks (Ball, 2012), who share what might be characterized as a global policy habitus (Lingard et al., 2015). These policy actors are fluent in the semantics of globalization and share a policy imagination that views international comparisons of national schooling system performance as being de rigueur.

Second, the strengthened influence of the OECD and PISA has contributed to a culture of testing that has influenced many nations. The spread of testing culture and the growth of data infrastructure in education (Sellar, 2014) have opened new opportunities for providers of educational testing services, creating new markets for what Ball (2012) has called "edu-businesses." In 2009 and 2012, Pearson plc, for example, played a role in the development PISA and is a key provider of services relating to NAPLAN in Australia (Hogan, 2014). Of course, Pearson is also heavily involved in the testing business elsewhere (see Ball, 2012: 124–128) and is by no means the only edu-business capitalizing on opportunities created by the "datafication" of education. We need to recognize, as Ball (2012) has clearly argued, that education policy analysis today must "extend its purview beyond the state and the role of multilateral agencies and NGOs to include transnational business practices" (93). Importantly, edu-businesses with global reach are seeking to position themselves as key players in the politics of mutual accountability in education (Hogan, Sellar, & Lingard, 2015).

We have shown here that, for various reasons, China has become an important reference society for the USA, England, and Australia for the purposes of externalization in national policy developments. At the same time, Shanghai is acting as a significant internal reference system for other schooling systems across China, a form of "indigenization" (Steiner-Khamsi, 2004), which is also looking to the "West" for ideas to reform its tradition of high-pressure exam-driven education. Referencing now works in multiple directions and across multiple spaces simultaneously and is largely about improving quantifiable school system performance. In the so-called global education race, the new Asian frontrunners are being keenly watched by, but are also watching, the other competitors, in the constant search for and justification of policy strategies to remain economically competitive and mutually accountable in an era of global governance in education.

4
CATALYST DATA

Introduction

In this chapter, we move to consideration of how a particular national regime of top-down, test-based accountability has had systemic effects in Australian schooling. This case illustrates how Novoa and Yariv-Mashal's (2003) global politics of mutual accountability plays out within one nation. National testing in Australia has emerged as an annual national spectacle, when the comparative performances of the different state systems of schooling performance on the national test are released and given substantial coverage in the media. Just as nations respond to PISA shocks of various kinds, so too do the various state-based schooling systems in Australia respond to their comparative performance. As with national responses to PISA results, state system responses are linked to concerns about "reputational capital" (Brown & Scase, 1997). This sometimes results in knee-jerk responses rather than more considered policy actions based on sophisticated analyses of the available data.

In previous chapters we have noted the complementarity between national testing and international testing, such as the OECD's PISA and the IEA's TIMSS and PIRLS. The OECD in 2011 conducted a review of assessment and testing in Australia (Santiago, Donaldson, Herman, & Shewbridge, 2011), which is significant to this argument about the complementarity between international and national testing. In this chapter, we look at the national complement in Australia to PISA and TIMSS and PIRLS, namely the National Assessment Program—Literacy and Numeracy (NAPLAN), introduced by the national Labor government in 2008. NAPLAN was established as a national census literacy and numeracy test at Years 3, 5, 7, and 9 for nearly all Australian schools. Related, the federal government also established a national statutory authority—the Australian Curriculum Assessment and Reporting Authority (ACARA)—to oversee this national testing and to create and manage a national website, My School, which makes publicly available the performance of the vast majority of Australian schools on NAPLAN, and enables school performance to be compared against national averages and the performance of similar schools, as measured on an Index of Community Socio-Economic Advantage (ICSEA). One function of ACARA is to manage the National Assessment Program (NAP), of which NAPLAN is the major component. However, PISA, TIMSS, and PIRLS also fit under this program—evidence perhaps of our argument about the complementarity of these two types of testing within the new global mode of mutual accountability in schooling systems, nationally and globally. ACARA also oversees moves towards a national curriculum (Lingard & McGregor, 2014). We note that to this point, NAPLAN has not been based in the Australian P-10 curriculum for English and Maths and the tests are focused on Literacy and Numeracy, rather than specifically on English and Maths. This elision, though, encourages the likelihood of a test-driven curriculum.

While NAPLAN is not a classical high-stakes test, insofar as it does not have immediate and direct effects on students, there is evidence to suggest that some nongovernment and some Catholic schools use test results on NAPLAN as a selection device with collateral effects on students. This chapter aims to demonstrate how the politics surrounding comparative system performance on NAPLAN have made it high stakes for education ministers, policy makers, and school systems, with consequent effects deflected down the line to the work of schools, principals, and teachers. As Baroutsis (2014) has shown, the media also pressure politicians and policy makers by prosecuting an argument that more accountability should be demanded of teachers.

Specifically, this chapter looks at the impact of what we describe as "catalyst data." In the case we analyze, NAPLAN test performance data at state system levels were being used by the federal government for accountability purposes across the various educational jurisdictions within Australia's federal political system. We developed this concept of "catalyst data" from a research project that forms the empirical backdrop to this particular chapter. Catalyst data were described by a senior policy maker interviewed in the project as data that encourage various stakeholders to ask questions about performance in the delivery of government services and, by implication, imply a need to make changes based on answers to these questions:

> We'll show you what's happened in terms of the data and it's a catalyst for you ... people like governments, the media, the community, academics, to ask the question: Why? Why is this so? What happened?

Here, this senior policy maker was referring to state and territory schooling system agreements with the federal government, concerning targeted improvements on national testing, as the *quid-pro-quo* for targeted Australian government funding on literacy and numeracy and for schools serving low socioeconomic communities.

While the concept of catalyst data was developed in an Australian research project, we argue that it has wider applicability and indeed is useful for considering some of the effects of what Ranson (2003) calls neoliberal accountability, which is illustrated in the following two chapters with reference to the North American context. PISA shocks, for example, might be thought of as involving catalyst data. Within nations, this mode of accountability is also linked to state restructuring and the so-called governance turn. As Webb (2011) suggests, "Neoliberalism centralizes and decentralizes the state when governments develop accountability 'interventions' to control public institutions" (736). This state restructuring plays out in vernacular ways in different political systems. The result is perhaps a global convergence in education policy at the discursive level, rather than implementation and practice levels. In this process, data become central to the structuring of the system; in effect they become the system structured around new state-school relationships central to neoliberal accountability.

In the Australian case, which is the focus of this chapter, what we see are new nation-state/provincial-state relationships in schooling, constituted through new data relationships and flows. In considering this phenomenon in England, Ozga (2009) observes,

> Data production and management were and are essential to the new governance turn; constant comparison is its symbolic feature, as well as a distinctive mode of operation. As a policy instrument data grew—and continue to grow—in strength, speed and scope. The shift to governance is, in fact, heavily dependent on knowledge and information, which play a pivotal role both in the pervasiveness of governance and in allowing the development of its dispersed, distributed and disaggregated form.
>
> (150)

The concept of catalyst data helps us to understand the pivotal role of data in new modes of governance. In science, a catalyst is commonly understood to be a substance that facilitates and sometimes speeds up a chemical reaction between other compounds, while remaining unchanged by this reaction itself. There is an obvious analogy here with the way in which (high-stakes) testing data facilitate systemic effects in schooling, particularly through comparisons and "reactions" between systems. These systemic effects are also deflected down the line to schools and teacher practices. However, catalysis also refers more broadly to processes of dissolution. In our use of the term "catalyst data," we want to echo both the technical and broader senses of the term. Performance data have catalyzed media and subsequent systemic reactions. In the context of Australia's federal system, such data are also contributing to a partial dissolution of the authority of state and territory education systems, by constituting a national space of measurement, comparison, and the associated allocation of funding. Here we see the emergence of a nascent national system of schooling, as an effect of the impact of globalization upon schooling policy in Australia and contributing to the creation of new spatialities associated with globalization (Amin, 2002). We note how this move was perhaps stronger under the previous federal Labor governments, but suggest that it continues under the conservative Abbott government elected in 2013. While this government has continued to focus on NAPLAN as a central driver of federal involvement in schooling and their so-called Students First policy, they have not continued the equity and redistributive focus of some of the previous Labor governments' policies (2007–2013).

There is a considerable body of research literature (for example Nichols & Berliner, 2007; Stobart, 2008; Taubman, 2009; Darling-Hammond, 2010) demonstrating the perverse effects of high-stakes testing upon teachers' pedagogical practices and upon students (Jones et al., 1999). We use the term "perverse," following its use in that literature and by our research interviewees in the research project that underpins this chapter. Both usages refer to the anti-educational effects that result when performance measures become targets for systems and schools. Performance targets potentially distort the work of teachers and schools. However, we do not mean to imply that these effects are simply an aberration in new accountability regimes; rather, we see them as almost the "new norm." They are endemic to these new modes of educational accountability.

Our focus is on the usage of national literacy and numeracy testing (NAPLAN) as a performance measure for state and territory education systems. Federal government "reward funding" has been allocated based on systemic NAPLAN performance in relation to targets agreed in a bilateral fashion between the federal government and the states and territories. The use of NAPLAN for this purpose facilitates comparative analysis of systemic performance and thus offers some potential to affect the reputational capital of the different jurisdictions. We examine the catalytic effects of this form of accountability on three state education systems (Queensland, New South Wales, and Victoria), where we will document some perverse outcomes of states setting and attempting to achieve performance targets and, in so doing, seeking to manage their reputational capital. However, the effects of this are not simply played out in and between schooling systems, but ultimately have real salience in the daily lives of teachers and students.

While Australian education systems provide the case for this chapter, we see this commensurate space of comparative measurement produced through national testing as analogous to that which has been constituted by LSAs. These also encourage the intensification of testing within national and provincial educational systems. While our focus is on the systemic effects of what has become in effect a high-stakes testing regime in Australian schooling, the research reported here has salience to the many nations around the globe that have introduced national testing programs associated with particular accountability, funding, and improvement regimes (for example Race to the Top under President Obama in the USA). The chapter focuses on the effects of high-stakes testing and the audit culture on policy makers and politicians within and across education jurisdictions, using Australia's federal system as an example.

The cases reported here are interesting insofar as what we are dealing with are intergovernmental relationships of mutual accountability within Australia's complex federal political structure. This case illustrates how political structures mediate neoliberal modes of accountability, as we also illustrate with regards to the Canadian cases reported on in the following chapters. The USA has also made a move to a common core for curriculum, accompanied by testing, but neither is imposed by the federal government (see Savage & O'Connor, 2014). The descriptor "national" in Australian education policy means a consensus or a compromise across the national and state and territory governments. In USA federalism, even the word "national" is a step too far, and thus talk of a "common core" in respect of curriculum. Of course, there is a total absence of such talk within Canadian educational federalism. While Canada has a federal political structure, it has no federal department of education nor a federal minister. The mode of accountability we discuss in this chapter is thus mediated in different ways in Canada, as we demonstrate in the cases of race and gender equity that are the focus of Chapters 5 and 6 respectively. In England, with a unitary form of government, the restructuring of the system via data flows has witnessed a strengthening of the hand of the national government and a weakening of the hand of local authorities in schooling (Ozga, 2009; Lawn, 2013), a good example of the ways in which new modes of accountability are linked to new center-periphery relationships within a particular political structure.

In what follows, we provide a two-part case study of policy developments in response to the national reform agenda in education and outcomes on NAPLAN. The first unit of analysis is the relationship between the federal government and three states in negotiating performance targets linked to reward payments for improved literacy and numeracy outcomes. At the heart of this unit of analysis is the interface between the Council of Australian Governments (COAG) Reform Council (subsequently abolished by the Abbott Conservative federal government), the three state systems of schooling, and the federal Department of Education, Employment and Workplace Relations (now Department of Education). The COAG Reform Council was created to monitor the pace of achievement of a range of national policies. We document some of the perverse effects that have resulted from tying federal funding, and very public media reporting, to systemic achievement in NAPLAN testing.

The second unit of analysis is the Queensland system and the ramifications of perceived poor state performance on the 2008 NAPLAN tests. This resulted in the commissioning of the Masters Review of Queensland primary schooling, the subsequent intensification of audit regimes (for example the introduction of Teaching and Learning Audits of all Queensland government schools), and the creation of statewide targets for improvement on NAPLAN. While the state Labor government that instigated this review and policy was defeated in late 2012, the subsequent Conservative government retained and strengthened the audit and accountability usage of NAPLAN data through the creation of a specific School Improvement Unit and each administrative region now has an assistant director focused on performance management. We focus on the work of one education region in Queensland and interviews conducted with staff there to show the effects of both national and state pressures for improvement. Overall, this unit of analysis demonstrates how national testing and audit regimes have become high stakes for state education systems, in the first instance by demonstrating effects across systems, while in the second demonstrating effects within the organizational structure of one system. Here we see catalyst data at work and how politics have ensured that NAPLAN has become high stakes.

Our analysis draws on approximately 50 research interviews with: (1) senior policy makers in state and federal systems and in relevant statutory authorities at state and federal levels; (2) personnel in international organizations, including the Organisation for Economic Co-operation and Development (OECD) and the International Association for the Evaluation of Educational Achievement (IEA); and (3) researchers and academics involved in debates about national and international testing agendas. To ensure anonymity, we have not named interviewees or their positions. We use quotes from these research interviews throughout this chapter.

In the following section of the chapter, we briefly revisit the audit and accountability literatures, some of which has been referred to in Chapter 1, and set the broad context of their place in education system reforms. We start with a focus on the emergent global education policy field that is being constituted through international comparative testing, which we have considered in some detail in Chapter 2. We then provide a brief descriptive account of Australian developments, which constitute a specific case of a more general policy development in schooling systems around the world; what we might see as a vernacular expression of a globalized education policy discourse. The two units of analysis dealing with the impact of NAPLAN testing as high stakes for systems are then outlined. We end by drawing out implications for thinking about similar developments in other national educational contexts and we link these to the effects of complementary international testing.

Situating the Analysis

The macro-political setting of both cases is the meta-policy of neoliberalism and related state restructurings (that is, the new public management and subsequent network governance considered in Chapter 1), as they work their ways out in educational policies within nations. However, a central point here is that these policies and state restructures, the so-called governance turn, have become globalized policy discourses associated with and advanced by international organizations such as the OECD. They are also linked to, and are expressions of, globalization in the period following the end of the Cold War and the emergence of a global economy framed by the precepts of neoliberalism. Think for example, of how both China and Vietnam, putatively communist regimes, now speak of "market socialism" to describe their economic approach. There is now research arguing that as part of these developments we are seeing the emergence of a globalized education policy field, using Bourdieu's concept of fields (Lingard & Rawolle, 2011), and that this field is being constituted through a "globalizing empiricism" (Torrance, 2006). As noted in Chapter 2, international measures of the comparative performance of schooling systems (for example the OECD's PISA and the IEA's TIMMS and PIRLS) are creating this global field as a commensurate space of measurement. Indeed, one of our international interviewees explained that through the expansion of the global coverage of PISA, the OECD aims "to have the broadest possible picture of the global talent pool."

Sassen (2007) has argued that globalization can be seen as the creation of a global infrastructure that facilitates the flows associated with the multiple circuits of the global economy. We see the creation of a global space of measurement of the comparative performance of national schooling systems as an important component part of this global infrastructure. National testing in Australia, and comparisons of individual school performance against statistically similar schools facilitated by the federal government's My School website, is likewise helping to constitute a national system of schooling through its technical infrastructure. Data infrastructures are thus centrally important in the global politics of mutual accountability in education. Grek et al. (2009a) and Lawn and Grek (2012) have argued similarly about the use of policy as numbers to create a European educational policy space and have documented the interweaving of these supranational and national policy developments.

The development of NAPLAN in Australia is also part of a globalized education policy discourse that argues that standards can only be driven up by such testing (Stobart, 2008). Furthermore, the development of national high-stakes testing around the globe is driven by and complements international testing programs and comparisons. One interviewee explained, in relation to the different functions of PISA and NAPLAN, that "you need to have those perspectives: a perspective that looks inward (NAPLAN) and one that looks outward (PISA)." This interviewee added that internal measures only register national improvement or decline and, therefore, comparative international measures are necessary to benchmark this performance and provide a broader comparative indication of improvement or decline.

Related to these developments have been a number of other phenomena, including the rise of talk about evidence-based (and evidence-informed) policy (Head, 2008; Wiseman, 2010), policy as numbers (Rose, 1999; Ozga, 2009; Lingard, 2011), and new forms of state accountability, as part of what Power (1997) has called the "audit explosion." Indeed, Power (1997) sees the hollowing out of the state associated with new public management—its steering at a distance approach—as actually generating "a demand for audit and other forms of evaluation and inspection to fill the hole" (44); he refers to this as a new form of the "regulatory state" (52). The subsequent development of network governance consisting of a complex mix of hierarchical and horizontal relationships, involving both the state and private sector (Ball & Junemann, 2012), has both depended upon and contributed to the significance of data and numbers. This restructuring has also opened up possibilities for greater involvement of edu-businesses in policy and data work (Ball, 2012). We return to this issue in the final chapter of the book.

An interesting literature has emerged on educational accountability, stretching from the critical and theoretical (for example Ranson, 2003, 2012; Suspitsyna, 2010; Ravitch, 2011; Webb, 2011) to the philosophical (for example Biesta, 2004; Harvey, 2010) and the more normative and policy pragmatic (for example Sahlberg 2010). Suspitsyna (2010) sees accountability mechanisms in education as technologies of governance, which *pace* Foucault have governmentality effects through ensuring that policy makers and principals and teachers in schools become self-governing. This position has been outlined in some detail by Rose (1999) in his account of neoliberal governance and the self-capitalizing and self-responsibilizing individual. Webb (2011) argues that at the broader societal level we are transiting from what Foucault called a "disciplinary society" towards what Deleuze (1995) described as "control societies," with the latter evident in the reality of ongoing incessant measurement and assessment. (As an aside, we note how prescient Deleuze was in commenting on the rise of performance pay for teachers, the emergence of continuous assessment, and the reconstitution of education as a business.) These numbers also provide a way for the state to manage risk, an aspect of what Thrift (2005) calls "knowing capitalism"; that is, capitalism becoming a project of knowing itself, with data being central to this self-knowledge. The next stage of this development is the enhanced influence of "big data."

In line with Webb (2011), we understand testing, audit, and accountability regimes as mechanisms tending toward the logic of "control societies" (Deleuze, 1995), enabling the continuous assessment of students, teachers, and schools and giving rise to feedback loops through which education systems are continually modulated in response to test results and their public representations (see for example Lyotard, 1984). Indeed, there is a way in which these data constitute the system and keep it operant. The emergence of adaptive learning technologies perhaps marks the fullest realization of this tendency to date, and is echoed in the move to online testing that will be introduced in Australia with NAPLAN and with the OECD's PISA in the future. In each of our units of analysis, we attend to the practices through which data are constituted and represented and acknowledge how data assist in making the nation and schooling systems legible for governing (Scott, 1998).

Statistical and scientific practices that inform and underpin high-stakes testing regimes such as NAPLAN are translated into representations that are conveyed by different media (for example charts, news stories, political narratives, reports). One interviewee described how "an optics problem" arises where visual representation of data renders opaque crucial decisions relating to its collection and analysis. Rose (1999) observes that single numbers in policy accounts do political work in hiding the technologies that have gone into their construction. Rose also argues that numbers help constitute the world, as well as represent it. As with single policy numbers, and following Latour (1999), the representation of testing results can be understood to involve a series of translations that simplify the phenomenon being tested (for example students' literacy skills) (see Gorur, 2013). This involves a process of reduction to generate standardized and comparable representations with an amplified capacity to have an effect as fact or evidence. As Porter (1995) has noted, "There is a strong incentive to prefer precise and standardizable measures to highly accurate ones" (29). For example, the My School website represents school performance on NAPLAN testing using color coding to indicate whether results for particular cohorts are better, worse, or on par with statistically similar cohorts. A complex technical process for determining levels of achievement, full of ambivalent analytical decisions, is ultimately represented in terms of "green" for good and "red" for bad. Through the high-profile media reporting of NAPLAN results, this process of translation, and attendant "optics problems," contribute to an affective politics, which manifests, for example, as moral panics in relation to declining literacy and numeracy standards or a "nervousness" amongst senior policy makers and politicians (Massumi, 2005; Protevi, 2009; Sellar, 2014). This is the effect of catalyst data.

We are particularly interested in the ways that representations and readings of NAPLAN data give rise to the emotions of anxiousness and nervousness among policy makers in response to media and political pressures for their system to be "seen" as improving and achieving at a high standard in comparison with other systems. Testing becomes high stakes for systems in part through this modulation of affectively registered pressure on policy makers. We also suggest that a similar phenomenon is evident in national (and provincial) comparative performance on international measures such as PISA, TIMSS, and PIRLS; for example, the various PISA "shocks" that have occurred in national systems (for example, Ertl, 2006; Takayama, 2008; Grek, 2009a) and that we have analyzed in Chapter 2. High-stakes testing is thus linked to an affective politics through which the work of educational governance is increasingly operationalized within education systems in control societies. This is one vector of governmentality and the self-governing of policy makers, school leaders, and teachers; what Rose (1999) calls "self-responsibilizing."

Contextualizing the Case

Australia has a federal political structure. Section 51 of the Constitution outlines the powers of the federal government and those not listed are regarded as residual powers of the states and territories. Schooling is one such residual power. During World War II the federal government took over income tax raising powers from the states, resulting in the high degree of vertical fiscal imbalance in Australian federalism; that is, the federal government has the bulk of the revenue, while the states have the responsibility for the delivery of large and expensive public policy domains such as schooling, health, and policing. This has often led to funding/compliance trade-offs between the federal government and the states. Since the centralist policies of the federal Whitlam Labor government (1972–1975), the peak moment of progressive Keynesianism in Australia, all public policy domains have had a complex mix of federal and state monies, involvements, and policies, with the nomenclature of "national," as noted earlier, often signifying a policy domain in which agreements have been achieved between federal and state governments. Since its formation in 1992, the Council of Australian Governments (COAG) (consisting of the prime minister, state premiers and territory chief ministers, and the president of the Australian Local Government Association) has been the primary forum for managing intergovernmental relations and national policy reform. Since the 1930s, there have been intergovernmental councils in most policy domains that cut across federal and state jurisdictions. The Standing Council on School Education and Early Childhood (SCSEEC), the current intergovernmental council for education, consisting of the federal education minister along with state and territory colleagues, was established in 2012 out of previous councils.

The significance of COAG has waxed and waned since its creation, but it took on a reinvigorated role after the election of the federal Rudd Labor government in 2007 (Carroll & Head, 2009). As one senior policy maker at the national level noted in an interview: "I think the standout for Rudd is that he actually went to an election on these issues" and "he won the election in November [2007] and held his first COAG in December. It was just astonishing. Then he held four a year for the next two years. Then he fell off the wagon." During the 2007 election campaign Rudd argued that "cooperative federalism" was important, as was the advancement of a range of national policy reforms, to ensure the global competitiveness and increased productivity of the Australian economy and to avoid blame shifting between the states and the federal government. This was intimately linked to the human capital framing of contemporary schooling policy. At that time, the pursuit of cooperative federalism was aided by the fact that there were Labor governments in all states and territories, a situation that has subsequently changed. From 2009, a new Intergovernmental Agreement on Federal Financial Relations (IAFFR) took effect, with the aim of reducing the plethora of specific purpose payments (Section 96 grants) to the states through consolidation of these payments into single larger payments. This gave the states more policy autonomy, but also brought audit pressures associated with accountability frameworks negotiated with the federal government. The COAG Reform Council is the statutory authority with responsibilities for assessment and reporting of state performance in relation to the IAFFR. We note that it was abolished by the Conservative Abbott federal government soon after it came to power in 2013.

Also pivotal to Rudd's 2007 election campaign was his commitment to a so-called Education Revolution, which was implemented through a range of national policies in schooling, including a National Curriculum, national testing (NAPLAN), a new transparency and accountability agenda evident in the creation of the My School website, and the establishment of ACARA. The Australian Institute of Teaching and School Leadership (AITSL) was also created to establish national standards and promote excellence in the teaching profession. As part of the broader IAFFR, a National Education Agreement was signed for schooling, outlining national outcomes, targets, and performance indicators to which the states and territories were party. The states also entered into National Partnership Agreements with the federal government in respect of specific schooling projects in three areas: Literacy and Numeracy, Teacher Quality, and Low SES School Communities. These National Partnerships included both facilitation payments to fund reform and reward payments, which were paid when targets set for improvement on NAPLAN were met. In schooling, NAPLAN was the key central performance indicator for the National Agreement and the primary data set for the establishment of reward targets for the National Partnership for Literacy and Numeracy. Our two units of analysis relate to this particular National Partnership.

Systemic Effects of Federal Funding Based on NAPLAN Performance

On the April 19, 2011, the *Age*, Victoria's daily broadsheet newspaper, announced that the "state flunks its own literacy, numeracy tests" and described how Victoria's schools had "overwhelmingly failed" to make progress toward targets for improving literacy and numeracy in schools, which were agreed to bilaterally with the federal government as the accountability mechanism for federal funding provided through National Partnerships. While the headline implied that Victorian schools were underperforming, the article itself conceded that Victoria had set "ambitious reward targets" and that its "failure" did not mean that it had performed poorly in comparison with other states. However, the headlines ultimately had the greatest impact on public perception. As one interviewee from the Victorian education department explained:

> I think the fact that in the end we performed much the same as all the other higher performing jurisdictions, *but it didn't present that way*, that we didn't get funding because we had a more difficult reward framework. Yet all you see in the headlines is that we did badly and others did well, it's a lot of reputational damage, so a lot of nervousness I think in preparing for this year.

At issue here are the processes through which targets were set and progress assessed in relation to the National Partnership for Literacy and Numeracy. While a core theme in the "Education Revolution" has been to increase transparency and accountability, the negotiation of reward funding frameworks for this National Partnership was not a transparent process for systems. Another interviewee in the Victorian education department explained, "It was all secret. There was no transparency around what Victoria was negotiating with the Commonwealth and what other jurisdictions were negotiating. You had no idea of whether what you were putting forward was in any way comparable with anyone else." This had important implications for setting targets and for the reporting and comparison of outcomes.

The opacity of framework negotiations appears reasonable given the intent of the National Partnership was that these frameworks negotiated by each jurisdiction would *not* be comparable. While the National Education Agreement explicitly specifies national outcomes against which state and territory governments would be assessed and compared based on their performance, the National Partnerships were bilateral agreements and "the diverse reform strategies being implemented in each state and territory are not intended to support a comparative analysis of performance" (COAG Reform Council, 2011: xiv). However, upon release of the COAG Reform Council assessments in 2011, systemic performance was compared in reductive and simplistic media accounts, subsequently raising the stakes for systems in terms of protecting their reputations. The key issues raised by interviewees in relation to this reporting of the National Partnership process included the different levels of "ambition" reflected in the targets set by each jurisdiction; the diverse nature of targets across jurisdictions; and disparities in the baseline data against which achievement was measured. We address each of these issues here to demonstrate the game playing that can be associated with target setting.

Under the terms of the National Partnership Agreement for Literacy and Numeracy, each jurisdiction was required to develop an Implementation Plan that formed the basis for bilateral negotiation of their reward funding framework with the federal government. This included setting targets in relation to four mandated measures of NAPLAN performance and negotiating unique local targets for improvement in other areas. We will focus on the mandated measures here. While there was flexibility for each system to set reward frameworks that reflected their particular circumstances and broad objectives, the National Partnership specified that targets needed to be ambitious and the Australian Council for Educational Research (ACER) was commissioned to assess the level of ambition. Notably, ACER considered that Victoria's proposed targets were not sufficiently ambitious and encouraged revision. One interviewee noted, "ACER, in fact, said our targets were not ambitious enough and we needed to push them up, which we did. Everybody signed these off and, of course, bingo, we didn't achieve."

Achievement in relation to the four mandated measures of NAPLAN performance was assessed for a set of schools nominated by each jurisdiction, with states and territories putting forward quite different sample sizes (see Table 4.1). States and territories also negotiated the specific data that would be used to measure their achievement. For example, Victoria opted for each year level (3, 5, 7, and 9) and area (literacy and numeracy) to be assessed in relation to each of the four measures (32 targets in total). In contrast, New South Wales opted to aggregate Year 3 and 5 results, across both literacy and numeracy, for a single assessment in relation to each of the four measures (4 targets in total). Queensland negotiated a total of 16 targets. Table 4.1 provides an overview of the reward frameworks negotiated by each of these systems. Tables 4.2–4.4 illustrate, in relation to the first mandated measure against which targets were set, the different structures of the targets, the different baseline data sets, and the results and assessments. An assessment of "A" was awarded where performance equaled or exceeded targets; a "B" was awarded where performance exceeded the baseline but did not reach the target; and a "C" was awarded when performance was at or below the baseline (COAG Reform Council, 2011: 9).

Victoria's nomination of 32 targets and a large sample of schools reflected a perception within the system that it had strong capacities in data gathering and performance measurement, and this was manifest as an intent to enter into the spirit of the federal government's transparency agenda and to lead by example in the National Partnership negotiation. A Victorian interviewee stated, "[T]here was a sense that we should do this properly, not play the game, not game the system first up." In contrast, the aggregated performance measures nominated by New South Wales, and the fewer resulting targets, were perceived to obfuscate performance rather than render it transparent. One interviewee wryly noted that

TABLE 4.1 2010 reward frameworks, New South Wales, Victoria, and Queensland (compiled from COAG Reform Council, 2011: 99)

Participating schools/ students	Assessed students and baseline year	Target groups	Target calculation
NSW — 4 targets for mandated measures				
147 schools 43 825 students 4% of NSW students	Measures 1–3: 12 442 Measure 4: 1 098 Baseline 2008	Years 3 and 5 Literacy *or* Numeracy Targets are aggregations of year levels and domains	Measures 1, 2, and 4: percent decrease in proportions at or below, or below Measure 3: scale point improvement
Victoria — 32 targets for mandated measures				
492 schools 184 506 students 22% of Vic students	Measure 1–3: 15 742 Measure 4: 335 Baseline: 2009	Years 3, 5, 7, and 9 Literacy *and* Numeracy	Measures 1–4: percent improvement in scores, based on 2009 gap between participating students and all Victorian students
Queensland — 16 targets for mandated measures				
279 schools 120 541 students 17% of Qld students	Measure 1–3: 12 745 Measure 4: 1 388 Baseline 2008	Years 3 and 5 Literacy *and* Numeracy	Measure 1–4: percent improvement on a projected decline, based on historical trend

TABLE 4.2 Mandated measure 1: New South Wales, targets and performance (compiled from COAG Reform Council, 2011: 19)

Target group	Baseline 2008	Target 2010	Result 2010	Assessment	Participation

Target calculation: A decrease of 5.0 percent of the proportion of students below the national minimum standard (equivalent to an increase of 0.6 percentage points in the proportion of students at or above the national minimum standard).

| Year 3 and Year 5 Reading and Numeracy | 88.5% | 89.1% | 90.5% | A | 98.9% (+0.2 ppts) |

TABLE 4.3 Mandated measure 1: Victoria, targets and performance (compiled from COAG Reform Council, 2011: 27)

Target group	Baseline 2009	Target 2010	Result 2010	Assessment	Participation

Target calculation: An improvement in the proportion of students at or above the national minimum standard equivalent to a decrease of 25 percent of the 2009 gap between students in participating schools and all students.

Year 3 Reading	92.3%	92.98%	91.5%	C	91.9% (−1.7 ppts)
Year 5 Reading	89.2%	90.20%	88.3%	C	93.1% (−0.6 ppts)
Year 7 Reading	91.4%	92.23%	92.9%	A	93.2% (−0.3 ppts)
Year 9 Reading	87.6%	88.95%	86.9%	C	87.5% (−0.9%)
Year 3 Numeracy	90.2%	91.10%	92.3%	A	91.5% (−1.5 ppts)
Year 5 Numeracy	92.8%	93.50%	92.3%	C	93.0% (0.0 ppts)
Year 7 Numeracy	93.7%	94.25%	94.1%	B 72.7%	92.8% (−0.4 ppts)
Year 9 Numeracy	94.2%	94.70%	90.9%	C	87.7% (−0.7 ppts)

TABLE 4.4 Mandated measure 1: Queensland, targets and performance (compiled from COAG Reform Council, 2011: 35)

Target group	Baseline 2008	Target 2010	Result 2010	Assessment	Participation

Target calculation: An improvement of 50 percent on trends observed from historical testing in the proportion of students at or above the national minimum standard.

Year 3 Reading	82.1%	81.5%	88.9%	A	95.2% (−2.5 ppts)
Year 5 Reading	78.0%	77.6%	81.2%	A	96.0% (−1.8 ppts)
Year 3 Numeracy	86.0%	85.9%	91.1%	A	95.0% (−1.9 ppts)
Year 5 Numeracy	85.1%	84.0%	88.4%	A	95.5% (−1.8 ppts)

"more aggregation leaves more flexibility for achievement." For example, it is not possible to determine exactly which aspect of literacy or numeracy across Years 3 and 5 contributed to the small increases achieved in New South Wales, or indeed if declines in some areas were masked by relatively substantial gains in others.

Different jurisdictions were also measured against different baselines: "The original establishment of the rewards framework was done on the basis of one year of NAPLAN data. . . . Nobody really understood how NAPLAN was going to behave, what it would show." New South Wales and Queensland used 2008 NAPLAN data as a baseline; however, Victoria used the 2009 data set. There was significant improvement nationally between 2008 and 2009, raising the possibility of an equating error between the two data sets: "that equating was not right, therefore everyone improves. So this ended up with, so with the COAG report saying Victoria are not getting funding . . . it really had nothing to do whatsoever with improvement really." Arguably, the 2009 data set provided a stronger baseline against which Victorian achievement in 2010 was compared. This made further improvement difficult: "the higher you are up the scale of performance the less it [NAPLAN performance] moves. It's a 'ceilinged' instrument." Aside from differences in the bilateral negotiations of targets by each system, the measurement of achievement against different baselines introduced a fundamental incommensurability that was largely elided in media reporting and in subsequent perceptions of comparative systemic performance.

Ultimately, Victoria's performance was variable in relation to its 32 targets and it received five "A"s, 10 "B"s, and 17 "C"s. New South Wales received three "A"s and a "B" for progress made in relation to its four targets. Queensland's achievement exceeded each of the targets it set and the COAG Reform Council granted them an assessment of straight "A"s. There were problems with this reporting of outcomes using "A"–"C" ratings, as described by one interviewee involved in the assessment process:

> [W]hen we say Queensland got all As and Victoria got mainly Cs, anybody who picked a report up like that would say gee, Queensland is way better than Victoria and Victoria must be terrible and that isn't the case because they're not comparative.

While the detailed performance reporting produced by the COAG Reform Council clearly specifies important differences in the reward funding frameworks negotiated by each jurisdiction, and the differences in data sets and measures, the "A"–"C" reporting enabled simplistic and comparative media reporting that had damaging effects for the spirit of the COAG reform agenda and the reputation of jurisdictions such as Victoria. This also had implications for the ways in which states and territories subsequently engaged with these kinds of processes:

> It's that "gotcha" thing and then we, it's almost like then you lose the jurisdictions . . . and this is what the [Intergovernmental Agreement] . . . is, it is meant to improve performance. It's meant to improve and if there is too much focus on the "gotcha", which there is in the media, then what we

find in our relationships with jurisdictions, which are incredibly important, is they go undercover and then they'll argue the toss about every small . . . every point and they'll totally not, it's not the spirit that you're trying to look for. You can really understand from their point of view.

Media reports of these assessments have encouraged systems to become more cynical and to focus on the comparative representation of performance over and above substantive improvement. For example, one interviewee from the New South Wales system told us that in relation to comparative data:

> We all use results as it suits us, and it was of concern to New South Wales when we noticed our relative decline in performance, that Western Australia was suddenly up there above us. All we could come up with was sampling error. We did talk to ACER to really interrogate their processes and it was revealed that yes, they didn't actually include remote schools in the sample.

We can see here how NAPLAN has become high stakes because of these accountability and comparison pressures and political, policy maker, and media responses. For Australia's schooling systems, this has included an intensification of debate over technical issues, including the application of political pressure to influence decision-making about testing methodologies and analysis. This is linked with efforts to massage results in order to preserve or improve public perception and thus to protect reputational capital.

"Gaming" the intended spirit of the reforms—that is, the setting and pursuit of ambitious targets for improvement—has been a significant perverse effect of this process. One interviewee explained that "as soon as you attach [performance measures] to rewards you create perverse incentives." For example, differences in the nature of the targets set by each jurisdiction were substantial. For each of the mandated measures Victoria set targets to reduce the gap between students in nominated schools and all students in the system by 25 percent (see Table 4.3). In contrast, Queensland set targets to reduce the rate of decline in performance (2006–2009), halving the gap between the baseline data and the projected decline in performance by 2010 (see Table 4.4). These targets were considered to be less ambitious than Victoria's, with one interviewee from another jurisdiction describing them as "not going backwards targets." Another interviewee suggested that the targets set by Queensland reflected a breakdown of the mutual accountability that state and federal governments shared for ensuring the integrity of the process:

> [A]lthough you could say gee, look at what Queensland did, in some regards I would put very much the responsibility back on the Commonwealth. It was the Commonwealth Department that agreed that Queensland could have these targets. Queensland didn't just say we've got them. . . . [I]f you

want to have a reform agenda well, you have to put the weight on accountability very much to make it effective. Then the weight goes very much in this instance I would suggest also on the Commonwealth's role.

While Queensland set targets that ultimately served its interests in terms of how its performance was assessed and reported, this distortion of the process was sanctioned by the federal government through its bilateral negotiation. The fact that Queensland benefited in terms of funding and public perceptions has led bureaucrats in other systems to believe that the National Partnership process and similar accountability mechanisms will be more explicitly "gamed" in the future. One interviewee argued that, for systems such as Victoria, "there will be a different dynamic and they will be much more hardnosed and much more cynical about playing the game." Another interviewee observed that now the process is perceived to be "definitely a game. It's a serious one because if Victoria doesn't meet these targets . . . we miss a lot of funding."

This analysis highlights a number of important issues. First, media reporting of systemic NAPLAN performance is placing pressure on policy makers in systems. This media reporting simplifies results into national league tables and is not particularly data literate, but as a senior politician noted to one of us, this means politicians and systems have to be seen to respond. In this way NAPLAN has become high stakes for systems and not just for the students sitting the tests, or the teachers and schools increasingly held responsible for their performance. These high stakes are manifest in the nervousness of policy makers, felt in anticipation of upcoming rounds of testing, and in new political pressures to address performance "crises." In response to this media and political pressure, and the significant funding tied to outcomes, "gaming" the National Partnerships is a rational and attractive option for states and territories. Our argument is that these features of this accountability mechanism have ensured that NAPLAN has become high stakes with consequences throughout systems and into the everyday lives of principals, teachers, and students. In the next case we examine in greater depth how system-wide performance "crises" have translated into an intensification of audit and accountability within state systems.

Systemic Effects of Poor NAPLAN Performance in Queensland

Queensland performed comparatively poorly in the 2008 NAPLAN assessment that was used as a baseline for the National Partnerships reward funding. This caused a political furor in the state, with huge media coverage by the *Courier-Mail*, the Queensland daily newspaper, and also by radio and television. There was also extensive national media coverage documenting state system performances and Queensland's poor comparative performance. We can see this as a "NAPLAN shock" driven by catalyst data. The immediate political response was for the then Labor premier, Anna Bligh, to appoint in December 2008 Professor Geoff Masters, CEO of ACER, to review the literacy, numeracy, and science performance of Queensland primary school students. Science performance was included because of the apparently poor performance of Queensland students in the 2007 TIMSS. Premier's Bligh's central role can be seen as an attempt to protect the reputational capital of Queensland, which branded itself as the "smart state" during the long period of Labor governments from 1989 until 2013 (see Adie, 2008), signifying a move away from the old "Deep North" anti-intellectual construction of the state. Masters provided "Preliminary Advice" to the Premier on January 25, 2009, and the final report, *A Shared Challenge Improving Literacy, Numeracy and Science Learning in Queensland Primary Schools* (hereafter the *Masters Report*) was released in April 2009 (Masters, 2009a, 2009b).

In the Preliminary Advice, one can see the political imperative and its temporality driving the need to quickly improve Queensland's test results on NAPLAN. For example, Recommendation 4 of the report states: "That last year's NAPLAN assessment materials—including test booklets, administration manual, marking guides, and details of the performances of last year's cohort on each test question—be made available for all Year 3, 5 and 7 teachers at the start of the 2009 school year for use in establishing students' current levels of literacy and numeracy development and to assist in identifying learning needs" (Masters, 2009a: 5). This is the use of NAPLAN materials as a "classroom resource" and the text suggested that, "These materials also may provide students with some useful test taking experience" (Masters, 2009a: 6). This is one common result of high-stakes testing, a focus on improving test literacy and teaching to the test, which at best is only a surrogate measure of the quality of schooling. To be fair, though, in both the Preliminary Advice and in the *Masters Report* there were recommendations for longer-term changes that reflected the temporalities associated with real and deeper educational change. What we are acknowledging here is the disjunction between political (and policy) time, framed by media responses and electoral cycles, and the much more protracted time of real and effective educational and school change. The Preliminary Advice recommended that the state government set a target so that "Queensland primary school students were performing at the level of students in the highest performing states in literacy, numeracy and science within the next three years." Importantly, in the context of negotiating the state's National Partnership reward framework, this recommendation was for comparative improvement. We note as well the methodological naiveté in this recommendation, as it assumes (erroneously) that Queensland is in sociodemographic and socioeconomic terms a commensurate unit of measurement with other states. This is most patently not the case.

We see in these developments a clear expression of the tight temporality of a political imperative and one with the added legitimacy of an expert review. This political imperative was obvious at the Premier's launch of the *Masters Report*, when in response to questions and discussion about why Queensland had done poorly on the 2008 NAPLAN, she explained that all of that evidence and associated explanations might well be true, including ones proffered by one of the authors of this book, but that there was a political urgency for her to do something, particularly in response to huge and negative media coverage, which was suggesting a problem with Queensland schools. The Premier noted that in this context she had a political problem and had to act, thus commissioning the Masters review—a good exemplification of the "mediatization" of contemporary education policy (Lingard & Rawolle, 2004).

Structural reforms have also followed from Queensland's poor NAPLAN performance in 2008. For example, from 2015 Year 7 has been moved into secondary schooling in Queensland, bringing schooling structures into line with those in both Victoria and New South Wales, while the earlier introduction of a new Preparatory year also aimed to help align the ages of Queensland students with those in other states. This appears to be an acknowledgement by the Premier that there were structural explanations for the 2008 performance. The government's commitment to the implementation of all Recommendations in the *Masters Report* also seems to suggest a commitment to broader change beyond the immediate enhancement of Queensland's comparative NAPLAN performance. What we see here, perhaps, is a mix of political tactics aimed at short-term test score improvement, as well as longer-term strategies. We also see an interesting mix of political and effective educational change temporalities.

These political tactics have had multiple effects, when placed in the context of the national reform agenda and the use of NAPLAN for allocating National Partnership reward funding. There have been perverse and gaming effects in the context of the Queensland system, with schools having quickly to improve Queensland's NAPLAN performance to meet the time frame of the political agenda. NAPLAN thus became high stakes for the system in Queensland with effects rippling down the line to regions and to schools. The impact of this catalyst data was very clear in the account provided by an interviewee at the federal level:

> I felt the interesting thing about Premier Bligh's response is that she did it on the basis of the 2008 NAPLAN ... across Australia everybody knew that Queensland looked very different from other States. I think Queensland would like to see itself close to and in comparison with States such as Victoria and New South Wales.... She brought in Professor Geoff Masters and did a review.... We can't say the Review had these results. But what we can say in 2010 ... is Queensland has improved. I know from a lower base, but better than other comparable institutions and governments. So you'd have to say something went on.

Later, this same interviewee commented:

> if you get the data right ... NAPLAN data is right, in the sense that it is extremely robust ... and the thing about it is you don't just do it once.... So it's not like you can say okay, let's just ride it out. The catalyst data says if you don't respond, it's not going away and furthermore it could even get worse over time if you don't act to do something now. So I think that's the weight of public accountability—with good data, it works, it's the benefit that it is there every year. It's against agreed and accepted data and good comparators and benchmarks or targets.

We can see here the political pressure on state systems and, in the Queensland instance, the taking up of this pressure by the Premier to improve Queensland's NAPLAN performance in a short timeframe.

The remaining analysis of this case will draw on interview data to show the effects in a regional office of the Queensland Department of Education. It shows some of the perverse effects of NAPLAN becoming high stakes for the system, including immediate structural effects such as the creation of positions in head office and in the region to handle political pressure from the premier's office. For example, an assistant director of general school performance was created to handle school data, especially NAPLAN. At the regional office, where we conducted research interviews, there was also a principal advisor of school performance position, or "our data guru" as one interviewee put it.

One specific development to flow from the implementation of the *Masters Report* was the creation of the Queensland Education Department's Teaching and Learning Audit instrument developed by ACER, the implementation of which was subsequently overseen by the assistant director of general school performance. Teaching and Learning Audits were conducted in each Queensland school in 2010 and this approach has been subsumed in a new school performance assessment framework, which includes regular school reviews. One interviewee at the regional office called these audits a "sort of fallout" of the *Masters Report*. In the foreword to the audit document, the director general stated:

> In keeping with the plan (Department of Education and Training's 2009–2013 Strategic Plan) Education Queensland has developed a new and comprehensive strategy to improve student performance.... The strategy encompasses extensive audit requirements for state schools in the area of teaching and learning with a teaching and learning audit being conducted in every Queensland state school in 2010.

The Teaching and Learning Audit consists of eight elements. Schools were ranked against each of these eight elements on a 4-point scale from Outstanding to Low. An interviewee in the regional office noted the strengths of the Audits: "it's really focused people on a Teaching and Learning agenda." In this particular regional office, research had been conducted on the correlations between a school's score on the Audit and their performance on NAPLAN. One interviewee explained that "we don't always see an alignment do we between audit and achievement" (an observation directed towards the regional director). This person also noted that they had only really found correlations between certain of the audit elements: "our initial feeling is that Two, Five and Seven are the elements that make a big difference here" in relation to performance measures such as NAPLAN; "the bang for the buck will come out of these three we think."

Several of the interviewees made the point that if schools scored poorly on one of the other elements and were pressured to improve on that by the system, this would not necessarily improve their NAPLAN scores. As the data person in the regional office stated: "you get your Teaching and Learning Audit and you've got two lows, so you feel this pressure that you've got to improve those two lows, you don't want to have a low, you want to move them, where in fact working on those two lows may have absolutely no effect on student achievement." Here we can see potential goal displacement. Improved audit scores become a target with potentially limited impact on NAPLAN, if the focus is not on elements which the regional office's own research had shown were correlated with test performance. This is interesting in an age of evidence-informed policy. The Teaching and Learning Audit purported to have been derived from international research evidence, but there is limited systemic research about its effects in respect of impact for improving NAPLAN performance. Here we are in agreement with a recent OECD report (OECD 2014), which showed that most education reforms in schooling systems around the globe are not subject to independent evaluations. It appeared that this region was the only one conducting research into the usefulness of the audit instrument for its stated purposes. As one interviewee noted, "So the system has not done any correlation of whether what you see in a Teaching and Learning Audit reflects in student achievement." We would make the more general point that school systems are now replete with data, but they seem to be used more for accountability and control purposes than for policy learning to drive effective reform.

The regional office interviewees also spoke of the state-wide performance targets set in response to the 2008 performance data, as well as in relation to the National Partnership reward framework, which we discussed above. Interestingly though, there was no mention of these national processes and pressures by those in the regional office. The pressure was seen to originate at the state level due to the premier's involvement, but as we have suggested the Premier's concerns were linked to the state's reputational capital and to the national reform agenda and critical media representations of Queensland's comparative performance on NAPLAN. One interviewee in the regional office commented: "I don't know if you're aware but in reaction to where Queensland performed in terms of NAPLAN 2008 the state set some state targets, which they anticipated would get us to a point where we'd improve and they were three per cent each year.... It's a state wide target not a school." This was a statewide improvement of 3 percent across the board in NAPLAN, irrespective of how schools performed on the 2008 tests. One interviewee in the regional office commented in relation to this, "an improvement in every part of NAPLAN—the silly percentage." The same interviewee went on to note how the region had decided to target two aspects of NAPLAN, reading and literacy, along with the target that "a hundred per cent of eligible kids will be above the National Minimum Standards." She continued that they then set local targets for different schools instead of blanket improvements targets for all domains of the tests and for all schools to improve by 3 percent: "You set a local target for improving the upper two bands with an emphasis again on reading and numeracy, but where reading and numeracy's ok, you could actually look at the other domains as well." Another interviewee heavily involved in data analysis observed, "to have a global target is ridiculous." The interviewees, though, also said this discrepancy between political targets set at state systemic level, as well as regional nuancing of these targets, caused some trauma for school principals, who were subject to different expectations and pressures from different parts of the system. What came through very clearly in the interviews was the need for more complex and nuanced target setting for individual schools on the basis of data, a very different approach to that of the political pressure for rapid and almost immediate improvement that led to blanket statewide improvement targets.

There was also much commentary on the limited statistical literacy of those leading schools and the need for a "data team in school leadership": "they actually don't understand target setting and stretching"; "they really struggle with targets" (see Alegounarias, 2011). This regional person also stated that, "sometimes like with all targets they go for the things that are easy to measure you know, as you would expect.... That's why spelling is a favourite for people, you know I can say how many more words I got right this week." These are some of the perverse effects the literature has noted when targets are set in relation to high-stakes testing (Stobart, 2008). There was also commentary about the ambition of target setting by middle-class schools and an observation that statistically similar school measures published on the federal government's My School website had made the region aware of this lack of ambition. They referred to these schools as "coasting middle class schools." Interviewees also described the conversion of targets to numbers of students at a given school and class level that must improve. This conversion to specific numbers at year levels "meant far more to them" (teachers and principals) than targets. An interviewee at the federal level had made this exact point to us about the local impact of national accountability around NAPLAN: "Have they (principals) ever said I have to lift 10 kids from there to there in national testing? They would never have done this without this [national accountability through NAPLAN]. So you need the architecture at every level."

Here we see the triage effects in classrooms (Gillborn & Youdell, 2000) and the focus on those close to achieving the required standards (Lipman, 2004) that result from target setting. Moreover, the reference to "architecture at every level" signals the new spatialities of data infrastructures. This region was running masters classes to improve the statistical literacy of school leaders, as well as a coaching program. The use of data as central technologies of governance was also reflected in the utilization of school data sets in interviews for the appointment of new school principals: "Data sets are a big deal, and they expect them to be able to speak cogently about the data in terms of how to utilise it ... tell you what the implications of that data are in terms of: what I need to work on, where the priorities are, why I make these choices."

The region was aware of these issues and was attempting to nuance them in research-based and educational ways, but all within a framework that had taken as given the agenda to improve test performance. To be fair, the region was also committed to trying to improve educational outcomes for all students, in both the underperforming middle-class schools and in disadvantaged schools serving poor communities. However, improved performance for one school necessarily means declining performance for another on the statistically similar schools measures, thus strengthening the ongoing fetish for improving test results redolent of Deleuze's depiction of control societies.

This unit of analysis has illustrated how reward funding tied to state improvement on NAPLAN, along with the politicization of NAPLAN performance through the close involvement of the Premier, had considerable effects within the Queensland system. We saw increased accountability surveillance through the Teaching and Learning Audits and their potential for goal displacement with improved audit scores becoming the focus of school reform. This pressure has been strengthened somewhat with the *Courier-Mail* (January 28–29, 2012) publishing a league table of all schools' scores on the elements of the Teaching and Learning Audit. We also see the disjuncture between the temporalities of political demands to improve Queensland's NAPLAN performance and those required for real educational change, as well as the perverse effects of target setting at the systemic level. This analysis also clearly demonstrates the potential triage effects of target setting and the pressures associated with improved NAPLAN performances on personnel in the regional office, which is further deflected down the line to principals and teachers. This is the impact of what we are calling catalyst data. Bligh's Labor government was defeated in 2013, but the new Conservative state government continued with these pressures on schools around NAPLAN performance and this mode of accountability. Indeed, it could be justifiably argued that the new government increased these pressures. This situation has also witnessed the creation of new positions at the central and regional offices focusing very much on managing the test performance of schools.

Catalyst Data: A Concluding Comment

The research-based narrative provided in this chapter has illustrated our concept of catalyst data. Accountability framed around comparative test performance has real effects in schooling systems and then into schools and classrooms. Introducing the education indicators in OECD's influential *Education at a Glance* report for 2011, current Secretary-General Angel Gurria drew attention to the role of these indicators as "catalyst[s] for change":

> At one level, indicators are no more than a metric for gauging progress towards goals. *Yet increasingly, they are performing a more influential role.* Indicators can prompt change by raising national concern over weak educational outcomes compared to international benchmarks; sometimes, they can even encourage stronger countries to consolidate their positions.
>
> (OECD, 2011b: 9, emphasis added)

Such data and indicators now prompt politicians, policy makers, the media, the schooling sector, and the public more broadly, to ask how schools and systems are performing and what needs to be done to improve performance. However, while they are being collected and reported in the name of transparency, accountability, and improvement, the analysis presented in this chapter demonstrates the wide scope for perverse incentives and effects to arise, especially when funding and reputational capitals are tied to performance measures and comparisons. Drawing on an observation from a senior federal policy maker and the analyses provided here, we defined catalyst data as data and indicators that: (a) pressure politicians, policy makers, and systems to respond to comparative measures of performance; and (b) have real and multiple effects beyond such measurement. These effects reflect and simultaneously constitute restructured schooling systems. In Australia, we have seen the emergence of a nascent national system of schooling structured around comparative system and school performance data produced through NAPLAN and associated policies. The comparison of each school's performance with that of statistically similar schools across the nation augurs an emergent national system of schooling. Indeed, NAPLAN as an effective policy tool has constituted the nation as a commensurate space of performance measurement of schools and systems. We have argued that this is a complement to the global commensurate space of measurement that has been constituted through PISA and other international large-scale assessments.

The first unit of analysis illustrates how NAPLAN has become high stakes for systems through reputational damage caused by the perception of poor performance. This process is analogous to the "shocks" to national systems that have arisen from PISA, as we point out in Chapter 2. In contrast to talk about evidence-based policy, the pressure and nervousness felt by policy makers and politicians in response to NAPLAN outcomes are more immediately motivated by concerns to improve or maintain the reputation of schools and systems and to secure funding, rather than the intended objective of improving literacy and numeracy outcomes in schools. With both units of analysis we have documented the affective dimension of responses to these pressures. Given the anomalies in the 2010 process for negotiating National Partnerships reward frameworks and assessing performance, it is understandable that systems would be inclined to massage the bilateral negotiation of targets to ensure achievability over ambition and to employ measures that obfuscate performance rather than making it transparent. This case provides clear examples of the fabrication encouraged in regimes of performativity (Ball, 2003b) and the negative and perverse consequences of target setting as a driver of educational accountability and the work of educational systems.

The second unit of analysis demonstrated that NAPLAN data also have the capacity to catalyze more substantial reactions, in the form of systemic reviews and structural changes. However, in Queensland these have been accompanied by, or have spurred, an intensification of audit and accountability within the system with perverse flow-on effects such as goal displacement, teaching to the test, and the naturalization of data as the most sensible medium for thinking about teaching and learning. While NAPLAN catalyst data have an undeniable capacity to produce reactions, these can permeate through systems in ways that are difficult to predict or control from the locus of the original policy agenda.

The analysis proffered demonstrates how comparative testing data in Australian schooling are helping to create new testing, assessment, and funding infrastructures that render schools and systems commensurate. These are facilitating an associated catalysis—in the sense of dissolution—of the autonomy and authority of state education systems towards a national system of schooling, despite federalism (Lingard, 2010). Agencies that collect, analyze, and report comparative data, in this case the federal government and ACARA, hold a considerable degree of control over the educational agendas of systems that are subject to comparison. The capacity to catalyze a reaction through the reporting of these performance data is also a capacity to dissolve, at least in part, the boundaries that have divided up the educational authorities being assessed, thereby constituting new fields of measurement and governance and an emergent national system of schooling. Of course, the Australian states and territories jealously guard their responsibility for education and do not readily cede this authority; however, the increasingly hegemonic logic of policy as numbers is creating conditions in which the catalytic effects of performance data, and associated perverse effects, are becoming increasingly intense within education systems.

This intensity travels to schools to encourage a purblind focus on simply improving test scores, which has real effects in the quotidian lives of schools, with "data walls" now a common experience for students and "data talks" a central element of teacher accountability within schools. This is a perverse effect of top-down, test-based accountability in schooling, as it works its way through the complexities of educational federalism in Australia. Here we see performativity par excellence distorting schooling and the professional practices of teachers who are the objects of policy and measurement, rather than active participants in policy processes. With this form of accountability, teachers have lost control of the field of judgment (Ball, 2003b).

While the cases we have dealt with here are Australian ones, we have suggested throughout the chapter the ways in which the analysis has applicability in other systems, particularly Anglo-American ones. We would suggest that what we have with this largely Anglo-American, neoliberal mode of educational accountability is what Verger and colleagues (2012), after the Portuguese sociologist Boaventura de Sousa Santos, call a "globalized localism." Further, we have not said much here about the involvement of edu-businesses in these developments and similar evolutions of data-driven accountability in other nations and education systems. However, in concluding, we must note the increasing involvement of "edu-businesses" (for example Pearson) in the testing and accountability agendas of governments (see Ball, 2012). As we will show in the final chapter of this book, Pearson now has interests in both national and international testing, such as NAPLAN and PISA respectively. This has been enabled by the state restructuring we refer to throughout the book.

5
PISA AND THE INVISIBILITY OF RACE

Introduction

In this chapter, we focus on the racially invisibilized discourses suffusing OECD's PISA through its marketing and mediatization of strong performing nations on the OECD's official website. We are thus concerned with another effect of the politics of global mutual accountability of schooling systems. Here we draw attention to the silencing of race at the heart of the neoliberal logics that enable such deracination. Specifically, this chapter deals with two of the videos jointly produced by the OECD and the Pearson Foundation (*Strong Performers and Successful Reformers in Education*), which are designed to showcase countries that have demonstrated strong performance on the 2009 PISA tests or have shown improvement following reform initiatives. We focus on both the Ontario and Finland videos and map their "racially articulated delimitations" in order to draw out their erasures, refusals, and evaporations, both in terms of addressing the materiality and significance of race and social class inequalities and how they are inextricably intertwined, but ultimately denied under current globalizing neoliberal conditions (Goldberg, 2009: 30).

The Ontario video is chosen because of the nature of Ontario's multicultural urban populations (OECD, 2011a; Tucker, 2011), and given the attention that Canada has received in OECD publications and in the literature as a comparative case with lessons for educational policy reform in the USA and elsewhere. We also focus on how Finland's education system is marketed by the OECD, given that it has become the poster child and reference society for educational reform in other nations. However, in following Simola, Rinnie, Varjo, and Kauko (2013) and others, we draw attention to this problem of benchmarking, international rankings, and hierarchical sorting of the world's education systems according to the logics of neoliberal governance for "enacting ideologies of technocratic rationality and causing countries with diverse traditions and cultures to assimilate their educational practices to seemingly unassailable standards of technocratic rationality, economic competitiveness and market growth" (613). Such referencing neglects the path dependency of reforms in specific nations.

Our focus in this chapter is on the significant role that visual media are increasingly playing in mediating and communicating policy productions, consumption, and dissemination (Fairclough, 2000; Koh, 2009; Lingard & Sellar, 2014), and the extent to which such mediatization is driven by a politics of neoliberal "governance by comparison" (Martens, 2007: 40; Novoa & Yariv-Mashal, 2003) and "policy entrepreneurship" (Ball, 2012: 12). Thus we focus our analysis on the political and ideological aspects of these "text saturated" videos and on the larger neoliberal accountability regime that relies on what Goldberg (2009) identifies as a politics of "deracination" and "racelessness." Our focus is on how the OECD's PISA functions as an instrument for promoting a form of color blindness in education policy, resulting in the erasure of race and of the cumulative effects of racial histories on visible minority populations in Canada and the USA. This erasure propels and enables a politics of comparison that is grounded in fundamental denial of racial inequality in the education system. As well, it draws attention away from "acknowledging the weight of racisms," as they are manifested in the persistent effects of the spatial concentrations of racialized poverty in urban locations in the North American context (Goldberg, 2009: 343; see also Gulson, 2011; Lipman, 2011; Rothstein, 2004).

Such historical legacies of racial inequality and, more importantly, their persistence, call into question the legitimacy and validity of comparing two disparate nations such as Finland and USA. Kamens (2013), for instance, highlights the problematics of drawing comparisons that can amount to comparing apples and oranges; then using these invalid comparisons as a basis for developing "typologies of the best and worst school systems," culminating in the installation of a global league table for ranking and benchmarking national education systems (124; see also Hargreaves & Shirley, 2012). The point is that such neoliberal regimes of accountability (Ranson, 2003) and comparative assessment are built, not only on fostering economic efficiency in the global education market place, but also lend themselves to a "best practice" model of educational reform that (implicitly) denies specific contexts and questions of race, social class inequality, and the path dependency of systemic reforms. For example, any point of comparison that tends to ignore or downplay the extent of outside of school effects, such as the increasing withdrawal of the welfare state, the income inequality gap, the impact of poverty and minimum wages on disadvantaged groups, lack of provision of health care and quality housing for all, and the concentrated urban spatiality of black impoverishment and disinvestment in specific national contexts, raises serious questions about a policy commitment to articulating and addressing inequities in education systems (Anyon, 1997; Berliner, 2006; Fine & Weis, 1998; Ladson-Billings, 2006; Lucas & Beresford, 2010; Luke, Green, & Kelly, 2010; Lipman, 2011). Ignoring or downplaying the extent and degrees of such structural distinctions across national contexts, and failing to account for their material effects and histories, even makes comparisons between Canada and the USA quite problematic. In some ways, the international policy influence of the OECD's PISA is actually dependent on a down-playing of such contextual, socioeconomic factors and an overplaying of policy and education system factors in the aetiology of system and student performance (Meyer & Schiller, 2013). We note also that this contextual denial is occurring at a time of growing inequality (Piketty, 2014).

As we illustrate in this chapter, holding Finland and Canada up as lessons for the USA is thus fraught with methodological, ethical, political, and epistemological conundrums. These conundrums result in a fundamental overdetermination and prioritization of inside school effects as a basis for educational policy reform (Berliner, 2013; Meyer & Schiller, 2013). Both the Ontario and Finland videos are important cases in terms of marketing education systems on the basis of a fundamental denial of the material effects of political economy and the erasure of race and poverty as clear obstacles to ensuring equity, without attending to a fundamental politics of economic redistribution and the history and persistence of racist ideologies (Anyon, 2005; Goldberg, 2009; Alexander, 2010; Lipman, 2011). As reiterated in Chapter 6, the effect is to lend too much emphasis to the source of school failure as residing in the lack of effective teachers, and the need for improved curriculum, while diminishing and diluting the overriding influence of the material effects of race and poverty in specific contexts. Accompanying such neoliberal reform agendas in the USA has been a strategic and deliberate disinvestment in public goods such as housing and health care in the interest of further marketization and gentrification agendas in major urban centers (Lipman, 2011).

The scale and extent of such differences in political and racial economy make any comparison between nations such as the USA, Finland, and Canada quite problematic. Such comparisons tend to downplay or minimize the overriding influence of these material differences. They throw into relief the problems and limitations of the OECD as a regulatory apparatus for shaping perceptions about educational reform and accountability in terms of the market and economic efficiency. It is in this sense that a certain neoliberal social imaginary has been fostered by the OECD's PISA results through a "governance by comparison" approach that generates truth claims and a particular way of seeing the world in which the material effects of race and poverty remain unmarked and are expunged from political and policy consciousness.

In this chapter then, we illustrate how this fundamental erasure or denial is manifested in the OECD's *Strong Performers and Successful Reformers* videos through the deployment of the category "immigrant," which functions as a proxy for "race," and also in terms of the erasure of race- and social class–based inequalities. We also note here how the production of these videos was sponsored by the Pearson Foundation, an indicator of the involvement of edu-businesses in these developments in accountability (Ball, 2012). We will return to a consideration of such involvement in the concluding chapter of the book and link it to the new network governance in education.

Neoliberalism, Mediatization, and "Racelessness"

In recent years we have witnessed educational marketization and the new formation of a complex network of state, business, and "policy entrepreneurship" with the increasing involvement of international actors such as the World Bank and the OECD in national education systems (Rizvi & Lingard, 2010; Ball, 2012; Dimitriadis, 2012). As Ball (2012) argues, "business is now directly engaged with education policy in a number of different ways and these engagements are part of a broader set of complex processes affecting education policy" (11). The new and improved cultural technologies of video, blogs, and twitter have been utilized to disseminate and communicate information about performance on PISA tests across nations and to showcase strong performers among the countries that participate in PISA. As Lingard and Rawolle (2004) argue, drawing on the work of Bourdieu, policy production is increasingly "mediatized," and with regard to OECD's PISA, we illustrate how it functions as a technology of neoliberal governance that takes the form of *media spins* and *sound bites*. Wiseman (2013) asserts that:

> In the educational community, the importance of media coverage is often overlooked when it comes to thinking about policy responses.... However, the importance of media is not lost on those who organize, plan and disseminate results from these studies. This is evidenced by the media kits, press releases and initial results announcement events that have become a staple of the PISA dissemination cycle.
>
> (305)

This emphasis on mediatization is evidenced most recently by the media coverage of Canada's ostensibly *poor* international math performance on the 2012 OECD PISA tests, with the results being published in December 2013 (CMEC, 2013a; OECD, 2013b). The national newspaper in Canada, the *Globe and Mail*, published a front page article entitled "National emergency as Canadians fall out of global top 10 in math"—a headline clearly designed to incite moral panic and crisis over Canadian's falling performance as one of the leading global players (Alphonso, 2013). This crisis discourse is further emphasized in the opening line of the article: "Canada has dropped yet again in international math standings, falling out of the top 10 and raising alarm bells about the country's future prosperity." Such media spins point to the very significant role that mediatization plays in fostering and supporting neoliberal governance and its instantiation in a global education policy field where measurable performance on PISA tests is tied to the logics of economic efficiency and capacity to compete in the global labor marketplace (Lipman, 2011; Rizvi & Lingard, 2010). In the USA, Lipman (2011) has shown how such a culture of performativity and the "economic logics in which it is rooted have produced a global convergence of policies rooted in neoliberal values albeit mediated by specific national histories" (18). However, it is important to note the racelessness or colorblindness of such media spins, which are rarely concerned to address questions of the persistent race achievement gap and the impact of rising income disparities on specific populations.

It is for this reason that we are concerned to focus particular attention on the media and forms of mediatization deployed by the OECD in its fostering of a project of *deracinated* neoliberal governance. We identify mediatization as an important element of the "policy dispositif" (Bailey, 2013), which has come to be a defining feature of the PISA effect and its far-reaching influence across the globe (Lingard, 2011). Bailey, for example, draws our attention to the Foucauldian notion of "dispositive." He defines dispositif as "a socio-technical formation of 'government'" for materializing a "dominant political rationality" (809). We would see PISA as a technical instrument deployed within the context of what Bailey identifies as a "strategic battlefield" or "struggle over the governing of education," thereby playing a major role in shaping, steering, and constituting a global education policy field according to a specific grid of norms associated with neoliberal rationalities or logics (809). Dispositif is thus a key concept for understanding the mechanics of "complex processes of policy enactment, policy advocacy, policy influence and policy practice" and illuminates the possibilities for exploring "how policy is disposed and performed in different material sites in different and contingent ways" (814). It is this focus on the technical and material forms of policy production and proliferation that we draw attention to in this chapter by focusing on the mediatization of PISA results as a central mechanism in the raceless technology of neoliberal governance and the global politics of mutual accountability.

The Foucauldian notion of governmentality as "a certain mentality" is central to Miller and Rose's (2008) conceptualization of a logics of governance operationalized through an "ensemble formed by institutions, procedures, analyses and reflections, the calculations and tactics, that allow the exercise of this very specific albeit complex form of power (Foucault, 1979: 20)" (27). It is the mediatization of policy discourses, as a central component of what Rose (1999) terms "the analytics of governmentality" (19), especially as it relates to certain styles or registers of "truth telling" and "rhetorical devices for adjudicating and certifying truth claims" (9), that concern us in this chapter, particularly in regard to the question of race and its erasure or purging from the "explicit lexicon of public administrative arrangements" (Goldberg, 2009: 342), governing the terms and limits set by the OECD (2011) for thinking about global educational reform initiatives.

We focus on two of the videos produced by the OECD and the Pearson Foundation, which showcase school systems that were chosen for their strong performance in the OECD's PISA. Among the nations included as reference societies against which the USA and other poor performing nations are compared are Finland, Shanghai, China, Singapore, Korea, and Ontario, Canada. The OECD website states specifically that:

> Starting from very different levels, a number of countries and regions have succeeded over the last few years in raising their students' performance substantially. They display some important common features. Their politicians and social leaders share with parents, teachers and students a strong belief in the value of education.... The best systems deliver strong and equitable learning outcomes across widely varying cultural and economic contexts. By showing what they achieve, the PISA tests *provide a mirror* to all countries and demonstrate what is possible. Others can learn from those that do well.
> (OECD, 2010c, our emphasis)

The use of the mirror metaphor highlights the function of the OECD's PISA as a global panoptic and regulatory mechanism. Such framing sets the terms and limits of the rationality behind the what Lingard (2011) identifies as a "rescaled political authority" (356) and the constitution of a space of equivalence, epitomized here by the technical deployment of the PISA instrument by the OECD as a disciplinary mechanism for constituting a commensurable space of comparative performance measures across the globe: "With the globalization of the economy, PISA's international comparative school system performance measures become in effect a surrogate measure of the potential international competitiveness of the national economy" (Lingard, 2011: 368). This global panoptic effect of such neoliberal regimes is highlighted by Kamens (2013), who draws attention to the regulatory function of PISA as a technology of governance that derives its force from its normative and normalizing capacity to set the terms and limits for what is to count as successful educational reform: "innovation can spread quickly through world society because there is no central authority that can control either the flow of borrowing or the pace of intervention" (125). However, Kamens further claims that such a regime of neoliberal governance has enabled and provided "the stimulus for nations to organize with others into blocks that offer various forms of self-protection and competitive advantage in a variety of domains," lending "increased prominence and visibility to certain members of the OECD":

> As other nations have emerged as global economic political successes, they too get added to the list of world models of economic and political success.

> As such, these nations are now important role models for other countries in the minds of their educated elite. Their institutions become mirrors that less successful societies use to judge their own progress in a wide variety of domains—for example, education, economic success, human rights achievements, successful democratization.
>
> (125)

Both Canada and Finland are held up as such exemplars or *mirrors* for other nations to gaze into, particularly in terms of learning from the reform strategies that have been instigated by these nations, and which have resulted in the improvement of their education systems and the performance of their students. Both countries are also heralded as having achieved a degree of successful democratization in their education systems through implementing certain policy initiatives and reform strategies committed to inclusive pedagogy directed at enhancing the achievement of immigrant students and supporting students with special education needs (see Hargreaves & Shirley, 2012). Canada, in particular, prides itself on its successful achievement of immigrant students, who are represented as performing as well as native-born Canadians. This is similar to the situation in Australia, where Language Background other than English (LBOTE) students are, superficially at least, seen to perform as well as native English speakers on Australia's national tests (Creagh, 2014). However, when the LBOTE category performance on these tests is disaggregated, this is not the case.

In this chapter we are concerned with erasures in drawing attention to the "visualization of education policy" and its reception regimes with regard to how both Ontario and Finland's education systems and their successes are represented through the work of "a politics of government," the effect of which is a certain degree of ideological closure and deracinated erasure (Koh, 2009: 283, 284). The video texts, therefore, are analyzed in terms of their capacity to shape and foreclose thinking about educational reform through careful semiotic design and "accessed voices," with key players being included strategically in the authorization and certification of particular truths about the educational reform policies that have motivated "best practices." As Koh argues, "because the selection of design is not innocent, we need to ask who we see and who is omitted, who is privileged within our scopic regime and who is disadvantaged and whose interests do the visual representations serve?" (285). Thus, we are concerned to draw special attention to the cases of Ontario, Canada, and Finland as high-quality/high-equity performers in terms of how the OECD deploys mediatization to set the terms for establishing certain scopic regimes for promoting its political agenda and in setting the terms of what is to count as successful educational reform and its visibilization in regard to the instantiation of a global league table.

The technical means and expertise embodied by OECD's PISA for making possible the ranking of "world class" education systems in terms of what

Ozga (2009) and Lingard (2011) have termed "policy as numbers," and, hence, for creating the nation as "a space of equivalence" (Porter, 1995: 37), have resulted in the generation of certain enclosures in relation to what is to count as evidence and equity (Miller & Rose, 2008: 69; Luke et al., 2010). As we illustrate in this chapter, such spaces of equivalence place race under erasure. We provide a cautionary narrative about how data are employed and the problematic ways in which the notion of equity is reconstituted with the effect of erasing race and the full import of class disparities from an analysis of the inequalities that continue to dog education systems (Lipman, 2004; 2011; Berliner, 2006; Ladson-Billings, 2006; Noguera, 2008; Lingard & Sellar, 2014). For example, Dimitriadis (2012) draws attention to the political aspects of the disaggregation of test-driven data and the employment of particular categories to show the concern for social equity, while hiding other important categories:

> Much of this test score data have been disaggregated by and through particular social categories, often in the push for something like social equity. Yet, these categories often present themselves as neutral and value free. The classification of knowledge is a power- laden process- revealing some things and hiding others.
>
> (56)

In the Ontario context, we highlight how the OECD, through PISA, employs the social category of immigrant as a basis for establishing a particular conception of social equity, while simultaneously masking racial inequality. Brüggemann and Bloem (2013), in a recent study of Roma students' achievement on PISA tests in Europe, challenged the results on the basis of the low sample of Roma students and OECD's failure to report the achievement of nonimmigrant minority students:

> PISA has also triggered discussions about educational equity, especially with regards to the achievement gap of students with a low socio-economic status or migration background. PISA and other international assessments have however failed to provide data about learning outcomes of non-migrant minorities. Hardly any data about learning outcomes of Roma pupils is available, even though the number of Roma in many European countries is considerable.
>
> (17)

The OECD's concern about social equity has also been discussed by Wiseman (2013), who argues that there is a legitimating myth of excellence and equity that is operating in most educational systems around the world and that this discourse represents the "global norm." He asserts that it is not that these countries are not striving to attain these goals of equity and excellence, but "they are legitimating myths because it is certain that no educational system has attained or can completely attain system-wide excellence or equity" (307). This "in-visibility" of race in public discourse in general, as Goldberg (2009) argues, is a result of globalization and the neoliberal shift in the role of the state from a welfare/pastoral state to a neoliberal state, which facilitates the movement of capital and information, and introduces self-responsibilizing into welfare systems (Rose, 1999). In such a scenario, Goldberg argues that the focus on meritocracy and "individualized merit and ability" has resulted in the idea of racelessness under neoliberal regimes:

> In diluting, if not erasing, race in all public affairs of the state, neoliberal proponents nevertheless seek to privatize racisms alongside most everything else. . . . Categories of race disappear as much from keeping account of discrimination as from producing the discrimination itself, thus leaving the condition it is supposed to articulate, to mark and express as well as identify and assess, as untouchable as it tends now to be untouched.
>
> (339)

In the following two sections we provide an analysis of the Ontario and Finland *Strong Performers/Successful Reformers* videos. Each video includes "accessed voices" from various authorities in the specific country in question, which speak to the particular reform strategies and the diverse approaches that have been developed to help to improve their education systems. These voices are interspersed with footage of teachers teaching in classrooms. In the following section we devote some attention to the Ontario video, given that Ontario has been identified by OECD as a high-performing/high-equity Canadian province in its PISA results and has been ranked top ten in reading among countries that participated in the PISA assessment. Ontario's achievement has been especially praised because of the performance of its immigrant populations on the PISA 2009 test.

The Case of Ontario and High-Performing Immigrant Students

The Ontario video opens with commentary from the premier, who sets the tone for the entire policy narrative on educational reform that is central to the marketing of Ontario as a strong performer with a commitment to "obtain[ing] measurable improvement." It is significant to trace initially how the question of student diversity is strategically inserted into a policy reform narrative that is centered on a commitment to raising achievement and graduation rates. This opening comment by the premier is followed by an assertion from the assistant deputy minister of education, who refers to Ontario's commitment to raising the level of achievement and to setting targets with the clear goal of having "75% of our students by age 12 reading and writing and using skills of mathematics with high levels of competency, and improving our graduation rate from high school to 85% of the cohort entering Grade 9 graduating within five years." Central to this policy narrative is the imperative to address diversity, a policy commitment that is articulated by the premier. He speaks to a sense of urgency on behalf of his government to raise achievement and graduation and makes specific reference to Ontario's student population "that is extremely rich in its diversity" with "close to four out of 10 Ontario students" being identified as immigrants. The question of student diversity explicitly articulated in relation to the category of immigrant is immediately tied in with the government's commitment to raising achievement.

Further commentary by the assistant deputy education minister follows, beginning with the assertion: "We need to deal with that diversity." She goes on to claim that central to achieving this goal is providing supports and resources to schools, as well as having the technical capacity to identify "children living in poverty in a particular school population" and the "proportion of children without either English or French as their first language." A series of four text slides is then introduced that functions in a legitimizing capacity and as grounds for validating the previous voices and the privileged construction of educational reform in Ontario that they endorse. Slide 1, for example, presents the percentage of students who met the provincial standard in 2002–2003 (54 percent) and those who did so in 2009–2010 (68 percent). Similarly, slide 2 presents the high school graduation rate for 2004 (68 percent) and for 2008 (77 percent). The documentary then cuts to slide 3 with these statements: "OECD Program for International Student Assessment (PISA). In 2009 Ontario ranked among the top 10 performances in reading." This is followed by slide 4, which reads: "4 out of 10 students in Ontario are immigrant children. Yet immigrant and Canadian-born children perform equally well in the PISA assessment." Slide 4 in this series includes this written text: "How might Ontario's policies help students to succeed in a diverse context? The Unionville High School experience."

Here it is possible to identify how both the sequencing of voices and slides provides a seamlessly coherent and indisputable account of school reform policy effects in Ontario. For example, the slides point to the fact that student achievement and graduation rates have improved significantly under Premier McGuinty's liberal government, but clearly mask the fact that achievement and opportunity gaps have widened for certain designated visible minority and economically disadvantaged populations in Ontario and in specific ghettoized neighborhoods (see Anisef, Brown, Phythian, Sweet, & Walters, 2010; James, 2012; McCaskell, 2011). As Koh (2009) points out with regard to the mediatization of such education policy for public consumption, there "is no conflicting point of view or any hint of disagreement" (291) in terms of the weaving together of the policy narrative surrounding educational reform in the Ontario context and the clear designation of student diversity in terms of the immigrant category, with all of its semiotic implications for denying and erasing the experiences of nonimmigrant visible minority populations. This erasure is further made possible by employing an explicit focus on a particular school location in Toronto with a very specific socioeconomic and immigrant population.

It is important here to provide some context to the Ontario case, particularly in relation to the history of neoliberal reforms in education. The Conservative government of Mike Harris (1995–2003) introduced major educational reforms, which resulted in the amalgamation of school boards (Toronto District School Board became the largest board in Canada, with over 250,000 students), the introduction of standardized testing and curriculum. The Conservatives also introduced funding cuts to education and changed the funding formula, which resulted in the province taking control of funding, so that school boards could not levy taxes on residents. They also launched a major assault on teachers' unions. Together these changes created a polarized environment and were resisted by teachers and their unions (Rezai-Rashti, 2009). The Liberal government of Dalton McGuinty came to power in 2005 with a mandate to fix the education system by reinstating the professional authority of teachers and providing sufficient support to improve the achievement of students and increase high school graduation rates. However, it is important to note that education reform strategies were still dictated by a neoliberal emphasis on achievement gaps and the prioritizing of standardized testing regimes without due attention being paid to more redistributive policy interventions (see Martino & Rezai-Rashti, 2012).

There is a need to move beyond the initial analysis of immigrant achievement data supported by the OECD's PISA and to provide a "secondary analysis" of Ontario as a success story that is attributed to the government's education reform and policy initiatives (Wiseman, 2013). Such a narrative is enabled through a certain degree of ideological closure that is operationalized through the employment of the category of immigrant as a proxy for race. In short, behind the strategic and deliberate use of such a category, there seems to be a tendency to make race and racial inequality invisible, or at least the effect is racial evaporation and dilution (Goldberg, 2009: 344), where once marked individuals "have no reference point, no measure, no determination" (345). For analytical purposes, such a reading, which attends to these sorts of ideological closures and erasures in the production and preferred reading of "documentary" visual texts, needs to be situated "in the complex interplay of institutional constraints, ideological underpinnings, political assumptions and priorities" (Koh, 2009: 284). It is in this capacity that we draw on Goldberg's (2009) argument about the current state of invisibility of race and its proxy articulation as being very much at work in the production of the Ontario *Strong Performers* documentary text for public consumption and marketing by the OECD:

> Its deepening invisibility is evidenced in its prevailing proxy articulations—its fixation, its pre-occupations—today in the powerful polities of the global north: migration and immigration, terrorism, contagious disease and viral spread.
>
> (359)

As already exemplified, it is by attending to both the structural and design elements of the video text and to a secondary analysis of Ontario's performance, as it represented in the documentary, that further insights into the reception regimes governing its "truth claims" and "authorial properties" can be further unraveled (Koh, 2009: 288). Such critical interrogation challenges the seamless and unproblematic notions of "high equity" and "high achievement" of students' performance in terms of how the province of Ontario is represented as an exemplary case. For example, Wiseman (2013) claims that in most cases "the initial results" are celebrated while the secondary analysis is ignored. He argues that this secondary analysis is not often made "accessible to the general public" or does not target the political agendas of politicians and policy makers. In other words, what is masked are the politics behind the classificatory systems that the numbers both enable and disguise (305).

Rose (1991), in drawing attention to the relations between numbers and politics, argues, "paradoxically, in the same process in which numbers achieve a privileged status in political decisions, they simultaneously promise a 'de-politicization' of politics, redrawing the boundaries between politics and objectivity, by purporting to act as automatic technical mechanisms for making judgements, prioritizing problems and allocating scarce resources" (647). For example, he speaks of the numerical and statistical "techniques of inscription and accumulation of facts about the population" that render it visible and make it amenable to administration as "a domain with a certain internal homogeneity and external boundaries" (676). Rose (1991) further explicates that numbers and their role in the generation of specific categories and classifications "delineate 'fictive spaces' for the operation of government, and establish a 'plane of reality', marked out by a grid of norms, on which government can operate" (676). It is in this sense that our analysis of the Ontario video text is compelled by an attempt to trace the *grid of norms* governing the particular policy viewpoint on education reform in Ontario that is articulated through "accessed voices" and the designation of Unionville as an exemplary case for supporting and validating certain evidentiary claims about the achievement of immigrant populations as a manifestation of a commitment to and realization of high equity.

The video draws attention to the successful experiences of students in Ontario by showcasing Unionville High School, located in the Greater Toronto Area (GTA), where there is a significant concentration of economically advantaged, high-income Asian immigrants. The video focuses on the ideological significance of the deployment of the category of immigrant as a means by which to erase or avoid the persistence of the problem of racialized poverty and its impact on black underachievement in Toronto urban schools. This erasure or avoidance, which is enabled by the use of immigrant as a statistical category, masks the political ramifications behind the selection of the particular case and the emphasis that is placed on such a school in the documentary. In addition, it highlights that such a selection is not an arbitrary decision but a carefully orchestrated one designed to "set up preferred reading pathways" that serve the interest of those government officials who initiated and are endorsing the reform strategies in the Ontario context (Koh, 2009: 286). As Koh argues with regards to the visualization of education policy, the selection of design is not innocent and questions about whose viewpoint is included, whose is omitted, who is privileged, and whose interests are being served in the service of establishing such "a scopic regime" need to be asked (285).

Unionville High School

A brief description of Unionville High School (HS) helps to provide some important details and contextual background about the population, its socioeconomic demographics, history, and the policy reforms that the video claims have been undertaken to improve the school's performance. Taking into account these factors helps to explain "a process of selection for ideological reasons" that enables a privileged viewpoint to be authorized and, hence, "the disjuncture between policy and practice" to be effectively managed and disguised (Koh, 2009: 287). In short, the selection of Unionville, rather than another more representative urban school in terms of economic and racial diversity, serves to support a particular interpretation of the positive effects of school reform policies that have been instigated by the Ontario Ministry of Education.

Unionville HS is located in the city of Markham, about 33 kilometres from Toronto. The demographic of the city is 34.4 percent white, 34.2 percent Chinese, 17.3 percent South Asian. Unionville is said to be one of the most affluent areas in the GTA with an average household income of $127,900 CAD, which is much higher than the Canadian average income of $54.089 CAD. In 2001 the Fraser Institute, a conservative think-tank that ranks all Canadian schools based on their performance on standardized tests, gave Unionville HS a score of 8.9 out of 10 (see Fraser Institute 2001). In the same year, Unionville HS was ranked at 36 out of 568 schools and 21 out of 349 in Ontario. In 2012 the school received a score of 8.8 out of 10, which indicates that there is no significant change in the overall rating of the school in terms of student achievement during this time period (see Cowley, Easton, & Thomas, 2012). These data indicate that the school has been a high performer since 2001. Overall, Unionville has one of the top scores in Canada based on provincial assessment results, with 91 percent of students who wrote the Ontario Secondary School Literacy Test for the first time passing compared to a 78 percent success rate for the province.

However, upon viewing the video, the impression is created that the students' achievement is connected to the Ontario government's reform strategies and policy interventions as they are explained by the principal of the school and teachers on the basis of its performance on the provincial EQAO (Education

Quality and Accountability Office) tests. All staff indicated that the Ontario government developed mechanisms for monitoring student achievement, with specific attention to collecting data on the progress of English language learners (ELLs), immigrant students, and boys' literacy. In fact, considerable attention early on in the video is given to the emphasis in Ontario that is placed on monitoring and assessing students, particularly with regards to tracking their proficiency in literacy and numeracy with Michael Fullan, as special advisor on education to the premier, Marguerite Jackson, chief executive officer of the Education Quality and Accountability Office, and Ben Levin, the deputy minister of education, being employed and accessed at strategic points in the text to shape this authorial viewpoint of the successful governmental intervention that has resulted in improved achievement. Almost every classroom setting that is inserted throughout the documentary as a backdrop for voice-over commentaries features significant representation of minority students, primarily from East Asian backgrounds, which is meant to represent the diversity of Unionville HS, while excluding any attempt to include those students of South Asian backgrounds or white students who comprise 17 percent and 34 percent respectively.

A significant portion of the video—almost half—is actually dedicated to presenting the voices of educators from Unionville and it ends with final comments from both the deputy and assistant deputy ministers. The latter reiterates how the "performance gap for our English language learners ... has been closed by about half of that gap" over the "five or six years that we've been working at this." The assistant deputy minister further adds that "the line on any of the graphs that shows performance of our new ELLs is a much steeper improvement piece, and the evidence of improvement, than the general population, and that is absolutely critical in a province where up to 40 per cent of our children are, in fact coming from places outside of our province." This gap talk and the question of evidence, as explicated in Chapter 6, raises some important and troubling questions about the relation between political problematizations of achievement gaps as they pertain to the improvement of immigrant and ESL (English as Second Language) students in Ontario and "attempts to make them calculable through numerical technologies" (Rose, 1991: 673). What is disturbing is the visibility of the immigrant and ELLs that is created throughout the video "to help configure the respective boundaries of the political and the technical" (Rose, 1991: 668–679) with regards to expunging the significance of the persistence of racial inequalities in the education system in Ontario, particularly with regards to the performance of black students, specifically those Caribbean and Somali-speaking students who have one of highest dropout rates in urban centers such as Toronto (Martino & Rezai-Rashti, 2012; TDSB, 2006).

This denial is further heightened through the selection of specific content and the visualization of diversity at Unionville HS in terms of its representation of the student body. For example, when the video moves to the actual school environment and to teachers who discuss their specific students, it cuts to shots of classroom contexts that are filled predominantly with Asian students to emphasize diversity and also ELL designation of the student population. The sequencing of scenes and accessed voices of the deputy education minister followed by educators from Unionville is important in shaping and reinforcing the video's point of view about the success of education reform strategies that have been implemented by the Ontario government to close "the achievement gap" for immigrant students. It is important to note that there is simply no mention of the significant race and social class achievement gaps that continue to dog the education system in Ontario. More importantly, the fact that this school is located in a neighborhood where the average income is over 100,000 dollars per year is simply elided. These exclusions are important in terms of securing the ideological closure that enables the government to claim success for its interventionist program. For example, just prior to being introduced to educators from Unionville, the deputy minister is featured and strategically inserted to reiterate the government's commitment to improving every school by concentrating on the bottom 10 percent or 15 percent and on how the government has ensured such learning success:

> And then because we knew there were *big achievement gaps* in Ontario among particular groups, we set out to do things particular to those. So for example, we have a big English language learning community in Ontario. And so we developed an English language learner's strategy because it turned that there was no consistency in practice in how we deal with donning the speaking students or non-French-speaking students across the province at all. (our emphasis)

This spin about the success of the government's interventionist strategy framed in terms of gap talk is built around its *Student Success Strategy*, which involved creating a new faculty position for the appointment of a Student Success Teacher in every school in Ontario. Hence, a slide follows the minister's commentary, entitled "Student Success Strategy," with the following text: "decrease dropout rates," "increase graduation rates." It also includes the above detail about creating the new Student Success Teacher position "to coordinate faculty attention on struggling students." The video then cuts to an image of a Unionville student glancing at what appears to be a worksheet—the close-up shot is cast above his right shoulder from behind—to create a sense of almost being transported to the classroom as a silent witness. At the same time, the voiceover of the Student Success Teacher is introduced for a couple of seconds before cutting to a visual of her at a meeting with a small group of faculty (clearly comprising those teachers who are involved in teaching this particular student) in which this particular student's language learning skills are being discussed: "Semester 1, he has ... he has period 1 off; he has art, Period 2; he has ... he is good at strings—his music mark is good.

So he will also get a credit after school. And I don't think he needs the language skills, he speaks quite well." The video then cuts to the principal of Unionville who talks about being excited about the Student Success initiative, followed by the camera cutting back to the Student Success Teacher whose commentary is interspersed with footage of her actually working closely with the previously mentioned ELL student in a one-on-one capacity. For example, at this point in the video, the Student Success Teacher reiterates that while ELL students "have been successful in their own country . . . they're not successful here with the transition to English, and so they fall behind and we have to find a way to make sure that they don't—that they can continue with the success they've had at school." A little later in the video, the Student Success Teacher is used to reiterate how Unionville is addressing the question of enhancing the educational achievement of its immigrant students. Her following statement is preceded by a commentary by the principal who mentions the "countless ways" in which learners are supported through a student success lens that involves "a collaborative effort" and "a full school initiative" that is made possible by the Student Success Teacher:

> We have weekly meetings. It brings our team together, and it allows us to track the students that we are watching, and it's made up of members from guidance, Special Ed, Alternative Ed, our literacy teachers, our administration- we all sit in . . . in that meeting. And we're able to review the students that don't seem to be successful.

The strategic focus on and amount of time devoted to the Student Success Teacher at Unionville really function politically to present her as the embodiment of the government's commitment to enhancing the achievement of immigrant students. This "success story" is further supported by the school principal, who is once again strategically inserted at this point in the video and paints a very different picture of the school community than the one provided by official statistics:

> Some students come across the table . . . they're failing all four subjects. They don't have money for transit pass. They're living with no parents in the country- the parents might be living in China. And that team will network-everything from the cultural settlement worker to the administrator, to, say, an Alt Ed teacher, to make connections and set up that program for success. That's the best example of a student success team, is looking at the child and looking holistically how we can support them.

Considering such statements and given that viewers are not being informed about the level of income and education of parents in this community, the impression is created that Unionville is a poor school with a high concentration of English language learners, some of whom do not have enough financial support to even pay for a public transit pass. However, as we mentioned previously there is a significant concentration of high-income earners in this neighborhood, with almost 70 percent having obtained higher-education degrees. In addition, this is one of the highest performing schools in Toronto and all of Canada and has been for some years.

Koh (2009) discusses the significance of "accessed voices" in documentary forms of presentation and points out that "documentary is essentially a filmic practice that re-presents and constructs a particular worldview" (287). He asserts that this form of presentation provides an insider's point of view that corroborates ideologically the institutional voices (deputy minister, special advisor to the premier of Ontario, and the chief executive of EQAO).

> Apart from the presenter's full commentary, the programme's point of view is also shaped by the "accessed voices" that comprise interviews with school principals, teachers and students. While these "accessed voices" give us an insider's point of view, their voices also function ideologically as institutional voices to provide a vicarious experience of the "real" because of their role as "eye-witness."
>
> (290)

All in all, the OECD video represents a strategically orchestrated viewpoint in which Ontario's success on PISA is directly attributed to the government's education reform policies and strategies. However, highlighting several different factors and other data sets raises some questions and challenges this "unproblematic" truth about the extent and nature of the Ontario success story and the reform strategies that have supposedly produced such high achievement on the PISA assessment.

Immigrant versus Nonimmigrant Minorities

As we have illustrated through our analysis of the Ontario video, PISA employs the category of immigrant in addressing the question of student diversity and achievement. No data on racial minority students who are born in Canada and persistently underachieve or drop out of school are provided. However, data generated by the Toronto District School Board (TDSB), which is the largest school board in Canada with approximately 250,000 students and with a high concentration of cultural and racial minority students, present a very different picture of minority student achievement (TDSB, 2006). Of the 25 percent of students who do not graduate, the report points to students of Aboriginal, black, Hispanic, and Middle Eastern backgrounds as those who are at risk: "those students have the lowest test scores (EQAO), the lowest rates of credit accumulation through secondary school, and the highest drop-out rates . . . the lowest rates of school attendance and the highest suspension rates" (3).

Using the category of immigrant to describe the education system's success is misleading here. Questions pertaining to immigration policy and the sorts of immigrants who are being granted privileged access to Canada need to be considered within the context of discussions regarding the achievement of immigrant students in the education system. For example, the change of immigration policy in recent years indicates that Canada's immigrants are among the highest educated and skilled and they are selected because of their contribution to the economic productivity of the country. The report by the OECD in 2006 indicates that "on average, first generation Canadian students had parents with as many or more years of education as native-born parents" (see Mehta & Schwartz, 2011: 150)—an important consideration that seems to be elided in the success story mediatized by the OECD in the production of the Ontario *Strong Performer* video.

In fact, one important consistency in Canadian immigration policy, and specifically with the Points System, is the emphasis on economic success. Throughout the 1990s, the economic imperatives underlying Canadian immigration policy became increasingly obvious. According to Beach, Green, and Worswick (2006), there was an obvious shift away from the family-class and an emphasis on family reunification to an emphasis on the economic-class, specifically skilled workers. Accompanying these shifts were policy changes under the Points System "away from specific occupational preferences and towards broader emphasis on educational credentials, language facility and young families, again with an eye to human capital and skills development of the host country" (3). Furthermore, in line with many of the recommendations made by Citizenship and Immigration Canada, changes to the Points System in 2011 gave greater significance to language proficiency (16–20 points) and younger workers (10–12), more points were to be awarded for nonuniversity credentials such as trades and technicians, and there was a reduced emphasis on work experience, preferring instead arranged employment.

In 2013, changes were made yet again to the Points System under the Federal Skilled Workers classification. Currently, there are six selection factors and a possible 100 maximum points. Potential immigrants require a minimum of 67 points to qualify to immigrate to Canada as a federal skilled worker. These selection factors are: (1) English and/or French skills (max 28 points); (2) Education (max 25 points); (3) Experience (max 15 points); (4) Age (max 12 points); (5) Arranged employment in Canada (max 10 points); and (6) Adaptability (max 10 points). Resurfacing in 2013 is the economic focus of the immigration policy, and the need to streamline and make more efficient immigration policies and procedures. According to research conducted by the Fraser Institute, Minister of Immigration, Jason Kenney, introduced many new changes to immigration policies that aim "in part, at lowering the fiscal burden through the use of more efficient selection processes, better information about candidate qualifications, speeding up the processing of refugee claims, reducing opportunities for fraud, increasing the financial responsibility of sponsors of parents and grandparents, and various other measures" (Grubel, 2013: iv).

Another significant factor to be considered is the variation in composition, context, and origin of immigrant groups that might explain the differences in educational attainment. A study by Dronkers and de Heus (2013) using the PISA 2006 results shows that the origin and destination of immigrants have a significant impact on their academic achievement. For example, they claim that the average score of 468 for migrant students conceals significant variations among migrant groups "ranging from a score of 404 for the Albanian migrants to a score of 571 for the US migrant pupils. Other high performers are the Chinese and Australian migrants (552 and 548 respectively)" (249). Dronkers and de Heus argue that the factors contributing to the academic success of migrant students are more complex than for native-born children. In their multilevel analysis of migrant student data from PISA 2006, which included students coming from forty-six different countries and living in sixteen destinations, they show that migrant students living in Australia and New Zealand (traditional migrant receiving countries) outperform migrant students in other countries. Dronkers and de Heus conclude that:

> Children from migrant communities that have higher levels of socio-economic capital than the native population outperform comparable children from communities with relatively lower level capital. This is to a large extent the case because children from these relatively high-status communities have higher levels of parental socio-economic capital and a better command of their destination country's language (composition effect).
>
> (263)

These sorts of insights, which raise questions about the apparently technical matters of measurement surrounding the deployment of the category of immigrant as a defining basis for establishing certain truth claims about addressing achievement gaps, point to the political decision making behind "a numericized public discourse" (Rose, 1991: 684). The statistical designation and targeting of immigrants as a generalized category serve not only as a basis for a deracinated neoliberal form of governance in constituting "a new visibility of the facts," but also as a means by which to mobilize a rationality of government in the service of attaining particular objectives (Rose, 1991: 678): "Numbers are not just 'used' in politics, they help to configure the respective boundaries of the political and the technical, they help to establish what it is for a decision to be 'disinterested'" (678–679).

It is in this sense that PISA functions as an instrument of government and as part of a *policy dispositif* that supports specific schemes and interventions such as those related to a rearticulation of what counts as equity with regards to addressing student diversity, a phenomenon that we have illuminated through our analysis of the mediatization of OECD's PISA results for Ontario. As Miller and Rose (2008) stipulate:

> Government, of course, is not only a matter of representation. It is also a matter of intervention. The specificity of governmentality ... lies in its complex interweaving of procedures for representing and intervening (cf. Hacking 1983). We suggest that these attempts to instrumentalize government and make it operable also have a kind of technological form (Foucault 1986). If political rationalities render reality into the domain of thought, these "technologies of government" seek to translate thought into the domain of reality, and to establish "in the world of persons and things" spaces and devices for acting upon those entities of which they dream and scheme.
>
> (32)

Thus the dream of educational reform and its supposed materialization through the policy schemes and interventions devised to realize student success and to map it through the strategic deployment of the immigrant category in Ontario are what we have been concerned to illuminate. What is interesting about this turnaround story that is attributed to the ministry of education's intervention and reforming of the education system is that it "produces an unproblematic 'truth' about school reform" (Koh, 2009: 291) that is sustained through ideological exclusion of important facts about the influence of socioeconomic advantage and what Gillborn (2008) terms "locked in inequality." He defines the latter as "inequality that is locked-in when historical advantages built through conscious discrimination in the past become institutionalized to such a degree that even the removal of all existing barriers cannot create a level playing field" (64). In other words, employing the category immigrant as a proxy for student diversity enables the video to ignore the full extent of race inequality in urban schools located in cities like Toronto with their "historical legacy of inequality in housing, education, wealth etc.)," which continue to afflict black ghettoized communities (Gillborn, 2008: 64).

In other words, what is maintained throughout the video is "a rhetorical continuity" about the Ontario government's school reform success strategies that is made possible by its focus on Unionville HS as a representative case, which ignores the fact that many economically advantaged immigrant students actually attend this school. More importantly, such a focus on the success of immigrant students hides and avoids the need to attend to the persistence of the significant achievement gap between white middle-class students and some specific minority groups, which remains intact despite the government's reform initiatives. It is this pernicious focus on and visibilization of the achievement of Asian immigrant students that deflects attention away from a consideration of the extent of the black–white achievement gap and, hence, the persistence of race inequality in the education system. As Gillborn (2008) points out, such illustrations that are concerned to portray overoptimistic accounts of the impact of school reform initiatives and policy interventions are actually a deception and hide "the true scale and locked-in nature of race inequality" (68). In fact, Gillborn (2008) further highlights how gap talk, with its focus on closing or narrowing achievement gaps, "operates as a discursive strategy whereby statistical data are deployed to construct the view that things are improving and that the system is moving in the right direction . . . [it] serves a particular strategic and political purpose" (65).

This logic and rationality of government with regards to thinking about achievement, therefore, is one that has pervaded and continues to colonize the policy discourse about educational achievement here in Ontario and Canada, as we explicate further in the following chapter. For example, CMEC (Council of Ministers of Education Canada) (2013a) continues to focus on the gender achievement gap and "boy crisis hype" as a persistent phenomenon at the expense of paying any attention to "the gaps between students of different races and classes [which] are much larger than those for students of different genders" (Mead, 2006: 9). In a recent publication entitled: "What is the potential for boys to catch up to girls in reading? Results from PISA 2009," OECD data are used to frame a policy discourse about the persistence of "a significant gender gap . . . with girls consistently scoring ahead of boys" (CMEC, 2013b: 1). It is in this sense, as Gillborn (2008) explicates in his work, that some critical attention needs to be devoted to questions of big data and how it is deployed. He shows "how apparently technical matters of measurement are actually political decisions because different methods produce diametrically opposed conclusions from identical data" (69). We take up this matter further in the following chapter, which deals specifically with the gender achievement gap.

This observation about the political uses of numerical data in terms of its calculative effects is highlighted by Berliner (2006), who argues that PISA doesn't do a very good job of breaking down the data by social class, race, and ethnicity with its potential for visibilizing "intercorrelations between poverty, ethnicity and school achievement" (963). He disaggregates 2000 PISA test score data for the USA to reveal that "our white students (without regard for social class) were among the highest performing students in the world . . . [while] our African American and Hispanic students . . . were among the poorest performing students in the international sample" (963). Berliner adds that if only "educational opportunities available to white students in our public schools were made available to all our students, the USA would have been the 7th highest scoring nation in Mathematics, 2nd highest scoring nation in reading, and the 4th highest scoring in science" (963). In the next section and in relation to an analysis of Finland as a reference society we explore the mediatized framing of the lessons to be learned about educational reform and the limits that are imposed in terms of drawing comparisons between nations such as Finland and the USA and also between the USA and Canada.

Finland as Reference Society

The Finland video, like the Ontario one, is also significant in terms of the spin it provides on educational reform and the lessons that it offers, as well as the mirror that it holds up to the rest of the world. Much has been written about Finland and its education policies since it emerged some years ago as a poster child for OECD's PISA and one of its highest performing nations (see Grubb, 2007; Sahlberg, 2010, 2011; Tucker, 2011; Hargreaves & Shirley, 2012; Silander & Välijärvi, 2013; Simola et al., 2013; Varjo, Simola, & Rinnie, 2013). While acknowledging that lessons about educational reform can certainly be learnt, despite the vast differences between nations such as Finland in terms of their histories, cultural contexts, policy trajectories, and alignments across state departments and jurisdictions, our interest is to illuminate the limits of such comparative analyses, particularly in terms of addressing the issue of racial homogeneity and the problematics of the urban (Ball, 2008). We use the Finland video to examine its potential for ideological closure in the "preferred reading path" that it sets for building a consensus about educational reform, which tends to prioritize inside school effects as opposed to ones highlighting the importance of social welfare and more redistributive policies. Sahlberg (2011) and Grubb (2007), for example, both draw attention to the importance of the welfare state and its alignment with educational policies that support economically disadvantaged youth in terms of the provision of health care and adequate housing, but such perspectives on the dynamics of inequality in terms of curtailing the capacity of schools to successfully ameliorate such structural disadvantages are either glossed over or simply ignored in discussions about the Finland case and its use to draw comparisons with nations such as the USA, for example (see Berliner, 2006, 2013; Grubb, 2007).

This phenomenon of ideological closure, as it is reflected in the OECD's mediatization and marketing of the Finland case, raises important questions about what Tucker (2011) refers to as "a certain interplay between empiricism and theory" (15). As Tucker stipulates, this integral relationship raises important issues about the questions that are asked in conducting research and the assumptions and theoretical constructs governing questions pertaining to causation. For us, it is the questions and the constructs that pertain to the role of the education system in addressing forms of inequality related to race and class disadvantage that interest us, and the extent to which they are muted in the prioritizing of educational policy discourses related to the steering of school reform agendas on a global scale through the OECD's PISA regimen (Lingard, 2011). It is for this reason that the "policy as numbers" approach to evidence-based policy making needs to be considered in tandem with fine-grained ethnographic empirical research that renders visible "the macro-level structural dynamics related to globalization and neoliberalism" and with analyses of how economic and social contexts impact schooling and the everyday lives and experiences of students, educators, policy makers, parents, and so on—a point that we will return to in the final chapter of the book (Lipman, 2011; Weis & Fine, 2012: 173).

The Finland video begins with a commentary from the Minister of Education, Henna Virkkunen, who emphasizes the commitment to egalitarian principles at the heart of the Finnish society and education system:

> I think one of the most important issues in Finland is that we want to have a system where all the pupils and all people have the equal opportunities and education, and it doesn't matter where you are living or are you rich or poor, or are you girl or boy. We want to give equal opportunities for everyone.

The opening images of the video focus our attention primarily on close-up shots of children and teachers in classrooms as we hear the voice-over of this commentary before cutting to an image of the Minister speaking and then back to the classroom — a strategy that is employed throughout many of the OECD visual documentary texts. The effect is to continuously direct attention of the viewer to the classroom and to an emphasis on the significant role of the teacher in educational reform. What emerges right from the outset is the Nordic emphasis on equality, which Sahlberg (2010) refers to as central to the "creation of a type of welfare state where basic social services, including education, became public services for all citizens, particularly for those most in need of support and help" (112). However, the significance of such a welfare state is not given any particular focus in the video, which is more concerned to emphasize teacher quality and teacher training as central to the Finish approach to ensuring good quality education. This blind spot is consistent with the fundamental rationality that is supported by OECD's PISA that socioeconomic hardship can be overcome by higher quality schools and teachers given that "it is possible to identify substantial numbers of resilient students in practically all OECD countries":

> In general, the accuracy with which socio-economic background predicts student performance varies considerably across countries. Most of the students who perform poorly in PISA share a challenging socio-economic background and yet some of their socio-economically disadvantaged peers excel in PISA and beat the odds working against them.
>
> (OECD, 2011a: 38)

Rothstein (2004) identifies a certain naivety in such reasoning and highlights how it can easily lead policy makers to lend too much emphasis to "simply improving the quality of teachers without having to worry about the social and economic causes of low achievement" (69)—a point we return to in the following chapter. But what is particularly interesting about the Finnish case, as marketed by the OECD, is not only the mediatized emphasis on improving teacher quality, which we will further document, but its blind spot in terms of addressing the significance of racial and cultural homogeneity, particularly in terms of drawing any comparisons with nations such as the USA or Canada, for example, where there are significant concentrations of visible minority and Latino populations in urban centers and evidence of ghettoized and racialized poverty, in addition to accumulated histories of racism and economic disadvantage (Rothstein, 2004). This absence is interesting, given Sahlberg's (2011) comments that while it is true that Finland "has remained ethnically homogenous," since it joined the EU in 1995 "cultural and ethnic diversification has progressed faster than in other European countries," and that there are schools in Helsinki where the immigration population is at 10 percent (68). However, such claims do not detract from other sources, which identify Finland as having one of most homogenous populations in all of Europe with Finnish comprising 90 percent of the overall population in 2010 (www.mapsofworld.com/finland/population.html). These details are important when drawing comparisons or attempting to use "big data" as a basis for providing lessons to other nations such as the USA, with its historical legacy of deeply embedded racisms (Goldberg, 2009).

Moreover, in the video there is a decided lack of emphasis on the specific role of the welfare state in Finland, which Sahlberg (2010, 2011) and others such as Grubb (2007) document as pivotal in supporting the work of teachers in schools and the education system in its capacity to address the educational needs of all students, and particularly those who are economically disadvantaged. With regards to examining the importance of noneducational services and the idea of supporting schools in the provision of such services, Grubb (2007) claims: "And any American educator suggesting that schools need non-school policies to overcome the effects of family background is now accused of violating the mantra that 'all children can learn' in contrast to the Finnish acceptance that both school and non-school services are necessary" (112). In addition, Sahlberg (2011) adds that "education system performance has to be seen in the context of other systems in the society, for example, health, environment, rule of law, governance, economy, and technology. It is not only that the education system functions well in Finland, but that it is part of a well-functioning democratic welfare state" (115).

So in tracing how the video represents Finnish education reform with the view to achieving an intended communication outcome with regards to orchestrating a particular policy narrative, to what extent are questions of the significant role of the welfare state and nonschool social support systems actually highlighted as central to Finland's educational successes? How are both semiotic resources and accessed voices employed in the service of privileging a particular way of seeing and producing certain "reality" effects (Koh, 2009: 287)?

Following the Minister of Education is a commentary by Timo Lankinen, the Director General of National Board of Education in Finland, who talks about the restructuring of the Finnish Education system since the 1970s, which has resulted in a fundamental decentralization of power to municipalities for educational governance. This devolution of delegated authority at the local level, combined with a focus on highly trained teachers, he infers, has contributed to fostering autonomy of decision making and increased professionalism for teachers and schools in terms of curriculum development and implementation, factors that are attributed to Finland's top performance on PISA. This message is emphasized visually and structurally in terms of the slide that follows the Director General's commentary and that states: "Finland has consistently been one of the top performers of all countries participating in PISA from 2000–2009." Following this slide the camera cuts to another classroom setting. A teacher is teaching a lesson, with comments from the Minister of Education being introduced as a voice-over, which then cuts to a visual of her talking to the camera. She further reiterates the benefits of the decentralized education system, with the municipalities having the delegated responsibility for running schools. The video then cuts to another slide stating that Finland's decentralization of education in the 1990s required a strong highly trained teaching force, once again emphasizing the role of teacher education and high-quality teaching as one of the central components of Finnish reform enabled by deregulation of top-down administrative authority to local municipalities. This slide is followed by another shot of a classroom setting featuring a teacher teaching a class that then cuts to a commentary by Pasi Salhberg, then Director General of CIMO (Centre for International Mobility and Cooperation) at the Finnish Ministry of Education.

Sahlberg's commentary further consolidates, encapsulates, and privileges an already established authorial view in the documentary regarding the emphasis and status that is given to teaching and the teaching profession in Finland, which Sahlberg highlights as a distinguishing feature, with teachers feeling that "they can use the knowledge and skills they learn in teacher education fully—that they have a role in curriculum planning and design; they have a very important role in assessing student performance." This commentary is followed by the director general of the National Board of Education reiterating Sahlberg's point about the teaching profession being highly regarded "coming only second to being a doctor or a lawyer." The documentary then cuts to the minister of education who also confirms this authorial viewpoint about the high status of the teaching profession in Finland, which she adds is also attributed to the fact that "all teachers are required to have a Master's degree from a university in Finland." Another scene of a teacher in a classroom follows this last comment that then cuts to an interview with the president of the Trade Union of Education in Finland who also mentions the high quality of teachers and teacher training in Finland. Interviews with a teacher, a professor from University of Turku, and another comment by

Sahlberg all serve to provide further insight into the nature of teacher education and in-service training and the investment in providing teachers with the support and mentoring needed to become effective in the classroom.

Later in the documentary, Sahlberg is introduced again to highlight the emphasis that is placed on early detection of difficulties that students might be experiencing in the school system; a policy priority that he believes sets Finland apart from many other countries where interventions are implemented only after the problems have emerged. Following this commentary is a slide entitled "Early Intervention" with this statement: "In Finland, there is an emphasis placed on early intervention. The percentage of students benefitting from part-time and full-time special intervention is highest from grades 1–3." The video moves from a focus initially on decentralization to a discussion about the status of the teaching profession, teaching quality, and the quality of teacher education to addressing the policy emphasis in Finland on early detection of learning difficulties and diagnostic assessment of student learning needs. In fact, Salhberg claims that both equity and quality of the education system in Finland is attributed to such policy intervention as reflected on student performance in "international studies."

The final part of the documentary video focuses on the Student Welfare Team, which meets on a weekly basis and comprises the subject teacher and other supportive professionals such as the school nurse, school psychologist, student counsellor, and principal depending on the nature of the identified problem that a particular student is experiencing. A vice principal's voice is accessed at this point in the video who claims that "these individual problems are dealt with, case by case, in this weekly meeting that every school in Finland has." This statement is followed by a comment by a student counsellor who supports this viewpoint: "The Student Welfare Group deals with any kinds of problems that we see in school having to do with problems at home or learning disabilities, multicultural problems. The main value of our Student Welfare Group is to interrupt, as soon as possible problems involved," which is tied in with the earlier point about the importance of early intervention.

The video ends with comments from the director of National Board of Education and by the minister of education, who both reiterate and tie together the various threads of the video, the former attributing "very small disparities between low achievers and high achievers" and success on PISA in Finland to "a virtuous circle surrounding teaching" that in turn is related to "excellent teacher education" and an emphasis on maintaining high standards for all students in the education system. This sequencing of accessed voices, slides containing key points, and classroom scenes are carefully orchestrated and have undergone a process of selection with the explicit intention of performing "a wider public pedagogy" (Koh, 2009: 287) in terms of fostering a particular policy narrative about educational reform inside Finland, but which is designed through its ideological closures to serve as a mirror for other nations.

In fact, right throughout the video these interspersed visuals of teachers in classrooms with primarily white Finnish students—although there is one classroom scene that includes a focused close-up shot of a student wearing the *hijab*—not only point to the whiteness of the education system, but to the policy emphasis of the strategically articulated narrative about the crucial role of teachers and schools in contributing to Finland's success on PISA. We in no means want to detract from the significant role of teachers and their influence, but it is the absence of a focus on drawing attention to the significance of the Finnish welfare state and its alignment of policy articulation across a number of administrative bodies and departments of existence that point to the limits of the reception regime that is established through the "rhetorical continuity" that is created as a result of careful editing, sequencing of images, accessed voices, and slides (Koh, 2009: 292). As Koh argues: "Editing is essentially a motivated practice, as edits of visual images connect spaces and times, themes and moods, sutured together to produce a seamless continuous flow" (292).

This editing effect with its ideological closure is reflected right throughout the video in the emphasis on teacher quality and schools in the extent of their support for student learning, early intervention, and diagnosis of student learning difficulties and needs. However, while drawing attention to the nature of the support teachers receive in the form of other professionals, such as school counsellors and school psychologists, it tends to underplay the broader significance of the extent of welfare support outside of the school system, which is a crucial factor in ameliorating social and economic inequalities that afflict some of the most disadvantaged students in the education system. As Schwartz and Mehta (2011) emphasize, "these are full service schools" that provide a daily hot meal for every student, health and dental services, in addition to offering guidance and psychological counselling services and other services to both students and their families who are in need (59). They reiterate that "none of these services are means-tested" and that health care, like education, is free in Finland (59).

The political ramifications of such a foreclosure are highlighted by a number of other OECD publications that are built on drawing lessons for the USA by a focus on top performers and turn-around nations on the basis of their PISA performance scores (OECD, 2011a). Such publications detract attention from a full consideration of the extent of poverty, income inequality, and race relations in a postwelfarist American context, which has resulted in what Berliner (2013) has identified as "an apartheid system of schooling," comprising racially segregated populations in inner-city schools. This phenomenon of the ghettoization of poor racial minorities in schools serving similar populations needs to be understood as set against a critical understanding of the impact of neoliberal education and economic policies that have worked in tandem to further disenfranchise such populations. The Finland video and other OECD publications, which tend to rely on the category of immigrant and to deny the full extent of the capacity of nonschool services to impact significantly on the quality of schooling for disadvantaged minority students, illuminate the severe limitations of drawing comparisons between nations that tend to focus, in an overdetermined way, on the influence of teachers and schools without also paying due attention to questions of the dynamic interplay of race and economic inequalities in countries such as Canada and the USA. There are, of course, significant differences in terms of the welfare state and its support in terms of provision of heath care, for example, that are important in any discussion of differences between these two nations, as indicated in the previous section.

At the heart of such deracination, in terms of policy discourses and narratives, is the question of the need to interrogate the data and interpretive frames governing how school achievement is being presented and mediatized through explicitly articulated exclusions. These foreclosures result in a fundamental politics of racelessness and de-emphasis of the significant role of poverty and the extent of income inequality in nations such as the USA. As Berliner (2013: 10) cogently argues: "For example, if national poverty rates really are a causal factor in how youth perform on tests, then Finland, one of the highest-achieving nations in the world on PISA tests, with a childhood poverty rate of about 4%, might perform differently were it instead to have the US childhood poverty rate of about 22%" (see Condron, 2011). Wilkinson and Pickett (2009) assert that it is not just poverty per se, but the extent of the inequality income gap that hurts nations. Further, as Lipman (2011) and Rothstein (2004) point out, this inequality is exacerbated by disparities affected by race relations in the USA. The USA has one of the greatest levels of income inequality of any OECD nation and Berliner (2013) argues that it is income inequality and not the wealth of a nation that "strongly predicts poor performance," with disproportionate access to neighborhood resources and quality housing, both of which contribute to further widening of the black–white test score gap (50).

So any comparison with Finland and the USA that fails to account for race and income inequality within the context of the withdrawal of the welfare state and the onslaught of neoliberal governance, with its encroachment on public housing and public education, especially in urban centers (Lipman, 2011), draws attention to the foreclosures that underscore such benchmarking and its comparative basis. However, as Wiseman (2013), points out with regard to the "strong performers and successful reformers," comparative policy responses that receive the most attention "from policymakers, the public and the media are related to improving teacher quality, developing accountability systems around standards, and creating opportunities for equitable education." In turn, this results in a degree of isomorphism among these top performing nations with their policy responses to PISA "rationally bounded into shared categories of expectations for reform, but which varies within the boundaries set by the legitimate expectations for each country's context and history" (Wiseman, 2013: 313).

However, we do not wish to deny the political significance and value of using Finland as a case in point to draw attention to the detrimental effects of neoliberal policies and agendas in other countries such as the USA, which have resulted in a degree of withdrawal of the welfare state and an instantiation of accountability regimes that fail to ameliorate racial and income inequality (Lipman, 2011). Finland has a low Gini coefficient of inequality and this should be acknowledged in any sensible usage of Finnish schooling as a reference system. However, the fact that Finnish PISA performance is not often used in this capacity, but as a means of placing emphasis on the role of teacher quality to the exclusion of addressing structural inequalities impacting on students and teachers in schools, is very significant. For example, Salhberg highlights that the Finnish way has involved a rejection of educational reform initiatives that have been supported by what he terms a global education reform movement (GERM), which is "characterized by increased competition and choice, standardization of teaching and learning, tightening test-based accountability, and merit based pay for teachers" (Sahlberg, 2011: 125). This policy reality then makes Finland an exemplary case for rejecting No Child Left Behind, Race to the Top, and neoliberal reform agendas in the USA (Berliner, 2013). In fact, according to Sahlberg, Finland's performance on PISA has actually protected it from the encroachment of neoliberal forces from within the country itself, which have been working to introduce more top-down and intensified accountability reforms. Moreover, despite the ways in which Sahlberg is used or accessed selectively in the PISA documentary, in his book he is clear about the lesson to be learned from Finland regarding the importance of the welfare state in guaranteeing high-quality education and the well-being of all students:

> The Finnish welfare system guarantees all children the safety, health, nutrition, and moral support that they need to learn well in school.... One lesson from Finland is, therefore, that successful change and good educational performance often require improvements in social, employment and economic sectors. As described by Stuart Kauffman (1995), separate elements of a complex system rarely function adequately isolation from their original system in a new environment. Therefore rather than borrowing only specific aspects of innovations from other education systems, more transferable aspects may be features and policy principles of a larger, complex system, in this case, the Finnish Model.
> (Sahlberg, 2011: 133)

Both the Finland and Ontario cases are useful in drawing attention to significant erasures and ideological closures in terms of how educational reform gets constituted and the lessons that can be learned. Our point is not so much that lessons cannot and should not be learned from these specific cases, but that certain key omissions pertaining to the impact of structural inequalities related to race and income disparity enable a specific policy articulation and rhetorical continuity and legitimation that underscores the marketing strategies employed by the OECD to push its own political agenda for driving global educational reform directives. More importantly, the lessons that are articulated and carefully orchestrated are ones that are built on a degree of deracination and erasure that is illuminated in these mediatized policy texts, which are "semiotically loaded and amenable to manipulation for a teleological end" (Koh, 2009: 294). The OECD documentary videos on successful educational reform initiatives in their design, therefore, need to be understood as providing examples of the mediatization of education policy making with "visual tactics being used to impose a consensual monolithic reading" about best practice that is driven by a deracinated neoliberal logic of accountability and quality assurance (Koh, 2009: 294; Power, 2004).

Conclusion

In this chapter we have drawn attention to the deracinated neoliberal social imaginary that is manifested through the OECD's PISA video series: *Strong Performers and Successful Reformers in Education*. We noted how this video series was partially supported by the Pearson Foundation, the philanthropic arm of Pearson plc that was abolished in late 2014 as Pearson mainstreamed corporate social responsibility. These are matters we will return to in the final chapter of the book, as edu-businesses now have a more significant role in policy processes in education in the context of network governance. We have also been concerned to draw attention to the conditions that have provided fertile ground for the growth and instantiation of a particular policy dispositif by turning a critical analytic focus on the role of PISA as a technology in fostering a global panoptic regime of "governance by comparison." This regime, as we have shown, results in a pernicious politics of erasure and denial, particularly with regards to addressing fundamental questions of race and the effects of poverty. Drawing on Koh's videological framework for interrogating the visualization of education policy, we used two of the documentary texts produced by the OECD—Ontario and Finland—as specific cases to raise some important questions about the rearticulation of equity through a reliance on employing the category of immigrant as a proxy for race, and student diversity, in the former video. In the latter video, we focused on the question of ideological erasure with regard to both illuminating the significance of racial-cultural homogeneity and the role of the welfare state. Our analysis, therefore, points to the limits of the comparative efficacy of these documentary texts in terms of the lessons to be learned. While there are clearly some important lessons to learn about educational reform, we have drawn attention to the fundamental limitations of the marketing of the Ontario and Finnish education systems in terms of the mentality of neoliberal governance that is reflected in how these nations are marketed through a strategic visualization of education policy.

What emerges though our analysis is a heightened awareness of the role of the OECD's PISA as a policy dispositif for the articulation and materialization of a "technicization of politics" that is grounded in a fundamental project of deracination. It is in this sense that the OECD's PISA needs to be understood in terms of a new terrain of networked governance, what Ball (2012) identifies as "new policy assemblages with a diverse range of participants which exist in a new kind of policy space somewhere between multilateral agencies, national governments, NGOs, think tanks and advocacy groups, consultants and international business, in and beyond the traditional sites and circulation of policy making" (10). Our aim in this chapter has been to highlight fundamental ethical, epistemological, and methodological concerns that call for a more careful and critical assessment of what comes to count as equity and successful educational reform. Such a critical project has continued to highlight the imperative to attend to the role of neoliberal rationalities and mentalities of government that come to both determine and define the limits for education policy reform schemes and interventions. As we have illustrated in the chapter, technologies such as the OECD's PISA have contributed significantly to transposing the education policy field into a global market arena of rescaled policy governance and articulation that relies to a significant degree on racelessness, denial, and erasure in its articulation and constitution of what is to count as equity and "successful" educational reform. These processes place sole responsibility for student outcomes on policy, schools, and teachers and in the process deny structural inequalities and the ongoing effects of institutionalized racism.

6
PISA AND THE POLITICS OF "FAILING BOYS"

Introduction

In this chapter we undertake an analysis of the gender achievement gap in Ontario and Canada, as an illustrative case of misrecognition in eliding systemic inequalities related to the effects of social class and racial differences in the education system. It further elaborates on the question of ideological closures and exclusions identified in Chapter 5 to raise some critical questions about what is to count as equity and evidence with regards to a policy focus on "failing boys" in the Organisation for Economic Co-operation and Development's (OECD) publication of the PISA 2009 results. We are particularly concerned with the politics of *truth telling* with regards to prioritizing a policy focus on the achievement of boys and also in terms of categories employed to define and measure socioeconomic disadvantage, practices that are governed by neoliberal logics of accountability and comparative performance measures (Meyer & Benavot, 2013; Wiseman, 2013). Here we see a refusal to engage with critical frameworks and empirical literature that offers a more nuanced account of the macro-level structural dynamics of systems of inequality as they are informed by an intersectional analysis of gender, race, social class, and sexuality in the lives of specific groups of boys and specific groups of girls (McCarthy, 1998; Weis & Fine, 2012).

We focus specifically on policy making processes and discourses from within the Ontario Ministry of Education and also the role of Pan-Canadian Assessment Program (PCAP) (CMEC, 2011), which is administered under the authority of the Council of Ministers of Education in Canada (CMEC), who through the mobilization of what Gillborn (2008) refers to as "gap talk," are concerned to steer educational policy designed to address boys' underachievement. Gillborn

(2008) argues that "talk of 'closing' and/or 'narrowing' gaps operates as a discursive strategy whereby statistical data are deployed to construct the view that things are improving and the system is moving in the right direction" (65). In this chapter, we highlight how "gap talk" is deployed politically to steer education policy in directions that eschew careful attention to performance gaps between multiple and intersecting categories of analysis such as race, ethnicity, gender, class, and geographical location. It is not that achievement gaps should not be the focus of policy intervention. Rather we argue that attention needs to be devoted to the categories in use and the epistemological frameworks that govern the use of numbers.

The attempts by CMEC to steer educational policy are particularly noteworthy, given that education in the Canadian context falls within the jurisdiction of the provinces and not the federal government. This is in sharp distinction with the Australian context where there is complex mix of federal and state government involvement in education, as we demonstrate in Chapter 4. We also see enhanced federal involvement in schooling in the USA with President Bush's No Child Left Behind and President Obama's Race to the Top and in the development of a Common Core for the curriculum. All of these policy developments are linked to test-based modes of educational accountability. Federal political structures then mediate accountability systems, but clearly do so in very different ways (see Savage & O'Connor, 2014 for a comparative account of federalism and schooling in the USA and Australia).

The chapter draws attention to the increasing use of numbers in policy and a particular global policy discourse; that is, a meta-narrative of failing boys, which is framed within a gender achievement gap discourse. In following Power and Frandji (2010) in the UK and Lingard, Creagh, and Vass (2012) in Australia, we illustrate the extent to which policy as numbers, as driven by forms of neoliberal governance in the education field in the Canadian context, has also contributed to powerful instances of *policy misrecognition*. This misrecognition has resulted in the displacement of a politics of redistribution and a failure to attend to racial inequality in terms of bleaching a more considered contextual analysis of schooling and the reality of the impact of material disadvantage on student participation and achievement in schooling. In short, we emphasize that such policy articulation, in terms of gap talk and the use of numbers, overshadows a commitment to addressing and tackling "the underlying causes of educational failure" related to what Power and Frandji identify as the "uneven educational outcomes" for various minority and economically disadvantaged populations, which can best be explained in terms of "maldistribution" (394). Such policy misrecognitions in Canada and elsewhere have actually displaced previous commitments by education policy makers to addressing racism and social class inequality. There is a similar elision at work in Australian education policy, where equity and social justice have become absences in contemporary policy, even in relation to the OECD's

PISA data regarding quality and equity in Australian schooling (Sellar & Lingard, 2014).

We draw on literature from within the field of policy sociology in education (Ball, 1994), which deals with the politics of numbers (Grek, 2009; Ozga, 2009; Lingard, 2011) and that addresses questions of biopower and classificatory systems in relation to neoliberal governance and accountability (Rose, 1999; Hacking, 2006; Miller & Rose, 2008; Ball, 2012; Lingard, Martino, & Rezai-Rashti, 2013). In so doing, our purpose is to highlight the political processes and practices that have enabled the phenomenon of struggling or failing boys to emerge as a target of policy making within the field of education in Ontario with its multispatial dimensions. We highlight the particular significance of this phenomenon of the gender achievement gap in the Ontario context, in relation to a global education policy field and regimes of neoliberal accountability and audit cultures as central to evidence-informed policy (Jordan, 2010; Wiseman, 2010). Consistent with our focus in Chapter 5, we elaborate further on the role of the media and how it functions as a particular technology in setting both the terms and limits of a social imaginary that endorses or fuels a neoliberal policy regime with all of its distorting consequences for measuring and understanding educational inequality. In short, we are concerned to foreground the effects of such policy frames and meta-narratives about failing boys in their capacity to displace a fundamental politics of redistribution, particularly as it relates to the persistence of race and class inequalities in education (Fraser, 1997; Gilborn, 2008; Rothstein, 2004).

Our analysis is set against a broader national and global policy context in which testing regimes such as PISA and PCAP serve as a legitimating basis for accountability-driven, evidence-informed policy in terms of defining, framing, and explaining the limits of educational inequality (Ball, 2003a; Jordan, 2010; Lingard & Rawolle, 2011). PCAP is administered by the Council of Ministers of Education Canada (CMEC), who set up a working group in 2003 comprising representatives from various jurisdictions and an external authority on measurement theory, to develop a large-scale assessment tool and program that has been administered to a sampling of 13-year-old students in all provinces and territories. Students were assessed in mathematics, science, and reading in 2003 and 2010 and this testing regime needs to be understood as part of federalism in Canadian schooling.

What is needed in analyzing data generated by LSAs, such as PISA and PCAP, is critical engagement with an informed research base and the onto-epistemological frameworks that underpin what Lucas and Beresford (2010) refer to as "the categories in use." As Savage and Burrows (2007) stress, we need to critically engage with the constitutive function of social data. Hacking (2006) refers to this phenomenon as "making up people" in the sense of creating categories in terms of constituting and classifying populations, which have implications for the framing of policy discussions on education and inequality, specifically as they pertain to questions of socioeconomic status, race, ethnicity, gender, sexuality, and their intersectionality:

> Empirical research offers little to social analysts and policy makers: theory is essential for drawing proper inferences from the research. Yet the wide set of plausible theories, and strategies of analysis that are not designed to eliminate nonviable theories, can ultimately render social science evidence of little value to policy.
> (Lucas & Beresford, 2010: 26)

In this chapter, therefore, we draw on both the empirical and theoretical literature pertaining to the gender achievement gap to highlight the problem of misrecognition and displacement in the failing boys policy discourse within the accountability systems of Canadian education. While our specific case is located in Ontario, Canada, our analysis has implications for providing further insight into OECD's influence as a technology of governance with its capacity for steering policy within nations and also at the provincial or local level. Furthermore, we elaborate on the nonviability of certain theoretical frameworks and epistemologies that underpin the authoritative assertions about the constitution and reconstitution of boys as the *new disadvantaged* (Lingard & Douglas, 1999) within the limits set by what has been termed by Ball (2012) as a neoliberal imaginary.

PISA, Equity, and the Gender Achievement Gap

The particular polemics about failing boys need to be understood in relation to the imperatives of globalization, the governance turn, and the neoliberal education policy regime that has come to define the nature of policy making within the field of education (Rizvi & Lingard, 2010; Ball, 2013). Within this new neoliberal education policy regime, Ball (2008), for example, identifies new managerialism, markets, and performativity as the three central technologies of governance (see also Lingard, Creagh, & Vass, 2012: 315–316). In Canada (and elsewhere) boys have emerged at the provincial, national, and global levels as a specific target of policy intervention in education and we argue this emergence needs to be understood and reconsidered in light of the global education policy field, with PISA functioning as another layer in the technology of governance in further directing policy makers' attention to a comparative focus on failing boys both within and across nations. Through PISA and its use in the Canadian context, for example, we see this rescaling and relocation of political authority in terms of policy effects within nations. As both Lingard (2011) and Grek (2009) have pointed out, it is important to understand the role of PISA as a technology of neoliberal governance that ushers in a culture of performativity and competitiveness among nations desiring to achieve "world class standards" (OECD, 2010a: 4) through the gaze of mutual accountability. As we have already illustrated in Chapter 5, the nation is constituted as a "space of equivalence" with Finland and Canada, specifically Ontario, being held up as exemplary in their performance on PISA tests. The OECD's tactics of promoting and marketing Ontario as a high-quality/high-performing jurisdiction is made possible through certain erasures and elisions pertaining to race and social class, and raises important questions of misrecognition and maldistribution for minority populations in the Canadian context (see Anisef, Brown, Phythian, Sweet, & Walters, 2010; Mundy & Farrell, 2008). However, while marketing Canada as a high performer, the political emphasis on disaggregating achievement data on PISA, which foregrounds gender, highlights the "relation between political problematizations and attempts to make them calculable through numerical technologies" (Rose, 1991: 673).

Such marketing of nations by OECD as top-performers draws attention to the ways in which political authority is being mobilized through a politics of numbers beyond the nation-state and a mode of global accountability in education, as we will illustrate below with reference to the Canadian case of CMEC and other networks, including the media, in their attempt to steer education policy regarding failing boys in the Ontario context. As Rose (1988) highlights, numbers in conjunction with the human sciences establish "a regime of visibility" and "a grid of codeability" for creating a navigable space of commensurability, equivalence, and comparative performance, thereby rendering the population amenable to administration, statistical mapping, and governance (187; see also Desrosieres, 1998). Power (2004), in fact, argues that "much has to be done to render diverse phenomena countable" or calculable, and that "measurement is based on classification systems that ignore 'inessential differences' and reduce complexity" (767). Those processes are an important step in creating performative systems of accountability based on outcome measures. This is not to argue against the importance of quantification, but rather to highlight, as Rose (1999) explicates, the politics of numbers and "the complex technical work" that is required to render phenomena amenable to measurement and, hence, government, particularly with regards to "the complex array of judgements and decisions that go into a measurement, a scale, a number" (208). Moreover, Lingard (2011) argues that numbers as inscription devices with their classificatory potential are not able to capture the messy, hybrid realities of people's lives today and can elide the complexity of schools in their variable contexts (see also Luke et al., 2010; Jordan, 2010; Wiseman, 2010).

Thus it is important to understand the role of PISA in terms of the execution of a neoliberal governmental rationality and analytics of governmentality, which is inextricably tied to norms for establishing grids of intelligibility that are rendered amenable to administration through calculable practices. Miller and Rose (2008), for example, point out that rationalities and technologies of markets have been extended "to previously exempt zones such as health and education" (18). They argue for an approach to policy analysis that takes account of the "complex and heterogeneous assemblage of conditions that makes it possible for objects of policy to be problematized, and rendered amenable to administration" (28). It is in this sense that we are interested to investigate how "boys" and broader questions of equity are treated as *objects of government*, which we set against this analysis of a rescaling of educational politics, policy making, and accountability. Our position is that there is a need to attend to the global, national, and local dimensions of education policy making. This project requires that we draw attention to the marketization of education, which is connected to cultures of performativity and accountability influenced by transnational policy actors, ministries, and ministers of education, the media, administrative bodies, and international economic organizations such as OECD.

Eschewing Important Questions of Equity and Redistribution

In its document, *PISA 2009 Results: Overcoming Social Background (Volume II)*, the OECD (2010a) aims to address equity in learning opportunities and outcomes and highlights the significance of socioeconomic background and the inequitable distribution of educational resources as key factors impacting student performance. However, the thrust of the data analysis in the second PISA 2009 volume is to draw attention to the fact that "educational equity can be achieved in diverse socio-economic contexts" (32). To support such claims, data are used to illustrate that countries with similar levels of income inequality do not necessarily show similar patterns of distribution in terms of learning outcomes and performance on PISA measures. Rather, what is more closely correlated is the performance of education systems and the share of poorly performing students, identified as those who fail to reach the PISA baseline Level 2 of reading proficiency (33). In short, the OECD (2010a) supports the position that, while there is a link between socioeconomic background and student performance, such an impact can be ameliorated by an effective school system, appropriate policies, and increased educational resources. Moreover, the data reveal that "there are students from disadvantaged backgrounds who show high levels of performance," which further supports the position that performance on PISA cannot be reduced solely to a student's socio-economic background (33). Within the context of such a framing and discussion of performance measures on PISA, equality in learning outcomes is defined as both the relative "difference between high and low performing students," and in terms of the proportion of those students who perform at a baseline level of proficiency. This enables attention to be focused on "the absolute proportion of students who fall below a baseline level of performance," which represents those students "who have not acquired the fundamental knowledge or mastered the basic skills that will enable them to progress further in education and beyond" (38). Thus both relative and absolute measures of equality in learning outcomes are flagged as important because of their capacity to "provide insight into *the extent to which a school system fails to provide* all students with equal and adequate levels of knowledge" (38, our emphasis).

While we do not deny that the quality of teachers and schooling can make a difference and may lead to better educational outcomes for some economically disadvantaged students, and that not all disadvantaged students necessarily perform badly, there is some concern that such a position can lead to an overzealous emphasis on school-based reform and the centrality of teachers at the expense of a more considered engagement with a broader societal politics of redistribution—a point that we explicate more fully later in this chapter (also see Condron, 2011). In fact, Wiseman (2013) points out how a focus on teacher quality and, hence, assumptions about the role of schools in raising achievement and addressing issues of educational equity, underscore the OECD's policy emphasis though the deployment of the PISA assessment regimen:

> As a result of this type of widely held and publicly affirmed causal assumption, the teacher-quality discourse among many countries' educational policymakers has taken a turn towards higher standards for teacher recruitment and selection (Beese & Liang 2010). And this assumed connection between teacher characteristics and student performance has a long history within large scale international assessments like PISA (Huber & Gordel 2006), even though the exact characteristics of teacher quality and their importance to student learning take decidedly different tracks in Finland and Singapore.
> (314)

Two aspects of this framing of equity and relative performance gaps within countries in terms of schools failing to ensure equality in learning outcomes emerge as troubling. The first relates to how gender is inserted into a grid of intelligibility regarding measures of educational equity. The second pertains to the *categories in use* that are deployed to measure the effect of socioeconomic background on student performance. For example, included in Figure 11.1.4 on page 34 of the OECD (2010a) document is a summary of PISA measures of educational equity for all OECD and partner countries ranked in terms of their mean scores. Gender as a category, disaggregated in terms of the percentage of boys and percentage of girls scoring below reading proficiency Level 2, comprises two of the columns represented with other criteria in separate columns, such as percentage of variance in student performance explained by students' socioeconomic background also being represented. What is foregrounded in the presentation and tabulation of such data is the stark gender achievement gap across nations, with more than twice as many boys (14 percent) than girls (6 percent) in Canada, for example, performing below Level 2 proficiency. In Finland and Australia the difference is even greater, with over three times as many boys failing to meet Level 2 proficiency and these are the results for some of the most highly ranked countries. In the UK, which performs just slightly above the OECD average mean reading score, the gender gap is still quite significant with 23 percent of boys and 14 percent of girls failing to meet Level 2 proficiency in reading. In the USA the numbers are 21 percent of boys versus 14 percent of girls. Such disaggregation of data to include a specific focus on gender elides a more thoughtful and nuanced consideration of race and class inequalities in performance gaps, which significant literature in the field has shown to be much greater than any gender gap, particularly in countries such as the UK, USA, and Canada (AAUW, 2008; Anisef et al., 2010; Berliner, 2006, 2013; Gillborn, 2008; Lipman, 2004; Mead, 2006; Rothstein, 2004; TDSB, 2006). The problem is that such measures of equity that direct attention to a gender achievement gap do so at the expense of a consideration of how other important socioeconomic and demographic variables interlock and overlap, with significant consequences for certain visible minority populations—both boys and girls.

This focus on the persistence of race inequalities of achievement as "a locked-in" phenomenon is highlighted by Gillborn (2008), as mentioned in Chapter 5. He discusses the effects of privileging both class and gender underachievement in terms of eschewing important questions of maldistribution. Gillborn argues for a more careful disaggregation of performance data and draws on data sources from within the DFES (Department for Education and Skills) in England, which are disaggregated by class, race, and gender to reveal the extent of different achievement gaps. The mapping of such data reveals the extent to which race and class achievement gaps are far greater than any gender achievement gap. However, Gillborn is concerned to draw further attention to the significance of an intersectional analysis of these achievement data, which uses a more sophisticated indicator of ethnic background to reveal important variations within these class- and gender-based trends. For example, a close reading of the data shows that white non-FSM (free school meal) students outperform their peers from the same gender from different ethnic groups with the largest disparity existing between white students and their black Caribbean counterparts: "White non-FSM girls outperform their Black Caribbean counterparts by 9.7 percentage points" while the achievement gap between "White non-FSM boys" and black Caribbean students is 17.2 percentage points (56).

Gillborn uses such disaggregated data to challenge the discourse of *white failure*, which was generated by the media coverage at the time in England and tended to portray white boys as being left behind by the education system. There was also much sensationalized newspaper coverage of white working-class boys specifically as "the worst performers in schools" (56), which tended to rely on moral panic and crisis associated with the familiar failing boys rhetoric, which has "tended to emphasize the scale of class inequalities as if they were a common factor," rather than unevenly distributed across race and ethnic lines (55). This focus on the practices of journalists in contributing to the mediatization of educational policy

(Lingard & Rawolle, 2004), as we will illustrate later specifically in relation to the Ontario context, is central to understanding the role of the media in how boys continue to be constituted as particular objects of government in that they are rendered as knowable and calculable subjects, and, hence, amenable to systematic and programmatic intervention (Miller & Rose, 2008: 30). Mundy and Farrell (2008) also draw attention to the role of the Canadian media and its emphasis on ranking Canada and its provinces, with little focus on issues of equity and pedagogy. They further elaborate that media "coverage is heavily focused on Ministries of Education, who typically attribute successes to the educational system, while laying failure at the feet of families or economics rather than their own policies" (210). This point further highlights the role of the media in the rendering of boys into such a discourse of moral panic and crisis (Titus, 2004) with its capacity to eschew important questions about the persistence of locked-in racial inequalities in education. As Gillborn (2008) illustrates, while both black and white students' achievement has improved over a period of 15 years since 1989 in England, the black–white achievement gap was far greater in 2004 (at 21 percentage points) than it was 15 years earlier (at 12 percentage points) (59).

Such an illustration of disaggregated data use and its capacity to draw attention to more complex interactions between gender, social class, and race influences, in terms of how they impact educational achievement for various populations, raises important questions about what counts as evidence and equity. Moreover, such data usage draws attention to important epistemological and political issues underscoring approaches to measuring, explaining, and defining inequality in educational policy and practice (Luke et al., 2010: vii; Martino & Rezai-Rashti, 2012; Mundy & Farrell, 2008). For example, while the OECD (2010a) does acknowledge the relationship between family and socioeconomic background factors and the unequal distribution of social and financial resources among various school locations, in terms of its impact on school performance, data are employed to show that there are indeed "weaker relationships between background characteristics and reading performance in some countries compared to others [which] signal that inequalities in educational opportunity are not inevitable" (43). Here we witness, once again, an exemplary instance of how international rankings and comparisons are used with implications for "new geographies of governance" particularly in terms of their capacity to steer policy related to educational and school based reform within nations (Lingard, 2011: 357).

More significantly, this focus on measuring certain background factors instead of others relates to the second concern mentioned above about how categories govern the measurement of such variables and their potential influence on students' reading performance. For instance, PISA involves the collection of "detailed information on various aspects related to the economic, social and cultural status" of students' families, and indicates that measurement is based on indices such as "the education level and occupational status of students' fathers and mothers and their access to cultural and educational resources at home" (OECD, 2010a: 43). However, it does offer the following cautionary note in drawing attention to what is not being measured:

> The relationship between socio-economic background and performance does not necessarily reflect inequalities that occur within the boundaries of the school; inequities also hinge on societal arrangements for family healthcare, income maintenance, housing and children, to name just a few factors. Indeed, some of these factors, or *their interaction with socio-economic background*, may have as much or a greater impact on performance than schools. *While PISA did not collect information about these factors*, it is worth keeping them in mind when interpreting the results reported here.
>
> (43, our emphasis)

In short, the OECD acknowledges that "the average performance of students depends on the education system and the overall social, economic and political institutions that influence student performance," which include "government institutions that improve children's material conditions, like housing, nutrition and health care," but that "differences in these conditions across countries are not taken into account" (56). These limitations have serious implications for being able to address the full extent to which any school is able to overcome socio-economic disadvantages and, hence, the locked-in inequality related to these structural determinants, which we know affect variously positioned populations differentially, given histories of race-relations and maldistribution in terms of access to resources such as good-quality housing in urban locations, employment, and so on (Anyon, 1997; Condron, 2011; Dumas, 2009; Lipman, 2004). Anyon (1997), for example, argues that school reform initiatives are simply not enough to overcome "decades of accumulated want and despair that impede students every day" in urban schools "until the economic and political systems in which the cities are enmeshed are themselves transformed so they may be more democratic and productive for urban residents, educational reformers have little chance of effecting long-lasting educational changes in city schools" (13). Failing to account for such socioeconomic factors and generational poverty enables overzealous attention to be focused on the role of school-based and pedagogical reform interventions in their capacity to improve the quality of education, while overlooking the devastating impact of generational poverty and its concentration in certain urban locations and among specific populations.

Rothstein (2004) challenges policy makers' common sense positions that schools can make a difference, which he indicates can easily slip into attributing the achievement gap to the fault of "failing schools" (and we would add, poor teachers) and with which he associates the current emphasis on high-stakes testing regimes and test-based accountability—a practice clearly related to the emergence of quasi-market forces in education associated with the rise of neoliberal governance and performance management systems (1). As Ball (2012) points out, "education is just one manifestation of a global reworking of the economic, social, moral and political foundations of public service provision and the development of new kinds of responses to social disadvantage" (15). Grek (2009) has well highlighted the role of PISA as a "governing device," which has enabled the OECD to constitute a space of equivalence for the emergence of a global education policy field (27). In short, the OECD (2010a) argues that "in a global economy, the yardstick is no longer improvement by national standards alone, but how education systems perform internationally"; they further argue that PISA is a means by which nations across the globe can be evaluated and can evaluate themselves in terms of ascertaining "the quality, equity and efficiency of school systems" (3) (Meyer & Benavot 2013). This is the new global mode of mutual accountability described by Novoa and Yariv-Mashal (2003). As we have witnessed, new spatialities of educational politics and political authority have produced a degree of competition amongst nations and have led to certain education systems in countries such as Finland, Canada (Ontario), and China (Shanghai) being marketed as exemplary models to be emulated by other nations, or at least as providing lessons for other nations to learn about what lies behind the success of each country (Tucker, 2011; Hargreaves & Shirley, 2012). What is interesting about this phenomenon is that the provinces of Alberta and British Columbia in Canada, while performing better on PISA than Ontario, have not received the same degree of publicity (EQAO, 2010). Ball (2012) refers to such situations as entailing policy entrepreneurship and networked governance of key policy makers within a context of heightened neoliberalism.

PISA as a Policy Steering Technology

With regard to the use of PISA results, there is some disturbing evidence that the data on reading performance lend themselves to being co-opted to drive particular educational reform initiatives that ignore important effects of poverty and their impact on the provision of quality education. Riddile (2010), in her article, "It's Poverty Not Stupid," for example, reports that the USA Secretary of Education, Arne Duncan, issued a statement upon the release of the PISA 2009 scores, which he claimed heralded "a massive wake-up call" because they "show American students holding relatively steady in the middle of the pack of the developed nations taking the international exam." Here we witness the effects of PISA as a technology of governance in steering educational reform and policy initiatives at the national level. In light of such data, Riddile claims that Duncan is advocating for "more charter schools, more reliance on competition and free market strategies, more testing, more use of test scores to evaluate teachers, more firing of principals and teachers, more closing of low scoring schools." As shown in Chapter 3, the USA is clearly responding to concerns about its ranking on PISA measures for designating "high performing education systems" across the globe, with the potential for nations to both being marketed and to market themselves as world leaders. Tucker (2011), for example, highlights that performance on PISA measures is about "compet[ing] in the global economy" (16), with scholars such as Mehta and Schwartz (2011) drawing specific attention to Canada, which "looks a lot like US but gets much better results," as having *high-quality* and *high-equity* systems (141; see also Luke, 2011).

Riddile (2010), however, includes commentary from the National Association of Secondary School Principals' (NASSP) Executive Director, Dr. Gerald Tirozzi, who offers a scathing critique of PISA by reusing the statistics to direct renewed attention to the correlation between performance on PISA reading scores and concentrations of school populations of students living in poverty, measured in terms of identifying those schools with a higher or lesser percentage of students who receive free and reduced cost lunch. He shows that schools with a less than 10 percent poverty rate had an average PISA score of 551, while those with a poverty rate of greater than 75 percent had an average score of 446. In fact, using these measures, Tirozzi shows USA schools with a poverty rate between 10–24 percent do better than 10 comparable nations (including Canada) with a top ranking PISA score of 527, and asserts that:

> The problem is not so much with our education system as it is with our high poverty rates. The real crisis is the level of poverty in too many of our schools and the relationship between poverty and student achievement. Our lowest achieving schools are the most under-resourced schools with the highest number of disadvantaged students.
>
> (Riddile, 2010)

This use of disaggregated data draws attention once again to the categories in use in the generation and analysis of data as numbers, as well as to the fact that "the very measurement of educational inequality itself is also not a given" (Lucas & Beresford, 2010: 25). As Tirozzi illustrates, how equity in education is defined changes how nations are ranked according to PISA reading scores and can lead to a shift in the reform focus away from blaming or reforming schools as a policy solution or problematic to one that requires serious consideration of a politics of redistribution. As Riddile (2010) argues, "Of all the nations participating in PISA assessment, the U.S. has, by far, the largest number of students living in poverty—21.7%." A similar argument is proffered by Condron (2011), who also draws attention to the grossly inequitable funding patterns of USA schools. Poverty and inequitable funding are bracketed out of policy discussion of what to do in response to comparative PISA performance.

Given the influence of such multispatial regimes of standardization and marketization within the context of the global policy making field in education, Rothstein (2004) also offers caution to policy makers, who in their concern to close the achievement gap for low-income and minority students, have directed inordinate attention to school reform efforts, which have focused on raising the quality of teaching with the effect of eschewing "the greater importance of reforming social and economic institutions if we truly want children to emerge from school with equal potential" (9). Such a position is consistent with that advocated by Fraser (1997), who argues for the need to move beyond a politics of recognition as a basis for addressing social injustice and directing attention to the politics of redistribution in looking to remedy, or at least ameliorate, socioeconomic disadvantage for minoritized populations (Power & Frandji, 2010). Rothstein, for example, highlights the need for reform strategies that are focused more broadly on redistribution and highlights the following salient points about socioeconomic disadvantage and its impact:

- The "full array of socioeconomic differences" need to be considered and cannot be measured solely in terms of income and parental education levels (52);
- No more than one-third of student achievement variation can be attributed to school effects that tend to be overstated (56)—differences in home literacy support, social class differences in childrearing practices, and differential access to out-of-school experiences such as summer camp, health conditions, housing and social mobility, racial discrimination, which are exacerbated by living in poverty and the accumulated, generational, and persistent effects of such factors over time for specific populations—and these cannot be overcome by contending that higher quality teachers and schools can compensate for such structural deficits: "simply improving the quality of teachers without having to worry about the social and economic causes of low achievement" cannot close the achievement gap for economically disadvantaged students (69);
- Low expectations that teachers and schools have of black and Latino students, while playing a role, cannot offer an adequate explanation of black underachievement—the cumulative effects of poverty, overcrowded and unstable or inadequate housing conditions, levels of support in terms of completing homework and for literacy learning outside of school, and how these are ambitions are exacerbated or frustrated by repetitive experiences of racism in terms of labor market access and success for these specific minoritized populations need to be considered (35);
- There are significant social class differences between blacks and whites with similar incomes—"income is an inexact proxy for the many social class characteristics that differentiate blacks from whites whose current year income is the same," because "blacks whose incomes are near the poverty line are more

likely to have been poor for several years than whites whose poverty is more often episodic" (47); and
- Significant differences also exist between blacks and whites with middle-class incomes—"white middle-class families are more likely than black middle-class families to have adequate and spacious housing, even when annual incomes are similar, because white middle-class families are more likely to have received capital contributions form their own parents,' whereas the black middle-class parents are more likely to be the first generation in their families to have acquired middle-class status (49).

Overall, Rothstein is concerned to emphasize the need for economic reform in achievement gap discourse, which must also address important questions of race and intersectionality as they relate to the cumulative effects of various socioeconomic determinants of generational poverty, health, well-being, adequate residential security and stability, childrearing, and access to educational experiences and opportunities outside of school, etc. For example, he claims that "if black students expect their academic efforts to be unrewarded, it is because the weight of historical experience has been that black efforts in fact have been unrewarded" and that, in spite of their "force of will and determination" to overcome the weight of such history, "teachers and schools cannot transplant ambition into students who are not ready to adopt it" (51). It is in this sense that Rothstein argues for an approach that takes into account both a politics of recognition and how it is intertwined with economic considerations and, hence, a need to attend to a politics of redistribution in addressing educational reform concerned to address the black–white achievement gap (see Fraser, 1997).

An intersectional analysis that takes into account questions of identity, culture, race, and social class is thus needed when interpreting test scores. Such an analysis would take into account background characteristics and differences related to long-term family income, provision of social and cultural capital through childrearing practices, quality of housing, access to health care services, nutrition and differential access to health amongst various populations, generational poverty, parents' educational levels and occupational status. This approach is consistent with Fraser's (1997) argument about addressing both a cultural politics of difference/recognition and a politics of social equality/redistribution, when it comes to dealing with injustices that are simultaneously both racial (cultural) and socioeconomic (economic) and that amount to "theorizing the ways in which economic disadvantage and cultural disrespect are currently entwined with and support one another" (12).

These discussions about the use of categories and interpretation of test score data, along with engagement with epistemological and conceptual matters regarding issues of redistribution and recognition, further highlight the need for methodologically sophisticated and nuanced considerations in the use of data and its analysis. In short, we argue that there is a need to attend more closely to the "theoretical bases of the categories in use" in interpreting test score data and in engaging with policy generating discourses about the achievement gap, particularly in terms of addressing "the complexity of defining and classifying persons along assumed equity-relevant dimensions" (Lucas & Beresford, 2010: 25, 27). In this sense, we support Connolly's (2008) position regarding the need for policy making discussions involving the measurement of achievement gaps to "engage adequately with substantive theoretical and empirical literature" (249), particularly "concerning the content of sociodemographic categories as well as the phenomena those categories collectively reference" (Lucas & Beresford, 2010: 73).

PISA, Gender, and Reading Performance

The OECD (2010b) draws specific attention to tackling both gender and socioeconomic inequalities, but in ways that ignore the need for the sort of disaggregation that has been illustrated by scholars in the field such as Gillborn (2008) and Rothstein (2004). The OECD asserts, for example, that "Girls outperform boys in reading in all countries assessed by PISA" and draws specific attention to "underachievement among disadvantaged boys" (85). While the OECD (2010b) acknowledges the importance of socioeconomic background on reading performance, and that such differences "are often compounded by racial and ethnic differences in achievement" (86), there is no focus on such disaggregated performance measures on PISA that, as Gillborn (2008) illustrates, would provide a more accurate picture of which boys and which girls are most at risk of underachieving (AAUW, 2008; Collins, Kenway, & McLeod, 2000; Lingard et al., 2012; Martino & Rezai-Rashti, 2012; TDSB, 2006). For example, such disaggregated data tend to highlight that middle-class boys perform much better than girls from disadvantaged backgrounds and that the race gap in achievement is much greater than any gender gap (Martino, 2008; Mead, 2006). However, the PISA focus is on highlighting that, *on average*, girls "have better reading skills than boys" and that particular attention needs to be focused on the wide gender gap among low achieving students, given that "boys greatly outnumber girls among those students who lack basic reading skills" and, hence, those who fail to attain Level 2 in reading proficiency (86). The effect of the use of such numbers is to illuminate the "fact" that this group of boys is most at risk.

However, in disentangling the influences behind both gender and class disparities in reading performance on PISA, the OECD (2010b) identifies *reading habits* and *interests* as key explanatory factors, claiming that "when boys enjoy reading, when they read widely and adopt learning strategies extensively, they can attain higher levels of performance reading than girls" (86). Much of the explanatory discourse behind boys' lower reading proficiency throughout the specific chapter devoted to the topic in the third *PISA 2009 Results* volume tends to highlight that "boys enjoy reading substantially less than girls" and, moreover, that they "have less extensive knowledge about effective summarizing strategies than girls," which, it is argued, "explains a large part of the gender gap in reading performance in most countries and economies" (89). It is mentioned that even in Finland, one of the high-ranking performing countries on PISA reading measures, "boys score an average of 55 points lower than girls."

In addition, disadvantaged boys are compared with socioeconomically advantaged girls in terms of their differential reading performance on PISA to assert that if these boys' enjoyment of reading matched those of the latter group, and if these boys had the same levels of awareness of effective summarizing strategies, the achievement gap would indeed be significantly narrower (OECD, 2010b: 95). Questions about comparing disadvantaged boys with advantaged girls, rather than disadvantaged girls with middle-class and more-affluent boys need to be posed, because they draw attention to the space of equivalences that are constituted through numbers. They also draw attention to PISA as a technology of governance for steering and endorsing educational policy making discussions, which further endorse a discourse of failing boys and moral panic in their capacity to eschew important questions of male and white privilege (Connolly, 2008; Gillborn, 2008). In short, the troubling nature of such framing of boys' literacy underachievement data is that it lends itself easily to being co-opted by a "recuperative masculinity politics" (Lingard & Douglas, 1999) and, in so doing, tends to eschew important questions of class privilege that exist for middle-class boys and those boys from more affluent backgrounds. More importantly, this emphasis on gender achievement gaps tends to oversimplify complex issues, not only in terms of eliding how race and ethnicity intersect with gender and social class to impact on groups of students differently vis-à-vis their reading achievement, but also in terms of lending itself to an overzealous emphasis on pedagogical reform that ignores the significance of structural determinants, such as access to resources and the material conditions with which many students in poverty have to contend.

These systemic influences, as Rothstein (2004) and Condron (2011) emphasize, cannot be compensated for by pedagogical and school-based interventions alone that are committed to motivating boys and engaging their interest in reading. For example, to emphasize that the 80 percent of gender achievement gap can be explained in terms of "the extent to which boys and girls enjoy reading and are aware of strategies to summarise information," and to further frame the problematic as a question of "the untapped potential of boys" as "represented by their unsatisfactory levels of internal motivation to read" (90), is to minimize the significance and impact of socioeconomic conditions and family circumstances. This impact is particularly pertinent for those most at risk students living at or below the poverty line, that is, those students who fail to attain Level 2 reading proficiency. Ultimately, closing the achievement gap, in fact, is reduced to a matter of "changing attitudes and behaviours" and to providing "equal access to high quality teachers and schools," the former being identified as "inherently more difficult":

> In the short term, this may require catering to boys' reading preferences, such as their relatively strong interest in reading newspapers and reading online, rather than designing a single model of engagement in reading. Over the longer term, *shrinking the gender gap* in reading performance will require the concerted efforts of parents, teachers and society at large to change stereotyped notions of what boys and girls excel in doing and what they enjoy doing.
>
> (OECD, 2010b: 99, our emphasis)

Here questions of gender identification are singled out for boys as inhibiting their engagement with literacy. While clearly masculinity intersects in very important ways with boys' engagement and participation in literacy (Alloway, Freebody, Gilbert, & Muspratt, 2002; Martino, 2001), such gender achievement gap talk suffers from many of the blind spots identified by Gillborn (2008), in terms of ignoring the significant variations that exist within broad class and gender based trends in achievement (55). More specifically, the question of how certain dispositions are acquired and the sorts of social, cultural, and economic capitals that are associated with high performance in reading and active participation in schooling are simply minimized (Bourdieu, 1986). In short, in its treatment and discussion of reading achievement, PISA tends to rely on a politics of misrecognition, rather than engaging substantively with a politics of redistribution. The former and latter are intimately intertwined in very complex ways (Fraser, 1997) and need to be a focus of government policy.

What is also important to highlight is that many of the most at risk students in school systems in Canada, for example, are not included in the PISA sample, because they have already dropped out of the system due to the cumulative effect of a range of sociodemographic and structural influences that intersect with race (see Anisef et al., 2010; TDSB, 2006). In addition, as noted by Mundy and Farrell (2008), Aboriginal students, especially those living on reserves, are often excluded from the PISA sampling. They rightly assert that the Aboriginal students' inclusion "might sharply impact appraisals of equity in the system, perhaps mitigating the high levels of praise for equity that Canada is awarded by the OECD" (210). For example, as Bouchard, Boily and Proulx (2003) indicate, "extremes in achievement do not divide solely along gender lines"; nor can social class differences be adequately accounted for without attending to significant questions of race and ethnicity, in addition to a consideration of the historical legacy of colonialism and its impact on Aboriginal populations in countries such as Canada, which produce conditions of locked-in inequalities that cannot be easily ameliorated through a reliance on school-based reform interventions: "In Quebec, for example, 77.4% of Aboriginals starting high school have already failed at least one year: In outlying regions, 87.9% of Aboriginal youth leave school before getting their high school diploma [Translation] (Larose et al. 2001: 153)" (Boily & Proulx: 57). Furthermore, such performance data also need to be coupled with an analysis of post-school outcomes and trajectories for boys and girls in terms of their participation in the labor market and earning capacity. Such data have the capacity to further highlight the scale of structural disadvantages for specific groups of both boys and girls (Collins et al., 2000).

Overall, this discussion and analysis highlight the extent to which the OECD (2010b) employs and frames an analysis of PISA performance data on the gender achievement gap in reading to steer educational policy making in a direction that is marred by significant blind spots, as it relates to prioritizing a discourse of failing boys (see also CMEC, 2013b). In this capacity, it needs to be understood as a technology of governance in terms of making up boys as a specific category and target (Hacking, 2006), which enables them to be made amenable to administration and policy making through an orchestrated use of numbers (Miller & Rose, 2008). Hacking highlights the role of statistical analysis and its function in the classification of "classes of people" or specific groups defined as having "definite properties." The ways in which boys are constituted within the commensurate space of the global policy making field and the global politics of mutual accountability, and the role of the OECD and specifically PISA, draw attention to both the use of numbers and onto-epistemological frames of reference that are deployed to render thinkable the problem of "failing" boys. In this capacity, PISA functions as "a vast statistical apparatus through which this domain [of underachieving boys] can be inscribed, tabulated and acted upon" (Miller & Rose, 2008: 36). The political effects of such a technology, in terms of treating boys as a target of government through a politics of misrecognition, is further highlighted in the following section with our analysis of the achievement gap discourse in the pan-Canadian context.

PCAP, Misrecognition, and the Gender-Achievement Gap

As already pointed out, the governance of education in Canada falls under the jurisdiction of specific provinces. However, CMEC was formed in 1967 by the ministers themselves "to provide a forum in which they could discuss matters of mutual interest, undertake educational initiatives cooperatively, and represent the interest of provinces and territories with national educational organizations, the federal government, foreign governments and international organizations" (CMEC, 2011: i). We note, though, among the rich countries of the world, Canada is the only one not to have a national minister of education or national education department. CMEC also claims to be "the national voice for education in

Canada" and, hence, positions itself as an administrative conduit for the provinces and territories "to work collectively on common objectives" (i). CMEC devised a Pan-Canadian Assessment Program (PCAP), which is designed to generate "comparative Canada wide data" on the achievement levels of Grade 8 students in mathematics, science, and reading and is specifically designed to "inform educational policies to improve learning" (1). Through such a statistical apparatus the ministers of education have strategically attempted to influence education policy as it relates to the problem of boys' underachievement. In conjunction with the federal government of Canada—namely the Department of Human Resources and Skills Development, and Statistics Canada—CMEC has also produced a report that details how Canadian results on the 2009 PISA study "measure up" (Human Resources and Skills Development Canada, CMEC and Statistics Canada 2010). Both reports are posted on the CMEC web site (www.cmec.ca) and are concerned to draw attention to gender achievement gaps. In fact, both reports highlight that girls continue to outperform boys in reading, and that boys tend to outperform girls in mathematics and science, although it is emphasized that in these latter two domains the gender gap is less pronounced (Human Resources and Skills Development Canada et al., 2010: 39).

What is significant about the PCAP results is that for each province test score data are disaggregated solely along the lines of gender and the two official languages of English and French. This specific focus on gender is justified in terms of "policy makers (including educators at all levels, parents, and other interested parties)" having a particular interest "in reducing disparities in educational performance" (29). Throughout the report, gender comparisons are noted for each of the subject areas across all provinces and territories. However, given this concern with the gender achievement gap, CMEC is concerned to emphasize that in mathematics, for example, while boys tend to do better overall, the gap is not as large as it is for reading performance, and, moreover, in some subdomains, such as "Patterns and Relationships" and "Data Management and Probability," girls have actually caught up to boys, so that there is no significant difference in favor of boys (31). In addition, the PCAP results also reveal that the mean score of girls in Science is significantly higher than the mean score of boys. A bar graph is also strategically included on page 128 of the report to represent gender and language differences in reading with regard to reading score comparisons on both the 2007 and 2010 PCAP tests. The graph shows that reading performance for both girls and boys has declined—by 7 points for girls (from 522 in 2007 to 515 in 2010) and by 12 points for boys (from 501 in 2007 to 489 in 2010). The representation of data in these terms draws attention to the extent to which the gender gap has widened over time. In 2007 there was a 21-point difference in mean scores between girls and boys, while in 2010 it had increased to a 26-point difference.

The use of such disaggregated data, and their representation in bar graph form, are designed to illuminate the phenomenon of failing boys. This immediately produces a significant blind spot in terms of significant disparities in achievement that exist for minority populations and in terms of socioeconomic background, which, as already pointed out, are far greater that any gender gap (Rothstein, 2004; Anisef et al., 2010; Jordan, 2010). In short, reducing achievement to a politics of gender disparities is to fundamentally misrecognize and eschew what counts as evidence and equity (Fraser, 1997; Luke, Green, & Kelly, 2010), particularly in terms of the need to consider economic disadvantage and intragroup variability regarding "the importance of race, class, and culture in measuring student outcomes" (Jordan, 2010: 150). As Jordan (2010) highlights, racial and socioeconomic equity are actually hindered when investigated through neoliberal and performance-driven educational accountability discourses (164). In this sense, as Rose (1999) points out, numbers are deployed as "inscription devices" and "actually constitute the domain they appear to represent," such as the problematic of failing boys thereby rendering boys as "representable" and "amenable to the application of calculation and deliberation" (198).

What is also interesting to note is that that the "measuring up" report, which was published in 2010 by CMEC and the Canadian government prior to the release of the PCAP report in 2010, reflects an exemplary instance of the rescaling of political authority that results in the constitution of a particular "policy habitus," which Lingard and Rawolle (2011) claim "enhances cross field effects between the global educational policy field and specific national fields" (496). In fact, CMEC (2011) explicitly states that one of the key purposes of PCAP "was to align itself with international assessments such as the Organisation for Economic Co-operation and Development (OECD) Programme for International Student (37). The cross-field policy effects, particularly in terms of the emphasis on the gender achievement gap, are also evidenced by the mediatization of policy (Lingard & Rawolle, 2004), with the role of journalists immediately reporting on the release of the PCAP results to spin a familiar discourse of moral panic about failing boys. For example, upon the release of the PCAP results a journalist for the *Globe and Mail*, Canada's national newspaper, published an article with the sensationalized headline: "Boys' poor results in reading feared to be spreading to math, science" (Hammer, 2011). The heading immediately mobilizes the rhetoric of disadvantaged boys, who are now also at risk of underachieving in other areas of the curriculum, where traditionally they have performed well. The notion of their failure "spreading" conjures up the specter of an epidemic that risks infecting boys across core curriculum subjects such as mathematics and science. In short, it is a phenomenon that is not confined only to reading: "The results raise questions whether struggles with reading are having a domino effect on boys' academic performance. Whether an isolated event, or a sign of something bigger, they raise a red flag for education" the journalist, Hammer, asserts. This newspaper report provides an exemplary instance of the mediatization of policy production, particularly in terms of endorsing a policy narrative about failing boys that is consistent with the one being promulgated through the use of numbers by CMEC, which functions to confer a certain degree of political legitimacy regarding the existence of a gender achievement gap.

The role of media within a network of cross-field policy effects has also been highlighted by coverage of the *Globe and Mail* newspaper on the subject of failing boys, which spanned an entire week in 2010. This particular topic was identified as one of the eight most pressing issues that will challenge Canada in the next decade, alongside the future of the military and the provision of public healthcare (Abraham, 2010). The article introducing the topic began with the following assertion: "There's a new gender gap in education: Around the world, boys rank behind girls by nearly every measure of scholastic achievement" (Abraham, 2010). Splashed across the bottom of the two full-page feature article was a series of graphs drawn from the 2006 PISA results, which disaggregated achievement data solely on the basis of gender for science, reading, and math across a number of OECD countries, including Canada. What immediately becomes apparent is evidence of a respatialization of authority as set against a particular policyscape (Ball, 1998), in which interplays of national and the global forces are mobilized around the recuperative masculinity interests proliferating a particular social imaginary about boys as the "new disadvantaged" through the mediatization of policy production (Lingard & Rawolle, 2004; Martino & Rezai-Rashti, 2012). As we have illustrated in this section, the mass media has functioned in very significant ways within a network of policy making effects and practices, as evidenced by both the role of CMEC and OECD to constitute a particular policy discourse in relation to the endorsement of a gender achievement gap and the mobilization of narratives about failing boys in the Canadian context.

Gap Talk in Ontario

As discussed in Chapter 5, Ontario (along with Finland, Singapore, and Shanghai, China) has been identified as having one of highest-performing education systems as measured by PISA (Luke, 2011; Tucker, 2011). It is also acclaimed to have achieved high equity, particularly with regards to immigrant students performing well in the education system. Luke (2011), for example, specifically attributes Ontario's success to "a distinctive commitment to equity, to multiculturalism" as "core Canadian values" (374). He also draws attention to the high quality of teacher candidates in universities and the investment in on-going professional development for teachers. In addition, Luke mentions the significance of a "less prescriptive curriculum" and "low-moderate emphasis on standardized testing," which he attributes to the push for educational reform that was instigated under Ben Levin, as "one of its key architects" (373) (see Dei & Karumanchery, 1999; Anderson & Ben Jaafar, 2003; Rezai-Rashti, 2003, 2009) for an alternative interpretation of education reform in Ontario). We have already explicated in the previous chapter how the OECD promotional video for Ontario, entitled "Making Sure Students from All Backgrounds and Origins Can Fulfill Their Potential," follows along these celebratory lines and markets Ontario as an exhibit or exemplification of achieving equity for all students, especially those students from immigrant backgrounds. Promotional materials of this kind are the conduit through which national educational performance is represented and policy ideas are shared in the global politics of mutual accountability. While there has indeed been a commitment to equity policy in Ontario that has been influenced by the *Charter of Human Rights* as an overarching framework for policy making both in education and across other fields of governance, the marketing of Ontario in these terms eschews and, we would argue, contributes to a fundamental misrecognition of the historical legacy of inequality that persists in Ontario for specific visible minority populations. The impact of standardized testing regimes and forms of neoliberal accountability mechanisms, such as those instigated under the previous Harris Conservative government and continued under the McGuinty Liberal government, should not be minimized or downplayed (Martino & Rezai-Rashti, 2012).

The Unionville immigrants who are represented in the Ontario promotional video are different from those living in other locations in Toronto in government-subsidized housing, where there are high concentrations of economic disadvantage and poverty. Analyses of Toronto District School Board data provided by Anisef et al. (2010), as well as data provided by the TDSB (2006), tend to offer a different picture of the situation in Ontario for minority students than that provided by OECD. Anisef et al. (2010), for example, document the phenomenon of early school leaving among immigrants in Toronto secondary schools and emphasize that this is "strongly influenced by socioeconomic status as well as such factors as country of origin, age at arrival, generational status, family structure, and academic performance" (104). Moreover, these scholars show that not all immigrants are successful in school and that "the substantially higher incidence of poverty" for certain immigrant populations means that they are "likely to face greater obstacles to academic success that may in turn have detrimental, long-term consequences" (104). In addition, a Toronto District School Board (TDSB) study found that students who speak Spanish, Portuguese, or Somali (the majority of these students are second- and third-generation Canadian) are at a higher risk than any other group of students of failing the Grade 10 literacy test. Furthermore, students from the Caribbean, Central or South America, and Eastern Africa have significantly higher dropout rates than the rest of the population (TDSB, 2006). This example of policy as numbers highlights the need to address which groups of students are most at risk and clearly data generated by local school boards such as the TDSB provide a more informed account of the structural inequalities that continue to impact on differently positioned populations in relation to their socioeconomic, ethnic, and racial backgrounds.

Such disaggregated data need to be set against a problematic policy making context within the Ontario Ministry of Education, which in 2009 launched its *Equity and Inclusive Education* policy that states "an explicit commitment to reducing achievement gaps" and includes the category of boys as a designated targeted population, along with "recent immigrants," "children from low income families," "Aboriginal students" and "students with special education needs" as being "at risk of lower achievement" (Ontario Ministry of Education, 2009: 5). Prior to the insertion of boys into official equity policy as a designated disadvantaged group, the ministry also produce a guide for facilitating boys' literacy engagement in Ontario schools, which endorsed, for the most part, problematic "boy friendly" approaches grounded in essentialist mindsets regarding the need to cater for stereotypical boys' interests as a basis for pedagogical intervention. The guide was also used as a template or policy frame for directing school-based research, funded by the Ontario Ministry of Education, as a basis for generating evidence informed policy for effective interventions in addressing the problem of boys' literacy achievement in schools. We have written about such policy initiatives with their implications for actually exacerbating questions of equity, which we have highlighted here as thwarting a politics of redistribution and a more sophisticated politics of recognition that does not resort to endorsing a recuperative masculinity politics (see Martino & Rezai-Rashi, 2012). We refer briefly to such policy interventions here only because they further highlight the importance of contextualization in producing a counter-narrative that interrupts the celebratory discourses of equity and multiculturalism that have come to characterize the ways in which Ontario is currently being marketed, based on its performance on PISA measures, as a high-quality, world-class education system. This has the effect of blinding the schooling system to ongoing inequalities in and through schooling.

Conclusion

In this chapter we have drawn on policy sociology and substantive theoretical and empirical literature to undertake an analysis of PISA's focus on equity and achievement gaps as basis for explicating the new spatial dimensions of the policy discourse of failing boys within the Canadian context. We have illuminated how the OECD's PISA functions as a technology of governance and a new mode of educational accountability, which is imbricated in policy making at the national and local levels, using Canada as a specific case in point. In the first part of the chapter we concentrated on OECD and PISA 2009 to provide a critique of the use of numbers, particularly in terms of endorsing a gender achievement gap, which eschews important questions of intersectionality with regards to race, culture, ethnicity, and social class. We have drawn attention in this analysis to the theoretical bases of the categories in use that are deployed by OECD in tackling gender and socioeconomic inequalities in reading. Our analyses highlight the categories in use behind the measurement of educational inequality, which as Lucas and Bersford (2010: 25) highlight, should certainly not be taken as a given.

In the second part of chapter we focused specifically on the use of numbers in the Canadian context and drew attention to how such numbers, particularly as they relate to the gender achievement gap, are implicated in a global education policy field, including global politics of mutual accountability in education, with OECD's PISA results as a pivotal reference point. This analysis has highlighted the extent to which national and provincial administrative bodies such as PCAP and the Ontario Ministry of Education function within a global web of networks in which Ontario features as a reference society and markets itself as a high-achieving/high-equity performer. In highlighting this global reworking of national and provincial policyscapes through a politics of numbers, we have drawn attention to the problematics of misrecognition that potentially result from the use of such comparative data sets, which fail to account for the complexity of socioeconomic disadvantage and its cumulative effects across generations for specific visible minority populations in the Canadian context. We conclude on the basis of our critique that the OECD, through PISA, is able to endorse a focus on school-based interventions and the role of quality education systems in their capacity to ameliorate socioeconomic disadvantages by ignoring significant structural dimensions of inequality and a politics of redistribution. In addition, we have been concerned to highlight how the respatialization of authority conferred by the apparent validity of PISA performance measures as indicators of achieving quality and equity is intertwined with broader effects of globalization and neoliberal accountability. It is through such technologies of governance, with their capacity for producing "a globalizing empiricism" (Torrance, 2006) that is central to commensurate global measures of the performance of schooling systems, that failing boys have been made more amenable to administration.

Overall, the critiques offered in this chapter suggest a cautionary note for education policy makers in respect of relying too heavily on PISA measures as a basis for decision-making regarding questions of equity as they relate to maldistribution. What is needed, then, is more engagement with data generation from the *bottom up*, which includes both quantitative and rich qualitative data that are generated at school board and local school level and disaggregated in multiple ways. Such data generation has the capacity to better account for the contextual specificity of schooling, as well as the influence of specific background characteristics and their effects for particular populations in specific school communities. There is also a pressing need for policy makers and schooling systems to more effectively utilize all of the analysis that the OECD provides on PISA performance. It is the positioning of a system within OECD PISA-based league tables of accountability that drive policy responses, rather than more nuanced and sophisticated analyses (Wiseman, 2013). What is also flagged as necessary, for both policy makers and those involved in the conduct of research into equity and social justice matters within the field of education, is the need for a detailed consideration of the extent to which onto-epistemological standpoints impact on both interpretive frameworks that are employed to generate and make sense of performance data and their methodological implications. As we have illustrated throughout this chapter, both the conduct of research and the sort of theoretically informed empiricism that comes to count as legitimate evidence are what need critical interrogation, particularly as they relate to gap talk within the within the system of global accountability in education.

7
CONCLUSION

Argument

Throughout the book we have documented and analyzed the phenomenon of globalizing educational accountabilities. These have been, by and large, top-down, test-based, hierarchical modes of accountability, aided by the creation of enabling data infrastructures and the enhancement of computational and data analysis capacities. We have shown some complementarity between global developments and national moves in establishing LSAs and the related multiple modes of accountability. We have also shown how these programs increasingly work together, with comparison having become central to educational governance in schooling systems, particularly in the Anglo-American world. The OECD has been very important in establishing and sustaining a global politics of mutual accountability in education, particularly through PISA. While the work of the IEA has also been important, it seems to us that the OECD's expansion of its quantitative assessment work (for example PISA for development and PISA tests for schools) is beginning to overshadow the work of the IEA in this respect.

We have seen the emergence of a global education policy field, partially constructed in relation to a global commensurate space of measurement. The OECD's role in helping to establish this space has been mainly through PISA and its enhanced scope (what it measures), scale (breadth of coverage across the globe), and explanatory power. The latter is very evident, for example, in the OECD's move to link measures of teacher classroom practices through TALIS with PISA scores, getting at what one OECD interviewee described as the "holy grail" of educational research. Globalizing educational accountabilities are thus helping to constitute a global education policy field, rather than being so much an effect of globalization (Sobe, 2015). Globalization manifests in new global infrastructures and data production, transmission, and analysis that these infrastructures enable. This is the constitutive work of data, numbers, and metrics; an important complement to their representational functions.

Much data generated by PISA and other LSAs could be of real policy use for nations and subnational systems. This is especially the case in relation not only to quality issues, but importantly in relation to equity. However, the evidence suggests that nations primarily respond to the initial globally choreographed release of PISA results, the accompanying global league tables of performance, and the emphasis on quality (Wiseman, 2013). This is an exemplar of the mediatization of education policy and of catalyst data at work. Much less attention is given to the very useful secondary analyses that the OECD provides, especially in relation to equity data, which thus have less catalytic effects in policy. This situation has allowed, for example, the Australian minister for education to state, based on PISA, that Australia does not have an equity issue in schooling. This is an observation clearly denied in all of the secondary analysis of PISA 2012 data (OECD, 2013a). It has also enabled a national consortium of Canadian Ministers of Education (CMEC) to unduly focus on a gender achievement gap without due consideration to how class and race intersect in important ways to influence participation in the education system (Rothstein, 2004; Lipman, 2011). The policy effect, as we have suggested, is most often for politicians and policy makers to use externalization to legitimate deeper implementation of policies that they already have in train. We have also argued that the OECD is part of this problem, because it tends to emphasize the significance of policy and the work of schools in the etiology of variable systemic performance, while downplaying structural inequality and contextual factors (Meyer & Schiller, 2013). At a time of growing inequality (Piketty, 2014) and austerity policies in many parts of the world, this is a little myopic. We have also seen the potential for this quantitative work to potentially drive out other very important qualitative research work conducted within the OECD's Education and Skills Directorate (for example, OECD, 2015). Certainly in the UK, Australia, Canada, and the USA, we do not see enough policy learning in respect of OECD data, particularly policy learning that recontextualizes policies and practices in recognition of the path dependency of policy reform within national and provincial systems. We also see neglect of how PISA data can inform policies focused on equity.

Throughout the book we have suggested that the new modes of educational accountability structured around testing have implications for issues of equity and social justice in education. Social justice reconstituted around test results reduces the meaning of this concept to refer only to the distribution of test performance in relation to social background, while social inclusion becomes redefined in terms of the achievement of minimum standards (Lingard, Sellar, & Savage, 2014). This reframes questions of social justice in education as technical question of how to improve performance and leaves unconsidered the role of current pedagogies and curricula in the production and reproduction of structural inequalities. We are witnessing in education policy a denial of the significance of context at a time when inequality is growing.

We thus have argued that the categories and data used by PISA need to be deconstructed (see Chapters 5 and 6), but also that sophisticated analyses of these data can be useful for policy purposes. We are cognizant of the potential contradiction here between, on the one hand, criticizing current categories and data usage, while on the other, pointing to the need for more nuanced usages of these data. In the latter case, as Lefstein and Feniger (2014) argue, we are caught within a mode of reason that must continue to grapple with "the methodological problems that plague the international comparative studies it seeks to critique" (846). We see this as a necessary evil, insofar as we argue for engaging with new data infrastructures in education, rather than critically dismissing them. We agree with Lefstein and Feniger's (2014) observation that the important issue for improving cross-national comparisons is understanding "how policy and culture interact with one another" and that to address this question we need more "systematic and elaborate data about the specific practices that are most consequential" (853; see here also Novoa &Yariv-Mashal, 2003).To this end, our position is one of seeking to improve and democratize globalized educational accountabilities.

Chapter 4 developed the concept of "catalyst data" to grasp the ways that data have real and significant effects, perverse and otherwise. Indeed, throughout we have suggested that data are central to the global education policy field. Moreover, in federal systems such as the USA and Australia, comparative performance measures on national testing are helping constitute a new emergent national space of schooling. Here we see the emergence of new topologies associated with globalization and comparison as a mode of governance. For example, the statistically similar schools comparative measure on NAPLAN in Australia constructs a new topological space where schools in different specific contexts are actually seen as being in the same abstracted space. We have also shown how catalyst data have effects within systems and how data flows now constitute the national system, just as globalizing accountabilities have helped constitute the global education policy field. With more autonomy granted to schools and school leaders, "systemless systems" (Lawn, 2013) are being constituted through data and kept operant in the way that Lyotard (1984) suggested.

In the Canadian cases, we have demonstrated how categories are very important in processes of datafication that underpin the creation of tests and metrics, which play a central role in the outcomes and representation of any analysis. Chapter 5 demonstrated this in respect of "race" through processes of deracination—the making invisible of race—associated with the use of the category of "immigrant." We know that, in terms of measures of equity, it is the intersection of social class and race that really matters. We thus need to disaggregate the category of immigrant and look at its intersection with social class and gender. Moreover, we have illustrated how the political deployment of immigrant as category has resulted in a fundamental erasure of non-immigrant racial minority groups. This has implications for the continuing need for anti-racism policy and curricular interventions in the education system (Leonardo & Grubb, 2014). In Australia, Creagh's (2014) research has shown how the category of LBOTE (Language Background other than English), used in analysis of performance data on national literacy and numeracy testing (NAPLAN), also elides social class–based and educational background differences within the LBOTE category. There are potential funding issues here as the analysis of results of the national tests shows that the LBOTE category do at least as well as the non-LBOTE category, while Creagh's analysis demonstrates that within category differences are significant and that consequently some of the poorest performers are hidden by the aggregated performance measure. These tend to be very disadvantaged recently arrived refugee children. Chapter 6 demonstrates the politics surrounding the "failing boys" discourse, a global policy discourse also enabled by a nonsophisticated and nondisaggregated analysis of the data and categories. What these two chapters together demonstrate is how significant categories are in the conduct of analyses, which calls for the need for a more theoretically informed empiricism that attends to the complexity of intersectionality in addressing race and gender achievement gaps in education. It is in this sense that they demonstrate the necessity of more sophisticated analyses that are explicit in their epistemological groundedness and attention to the politics of the intersectionality of race, gender and social class.

We have attempted throughout to exemplify the sort of work Savage and Burrows (2007) have suggested is needed in the social sciences today, as big data emerges and private sector companies develop their data analytic capacities in a challenge to the distinctive mission of empirical sociology. Globalizing accountabilities are part of what Thrift (2005) calls "knowing capitalism," and in this context we have sought to pursue Savage and Burrows's (2007) call to "renew the critical project of sociology by challenging current practices in the collection, use, and deployment of social data" (896). We have also sought to highlight the need for a sustained anti-racist critical analysis that attends to questions of datafication in global education accountability systems that support a politics of racial neoliberalism (Goldberg, 2009).

Throughout the book we have implied that the OECD's education work, especially its international large-scale testing, functions almost as a "global panopticon" or as a practice of "global panopticism," to use Foucault's concepts developed in *Discipline and Punish* (1995, originally 1975 in French). In adding the descriptor "global" here to the concept of panopticism, we are speaking perhaps of what has been referred to as "superpanopticism" (Poster, 1990) or the "international society of the spectacle" (Novoa & Yariv-Mashal, 2003). We have thus extended Foucault's concept beyond an institutional and carceral focus to global spaces and new topological spaces. We think that the concept of "global panopticism" is a useful way to think about globalizing educational accountabilities, but we also want to add some riders here on this usage, drawing on contemporary surveillance studies and critiques of broader applications of the concept (Yar, 2003; Caluya, 2010). In response to these critiques, we note that any Foucauldian analytical concept cannot be straightforwardly applied or simply wrenched from its specific historical and material context. To do so would be to fundamentally misunderstand the political function and use of a Foucauldian interpretive analytics derived from his genealogical studies. Throughout this book, we have attempted to map the disciplinary effects of PISA as a technology of governance and have been careful to move away from implying that panopticism is simply operating in any straightforward or hierarchical manner. We have illustrated that the concept of global panopticism has some explanatory potential for understanding the policy effects of global testing and accountability regimes. This analysis draws attention to the disciplinary effects of such regimes without reducing these effects to forms of regulatory surveillance. The genealogical approach that Foucault employs, in spite of its historical and material specificities, is designed to offer analytic insights into the operation of power relations that have purchase beyond the specific historical dynamics that Foucault mapped. As with all theoretical constructs, there is always some generalizability, but we are cognizant that such conceptual tools also have to be honed and must take into consideration the complexities and contingencies of new contexts.

Deleuze (1995) would suggest that we have moved from Foucault's disciplinary society to what he calls a society of control, a society in which we experience continuous evaluations and assessments. This move results from the reality that the family and the school have to some extent lost their disciplinary salience as normalizing institutions. What increased computational capacities and data infrastructures enable is not only the rise of big data, but also continuous assessment and "the informationalization of social control" (Yar, 2003: 255). We have some sympathy with that argument. In moves to have PISA and NAPLAN in Australia conducted online, with quick feedback loops in terms of data collection and analysis, and more sophisticated branching testing that allows for individual differences to be taken into account, we see the potential move to continuous assessment redolent of a control society and the rise of big data in education more broadly.

Rose (1999) speaks of a play between disciplinary and control societies and we think our analysis supports such a position. But what we see, and what our analysis has shown, are strong tendencies in the direction of intensifying control society modes of power. In terms of continuous assessment, Rose (1999) notes,

> One is always in continuous training, lifelong learning, perpetual assessment, continual incitement to buy, to improve oneself, constant monitoring of health and never-ending risk management. Control is not centralised but dispersed; it flows through a network of open circuits that are rhizomatic and not hierarchical.
>
> (234)

So, with our usage of global panopticism we do not want to suggest a simple top-down, one-way gaze of the "global eye"; indeed panopticism was never conceived to function in this way. Instead, we need to acknowledge the possibilities for the gaze to turn in many directions; while regulatory power is always at play, visibility is not only about control, subjectification and vulnerability (Yar, 2003: 258). Think here of international NGOs such as *Transparency International*, which could be seen to mobilize an alternative bottom-up global gaze. As Foucault (1995) noted, those "subjected to a field of visibility" assume "responsibility for the constraints of power" (202). We need to recognize that nations pay to participate in PISA and in other OECD programs. Historically, the OECD created PISA under pressure from the USA, as nations desired international comparative testing of their school systems as a surrogate measure of the putative competitiveness of their national economies within the global economy. This is the human capital framing of education policy, one proselytized by the OECD, but also readily embraced by political leadership within Anglo-American nations. There is always the possibility for a resistant gaze. There is also the possibility, as suggested above, for progressive usage of PISA data. The same is the case with all test data used for accountability purposes; for example, equity aspects of such data can be used in an "opportunity to learn standards" manner to make demands of politicians.

In the next section, we consider some possibilities for richer modes of accountability that are more educative in impact and, indeed, take as their raison d'être the broader purposes of schooling in respect of social justice, citizenship, democracy, and learning.

Rich Accountabilities

The central argument of this book is that educational accountabilities are being reworked in the context of new spatialities produced by globalization, datafication, increased computational capacities, and new modes of governance. This context has also opened up spaces for edu-businesses in the new networked governance within nations and globally (Ball, 2012; Ball & Junemann, 2012). We have critically analyzed some of the effects of these reworkings, particularly in relation to some of the perverse effects of accountability, growing democratic deficits in educational governance, and the elision of structural inequalities. We have thus given significant focus to what Lyotard (1984) characterized as the potential "terror" of performativity and its manifestation in performative accountability systems in education. Terror, in this case, can be defined as the pursuit of efficiency gains by reducing opportunities for the exercise of "voice" (Hirschmann, 1970) to contest and rework the logic of accountability regimes. Of course, as Ball (2003b) observes, even when opportunities to debate and shape what counts and what ought to be counted in accountability systems—that is, control over the field of judgment—are limited, resistance may take more subtle forms that reduce efficiency, such as the fabrication of performance. Here the aims and outcomes of performative accountability systems enter into a counterproductive feedback loop. People become focused on being seen to perform, rather than actually achieving organizational goals. For example, in Australia, NAPLAN was introduced putatively to improve educational standards, but the focus now in many systems and schools is on improving NAPLAN scores, encouraged by systemic emphasis on improving such scores, often driven by politicians. This is performativity par excellence.

Beyond the increase of performative "terrors," we see some more interesting possibilities in the "new wave" of educational accountabilities. In a suggestive observation regarding the current use of educational data, Henig (2013) points to important opportunities that new modes of accountability have opened up, but which we may presently be missing:

> Wariness toward the corrupting potential of interest group politics has led us to harness data tightly within administratively designed incentive systems; in the process, are we missing opportunities to inject data more forcefully into the public sphere, encouraging democratic accountability by parents and citizens who become, over time, more confident and knowledgeable about how to used data to collectively define priorities and select educational strategies?
>
> (xii)

In our current moment, we believe it is important to be engaging in the reconceptualization and redesign of accountability systems in order to: (1) make explicit, contest, and broaden the values and goals that underpin them; (2) draw on broader sources of quantitative and qualitative information, thus making "count" a broader set of educational inputs, processes, and outcomes; and (3) ensure that accountability systems inform meaningful and educative changes to practice. Of course, this raises a complex set of questions regarding how to make educational data public across local, regional, national, and global scales. It is possible to imagine parents and citizens engaging with school-level data in more knowledgeable and potentially influential ways, although these mechanisms require further development, but what possibilities are there for educational stakeholders outside of a small international elite of politicians, policy makers, and business people to shape the educational accountability mechanisms operated by international organizations and edu-businesses? This lack of possibilities is why some have spoken of a democratic deficit regarding these developments.

One of the central challenges for developing more democratic and meaningful modes of accountability, or what we might call ""rich accountabilities" is finding a productive balance between the value of large-scale generic data sets for system-level policy and governance purposes and the need for idiosyncratic knowledge specific to local contexts to inform local policies, pedagogies, and curricula. PISA has become a target of criticism because it emphasizes what is measured and contributes to a growing reliance on quantitative measures in education, thus potentially narrowing our views about the value and purposes of education. However, PISA and other LSAs, such as PCAP in Canada or NAPLAN in Australia, generate large amounts of data that can have system-wide relevance and can be relatively easily collected, analyzed, and represented. There is a missed opportunity here, because much of the data made available through these tests is not utilized for policy learning purposes. In our view, systems are replete with data, but are often not making fulsome and effective policy usage of these data sets. In some ways, this is because the data are used for control rather than enabling better educational outcomes.

In a project that two authors of this book are presently conducting (Lingard and Sellar), we have been working with schools and their communities to develop richer forms of school and system accountability. One strategy employed in this project, drawn from work conducted by Whatmore and Landström (2011), was the establishment of "competency groups": groups of interested local stakeholders, who sought to gather information that could be used to develop a view of what local communities expect from schools and how they might tell whether these expectations are being met. While closely aligned with the values that these stakeholders felt should underpin schooling in their communities, the data gathered by this group were highly context specific and often did not relate to outcomes that are measurable using tests. These idiosyncratic accounts are thus open to a different criticism to that often levelled at LSAs: these accounts do not necessarily produce information that can usefully inform policy at the system-level. Experiments with richer modes of local school accountability have gathered a large number of idiosyncratic accounts about schooling, often in narrative form and with little application beyond a particular context. However, these accounts often touch upon what are felt to be the most important aspects of education for communities, which are most often overlooked by LSAs, school-level student tests, and other forms of reporting.

It is easy to make simplistic assessments of the value of these different approaches to accountability and to simplistically critique their respective shortcomings. For example, some advocate for the utility of numbers for monitoring and improving schools and systems, while others prioritize "unquantifiable" aspects of education that can only be communicated in rich narratives. Debates for and against student testing often align more closely with one of these two positions, emphasizing the pragmatic need for data to inform policy or rejecting the reductive and perverse consequences of "policy as numbers" and emphasizing professional judgment. However, by treating the question of school accountability complexly, we can begin to see important relationships between these different approaches, including relationships of complementarity rather than contradiction. Here we are touching on multilateral modes of accountability that combine informed analysis of LSA data with deeply contextualized local narrative accounts. This combination means that the broadest goals of schooling at both systemic and local levels would inform processes of accountability. There is also a need to rethink the directionality of accountability relationships. For example, relationships of accountability can operate from schools to systems, as well as from systems to schools; from schools to communities as well as communities to schools. In Ranson's (2003) words, this would see "answerability" working multilaterally.

Here we will offer some brief comments toward a model for thinking about richer forms of educational accountability that work across large-scale data infrastructure and local knowledge and values. School accountability can be understood as a relationship between three elements: information (or data), practices, and values. Importantly, accountability systems must operate differently in different contexts, and the approach we sketch out here should be seen as a set of axioms that can be enacted in diverse ways, rather than a prescription for specific approach to accountability. Our desired mode of accountability is based on the necessity of strengthening school-community relationships, seen as important for both enhancing educational outcomes and enabling more democratic modes of accountability. Our argument here, then, has both educational and democratic rationales.

First, when used thoughtfully and for appropriate purposes, information generated by LSAs and other forms of student testing can provide a useful resource for monitoring schools and systems and for developing policies and programs. This is as true for PISA data as for national testing. However, this information is valuable only in relation to a set of educational values and purposes, and in relation to practices that may be changed by generating this information. What matters most is who controls the field of judgment in which information is produced and used. The important question that must be asked in relation to information produced for educational accountability is: What information is required to demonstrate that practice is producing valued outcomes or effecting valued changes to practice? A richer approach to accountability would include a variety of stakeholders in answering this question.

Second, changing policies and practices is often the primary focus for conducting LSAs and introducing other accountability systems. Information can be used to change practices such as teachers' curriculum design and pedagogies, parents' decision making, school leadership, system administration, policy making, and so on. While any information can act as a catalyst for change, as we have shown in Chapter 4, the big risk for accountability systems, particularly those with high stakes, is the encouragement of performativity and strategic and perverse behaviors. It is thus important to ask: How are judgments about different kinds of information translated into practice? Practice can be changed in ways that produce different information, but that do not necessarily make a desired difference in educational terms (for example, encouraging fabrication). While large quantitative data sets can provide an important source of information, the judgments made in relation to these data often benefit from being made as closely as possible to the practices that will be changed. This would allow for the analysis of systemic data at a contextual level applicable to a school or group of schools. This would also allow other information—contextual information, narratives, professional expertise, and so on—to inform the judgment and to provide richer catalysts for change.

Third, values always guide the use of information gathered through LSAs or more local and dialogical approaches. The question is whether these values are purely technical criteria—for example, the pursuit of "the best possible input/output equation" (Lyotard, 1984: 35)—or whether a broader set of values from diverse stakeholders can shape what information is collected, how it is analyzed, and how it is used to change practices. The German theorist of pedagogy, Klaus Mollenhauer (2014), argued that "bringing up children is . . . first and foremost a matter of passing on a valued heritage, of conveying to children what is important to us" (9). Any approach to educational accountability should embed opportunities to contest, discuss, and debate the value and purposes of schooling. The important questions to ask here are: What values shape the production of information about school performance? And do these values reflect what is most important about education as a social practice?

Each of the three elements considered here should feed into the others: values should frame the production of information and thus its usage to change practice; information should change values and practices where appropriate; and practices should generate information and pass on the values that are most important to us. None of these elements can be ignored in the task of reconceptualizing and redesigning educational accountabilities. As we have argued throughout, educational accountabilities, and particularly globalized accountabilities, are about comparisons and these are central to contemporary modes of educational governance. The Belgian philosopher of science, Isabelle Stengers (2011), suggests that practices of "comparison must not be unilateral and, especially, must not be conducted in the language of just one of the parties" (56). Richer forms of educational accountability require discussion about which information or data, which practices, and which values "count" and ought to be "counted." In turn, this requires mechanisms—more sophisticated infrastructures—for enabling interested stakeholders to become informed about educational data and to participate in these multilateral discussions.

While critical of the perverse and narrowing effects of globalizing educational accountabilities, we are cognizant that a "folk politics" of simple resistance to and rejection of the "new wave" of educational accountability is unsatisfactory. Often this is a critique of the neopositivism that seems to underpin evidence for policy in education today (Lather, 2013) and of the negative effects of testing. However, importantly, Piketty (2014) reminds us that, "Refusing to deal with numbers rarely serves the interests of the least well-off" (577). Important elements of developing richer modes of educational accountability include ensuring our desired values underpin the data collected, and then increasing the data literacy of teachers, school leaders, and administrators. We stress, though, that we must not ignore values, narratives, and professional judgment, which are not easily measured or translated into policy-relevant forms of information or data, but which are necessarily at the center of richer and more complex modes of educational accountability.

In many respects, globalizing educational accountabilities present us with two diverging possibilities. Lyotard (1984) observed this ambivalence at the heart of what he called, now more than 30 years ago, the "computerization of society":

> It could become the "dream" instrument for controlling and regulating the market system, extended to include knowledge itself and governed exclusively by the performativity principle. In that case it would inevitably involve the use of terror. But it could also aid groups discussing metaprescriptives [values] by supplying them with the information they usually lack for making knowledgeable decisions.
>
> (67)

These two options remain salient in our consideration of contemporary usages of educational data and data infrastructure. The development of richer modes of global educational accountabilities will require pursuing the second path; that is, linking up, local, regional, national, and global experiments in democratizing the data infrastructure that underpins educational accountability by enabling the values that guide these systems to be contested and revised, and by enabling information to be put to work in meaningful and productive ways. However, we recognize the difficulties of achieving this on a global scale.

Edu-business

At various points throughout the book, including when introducing the big ideas underpinning our analysis of globalizing educational accountabilities in Chapter 1, we have mentioned the growing significance of edu-businesses in education today, connected to the emergence of network governance and top–down, test-based modes of accountability. Network governance in education has emerged from the early state restructurings associated with NPM and has also been enabled by the computerization of society, globally; the globe is on our computers, as Spivak (2012) would say.

The emphasis with these governance changes has shifted from inputs (resources, ideas), to specific policy domains, to an emphasis on outputs and outcomes, as measured through performance indicators and data of various kinds. As Ozga (2009) notes, this restructuring gives the appearance of deregulation, but "is equally marked by strong central steering through various policy technologies"

(150); data management is essential to this new mode of governance. The state remains important in these developments, but now functions in very different ways, including, as we have shown throughout, being located within the global education policy field. The emphasis on outcome measures has seen new accountability regimes helping to constitute a systemless system. As Ranson (2003) has noted, today, strengthened data-based accountability "constitutes the system itself" (459).

These state restructurings are linked to neoliberal policy settings with the focus on school choice, competition between schools in an education quasi-market, and the use of performance data to facilitate school choice. However, they also have their own origins in moves to make the bureaucracy more flexible and nimble in response to the speed of change today and the global interconnectivities of politics. There is also the issue of a lack of trust in professionals underpinning these new accountability regimes (O'Neill, 2002, 2013).

Network governance has emerged as an admixture of hierarchical and horizontal relationships framed by the state within nations and also globally. Along with test-based modes of accountability, this has opened up new spaces for the involvement of edu-businesses. The standardization associated with testing further facilitates the involvement of edu-businesses in network governance; in that context, the products and services that edu-businesses can supply have broader applicability and thus greater potential profitability.

The first point that we want to stress here is how this restructuring of the state has opened up spaces for the participation of edu-business across the policy cycle in education and in respect of the three message systems of schooling: curriculum, pedagogy, and evaluation (Ball, 2012). The second point is that data-driven systems and test-based accountabilities also open up profitable spaces for edu-businesses to provide services (and products) in respect of test construction, psychometrics, data analytics, computational services, research *for* policy, policy evaluations, management of testing, accountability regimes and data infrastructures, professional development, and various other commercial products. What we see is the partial and potential privatization of education policy and the education policy community (Mahony, Hextall, & Menter, 2004). In respect of network governance and the role of edu-business, Ball (2012) suggests that this means,

> the production by education and consultancy companies of policy "texts" and policy ideas *for* and *within* the state, that is, the export of "statework" to private providers and "agencies", and the formation and dissemination of new policy discourses arising out of the participation of these companies in report writing, evaluations, advice, consultancy and recommendations.
> (99)

In this context, Burch (2006, 2009) describes the explosion of edu-business involvement over the last decade or so, as they seek to capitalize on a burgeoning industry with high profitability. For example in 2013, Pearson plc, the largest global edu-business, had worldwide sales of more than £5 billion across more than 100 education brands (see Ball, 2012: 124–128). We note how edu-businesses stretch from the largest organizations, such as Pearson, through to smaller national firms and individual education entrepreneurs, who help schools manage and sometimes massage their performance data.

Edu-businesses are involved in network governance across multiple spaces. For example, Pearson, whom we will focus on here (see Hogan, Sellar, & Lingard, 2015), has the contract to develop aspects of the PISA 2018 framework and has been involved in previous rounds of PISA.

The Pearson Foundation, its now defunct philanthropic arm, has together with the OECD supported the production of materials for disseminating policy learning from high-performing systems on PISA. For example, the Pearson Foundation supported the production of the *Strong Performers and Successful Reformers in Education* (OECD, 2011a) materials. The large USA-based publishing company, CTB/McGraw Hill has been endorsed by the OECD to manage PISA tests for schools in the USA. Fairfax County in Virginia, USA, has taken up PISA tests for schools in a significant way. This is also an example of a new topological policy space, whereby the OECD has reached into schools and a particular schooling system within the nation. Furthermore, with PISA tests for schools, individual schools can now compare themselves with other national systems and other schools located elsewhere around the globe. We note how it was an American NGO, America Achieves, which pushed for the creation of these tests with the OECD, not national governments. Private companies and research organizations have been accredited by the OECD to manage PISA-based tests for schools in different nations.

In abolishing its philanthropic arm, Pearson has mainstreamed what has been called "corporate social responsibility." This has been an important element of Pearson's new business strategy, in which profit-making and corporate social responsibility rationales have been brought together. On this very point, in its 2012 Annual Report Pearson noted, "commercial goals and social responsibility are mutually reinforcing" (Pearson plc, 2012: 34). This is what has been called "philanthrocapitalism" (Bishop & Green, 2008), where doing "good" is seen to be profitable.

Schooling systems in the USA have long been replete with testing and the involvement of edu-businesses. Indeed, we need to acknowledge that edu-businesses have long had legitimate roles in relation to the production of school textbooks and so on. However, President Bush's No Child Left Behind and President Obama's Race to the Top have strengthened the place of testing in the USA and helped reconstitute federal relations with schooling systems. Burch (2006) has shown how No Child Left Behind opened up opportunities for edu-businesses in relation to test development, test preparation, data analysis, data management, and related products. Pearson has been heavily involved in much of this and still makes more than half of its annual profits in North America, despite its expansion into the developing world and into China. Diane Ravitch, the assistant secretary of education in the Bush administration, is now an outspoken critic of what she calls the "Pearsonization" of American schooling. In a 2012 blog, Ravitch wrote about the "The United States of Pearson" and noted:

> It is widely recognized by everyone other than the publishing giant Pearson that its tentacles have grown too large and too aggressive. It is difficult to remember what part of American education has not been invaded by Pearson's corporate grasp. It receives billions of dollars to test millions of students.... With the US Department of Education now pressing schools to test children in second grade, first grade, kindergarten—and possibly earlier ... the picture grows clear. Pearson will control every aspect of our education system.

We note that Pearson have an integrated global business strategy, focusing on support for low-fee, for-profit private schools in developing nations (particularly in sub-Saharan Africa through the *Pearson Affordable Learning Fund*) and providing services and goods linked to testing and accountability, capitalizing on the opportunities made available by the globalized localism, GERM. There is, of course, the likelihood that what will work in each will be adapted for usage in other contexts. In Australia, Pearson helps a number of states manage NAPLAN.

In seeking to become the world's "leading learning company," Pearson employed Sir Michael Barber as chief education advisor—a former academic, senior policy maker in Blair's New Labour government, and one of the authors of the influential McKinsey Reports. Barber is a "boundary spanner" (Williams, 2002), working across the public/private sectors and has brought all of his "network capital" (Urry, 2007)—connections globally in both public and private sectors linked to education—to Pearson, and this will contribute to their expanding work in both the global north and the global south. We make the point here that movement across public/private sector employment is an element of network governance.

As part of its new business strategy, Pearson has developed its *Efficacy Framework* that attempts to ensure the effectiveness of all their education services and products by developing an evidence-base for them. As part of the *Efficacy Framework*, Pearson has also developed the *Learning Curve* reports and associated data bank, which utilize OECD, IEA, and other data to provide meta-analyses of what will work in education. These developments are part of Pearson's own move towards accountability to its shareholders, but also to governments and others who utilize their products and services. We note that Pearson, with the *Learning Curve*, are using publicly available data sets that have been paid for by tax payers within nations; nations pay to participate in PISA and TIMSS and PIRLS. In an open and democratic way, the OECD and IEA make all of their data openly available for usage by researchers and others. We see Pearson here through both the *Efficacy Framework* and the *Learning Curve* as providing research for policy. Pearson is working to establish policy problems to which they will proffer policy solutions, as they seek to help establish global policy agendas in education. We can see in all of this how data and testing are central to these strategic business moves.

While we have said more here about Pearson than other edu-businesses, we reiterate that there are large numbers of companies globally and nationally moving into this domain and even individual policy entrepreneurs. We note how Rupert Murdoch's New Corps has been broken into an entertainment business and an education division called Amplify with Joel Klein, former Commissioner for Education in New York, as CEO. In New Corps' 2012 Annual Report, Murdoch noted, "When it comes to K through 12 education, we see a $500 billion sector in the US alone that is waiting desperately to be transformed by big breakthroughs."

Other consultancy firms have been involved in policy advocacy. The influential McKinsey Reports are good examples of the production of policy texts and policy ideas for schooling systems as a basis for reform. These two reports—*How the World's Best-Performing Systems Come Out on Top* (Barber & Mourshed, 2007) and *How the World's Most Improved School Systems Keep Getting Better* (Mourshed, Chijioke, & Barber, 2010)—have been exceedingly influential with education policy makers and politicians across the globe. What we see with these types of reports is the emergence of a new type of policy genre that increasingly relies on LSAs (Coffield, 2012). These texts bowdlerize research *for* policy and also the actual stages of the policy cycle. However, we would suggest it is this simplification that makes them so attractive to policy makers in systems across the globe (Coffield, 2012). They sit in stark contrast to the more complex recommendations of academic research *of* policy and fail to recognize the complex mélange of research, politics, and professional knowledge that frame policy (Head, 2008). With this new policy genre we see how significant international comparative performance data are for edu-business. Further, as Coffield (2012) observes, "These reports are the work of 'global' policy analysts, remote from both the complexities of classrooms and from the discomfiting findings of researchers which pose such difficulties for politicians in search of quick 'transformations' of school systems before the next election" (145).

We also note that leading figures in transnational edu-businesses such as Pearson, and consultancy firms such as McKinsey, now have more ready access to policy makers than do others, and Pearson, amongst others, is seeking to set policy agendas. There are significant potential issues here to do with the lack of democratic constituencies for edu-businesses. Teachers and their representatives are largely excluded from these policy moves; they are seen as the objects of policy developed elsewhere, not legitimate participants in policy processes. We might then see a democratic deficit in these developments: this is a coming issue in respect of globalizing educational accountabilities. There is, of course, opposition to some aspects of these developments. We note in this respect the oppositional work of the American Federation of Teachers in the USA, that of Diane Ravitch already mentioned, and globally, opposition from Education International, the global federation of teacher unions representing more than 30 million teachers worldwide.

In Closing

The globalization of educational accountabilities is part of a changed policy context that demands attention to the interplay of new spaces, new data analytics, and new modes of governance. This book has taken up the methodological challenge of analytically working across these new spaces. We have sought to understand how relational infrastructure and new configurations of power are helping to change the education policy landscape globally. We have been concerned to foreground how specific technologies of scalar governance and the globalizing of educational accountabilities have functioned, and continue to function, in a panoptic capacity through a series of dispersed networks and operations of power. Much remains to be done in this regard, especially to track the growing influence of edu-business in education policy. If, as Ball and Junemann (2012) argue, the topology of policy is now changed, and we certainly agree with this diagnosis, then it is time for policy sociology in education to change too.

While there is much interesting and innovative research being undertaken in this domain, we see the need for further development of critical approaches that bring together sophisticated theorization of data in education and new modes of engagement with these data. In other words, it is important to challenge the ways in which prevailing data usage in education shapes perceptions and practices. At the same time, it is important to develop alternative uses that open up data to new analyses, new audiences, new possibilities for informed decision making, and more intelligent applications in policy making. We are thus wary of political mobilizations that reject data-focused methodological and technical developments in education, based on their alignments with certain modes of governance, their opening up of opportunities for commercial activity, or their narrowing of the values and purposes that guide education as a social practice. While we are critical of such developments, we see contestation over new methodologies and technologies, and experiments with putting them to work in more horizontal and democratic deliberations about the purposes, practices, and outcomes of schooling, as important ground to occupy in the present. We also see a pressing need for alternative information sets and multilateral relationships in emergent modes of accountability. We thus see globalizing educational accountabilities as a phenomenon in which critical policy scholarship has a stake and an active role to play.

REFERENCES

AAUW (American Association of University Women). (2008). *Where the girls are: The facts about gender equity in education*. Washington, DC: AAUW Educational Foundation.

Abraham, C. (2010, October 15). Part 1: Failing boys and the powder keg of sexual politics. *Globe and Mail*. Available www.theglobeandmail.com/news/national/time-to-lead/failing-boys/part-1-failing-boys-and-the-powder-keg-of-sexual-politics/article1758791/ (accessed November 15, 2014).

Adie, L. (2008). The hegemonic positioning of 'Smart State' policy. *Journal of Education Policy, 23*(3), 251–264.

Alegounarias, T. (2011, July 14). *Weighing and distributing the good of schooling*. Paper presented at the Australian College of Educators National Conference, Sydney, Australia.

Alexander, M. (2010). *The new Jim Crow: Mass incarceration in an age of colorblindness*. New York: New Press.

Allen, J. (2011). Topological twists: Power's shifting geographies. *Dialogues in Human Geography, 1*(3), 283–298.

Alloway, N., Freebody, P., Gilbert, P., & Muspratt, S. (2002). *Boys, literacy and schooling: Expanding the repertoires of practice*. Melbourne: Curriculum.

Alphonso, C. (2013, December 3). 'National emergency' as Canadians fall out of the global top 10 in math. *Globe and Mail*. Available www.theglobeandmail.com/news/national/education/canadas-fall-in-math-education-ranking-sets-off-red-flags/article15730663/ (accessed November 14, 2014).

Amin, A. (2002). Spatialities of globalization. *Environment and Planning, 34*(3), 385–399.

Anagnostopoulos, D., Rutledge, S. A., & Jacobsen, R. (Eds.). (2013). *The infrastructure of accountability: Data use and the transformation of American education*. Cambridge, MA: Harvard Education Press.

Anderson, S., & Ben Jaafar, S. (2003). *Policy trends in Ontario education 1990–2003*. Ontario Institute for Studies in Education. Available http://fcis.oise.utoronto.ca/~icec/policytrends.pdf (accessed November 14, 2014).

Anisef, P., Brown, R. S., Phythian, K., Sweet, R., & Walters, D. (2010). Early school leaving among immigrants in Toronto. *Canadian Review of Sociology, 47*(2), 103–128.
Anthias, F. (2012). Intersectional what? Social divisions, intersectionality and levels of analysis. *Ethnicities, 13*(1), 3–19.
Anyon, J. (1997). *Ghetto schooling: A political economy of urban educational reform.* New York: Teachers College Press.
Anyon, J. (2005). *Radical possibilities: Public policy, urban education and a new social movement.* New York: Routledge.
Appadurai, A. (1990). Disjuncture and difference in the global cultural economy. *Theory, Culture and Society, 7*(2/3), 295–310.
Appadurai, A. (1996). *Modernity at large: Cultural dimensions of globalization.* Minneapolis: University of Minnesota Press.
Appadurai, A. (2001). Grassroots globalization and the research imagination. In A. Appadurai (Ed.), *Globalization.* Durham, NC: Duke University Press.
Appadurai, A. (2006). *Fear of small numbers: An essay on the geography of anger.* Durham, NC: Duke University Press.
Apple, M. (2001). *Educating the right way: Markets, standards, God and inequality.* New York: Routledge.
Au, W., & Ferrare, J. (Eds.). (2015). *Mapping corporate education reform: Power and policy networks in the neoliberal state.* New York: Routledge.
Bailey, P. (2013). The policy dispositif: Historical formation and method. *Journal of Education Policy, 28*(6), 807–827.
Ball, S. J. (1994). *Politics and policy making in education: Explorations in policy sociology.* London: Routledge.
Ball, S. J. (1998). Big policies/small world: An introduction to international perspectives in education policy. *Comparative Education, 34*(2), 119–130.
Ball, S. J. (2003a). *Class strategies and the education market: The middle classes and social advantage.* London: Routledge.
Ball, S. J. (2003b). The teacher's soul and the terrors of performativity. *Journal of Education Policy, 18*(2), 215–228.
Ball, S. J. (2008). *The education debate.* Bristol: Policy Press.
Ball, S. J. (2012). *Global education inc: New policy networks and the neo-liberal imaginary.* London: Routledge.
Ball, S. J. (2013). *The education debate* (2nd ed.). Bristol: Policy Press.
Ball, S. J., & Junemann, C. (2012). *Networks, new governance and education.* Bristol: Policy Press.
Ball, S. J., & Youdell, D. (2008). *Hidden privatisation in public education.* Brussels: Education International.
Barber, M., & Mourshed, M. (2007). *How the world's best performing school systems come out on top.* London: McKinsey.
Baroutsis, A. (2014). *Troubling news: Challenging politics, perceptions and practices of newspaper constructions of teachers* (Doctoral thesis, University of Queensland, Brisbane, Australia).
Beach, C., Green, A., & Worswick, C. (2006). *Impacts of the Point System and immigration policy levers on skill characteristics of Canadian immigrants.* Kingston, ON: Queen's University Economics Department.
Beech, J., & Larsen, M. (2014). Spatial theorizing in comparative and international research. *Comparative Education Review, 58*(2), 191–214.
Bendix, R. (1978). *Kings or people: Power and the mandate to rule.* Berkeley: University of California Press.

References

Berliner, D. (2006). Our impoverished view of educational research. *Teachers College Record, 108*(6), 949–995.
Berliner, D. (2013). Effects of inequality and poverty vs. teachers and schooling on America's youth. *Teachers College Record, 115*. Available www.tcrecord.org.proxy1.lib.uwo.ca/library (accessed October 20, 2014).
Bernstein, B. (1971). On the classification and framing of educational knowledge. In M.F.D. Young (Ed.), *Knowledge and control: New directions for the sociology of education* (pp. 47–69). London: Collier-Macmillan.
Berry, D. (2011). Introduction: Understanding the digital humanities. In D. Berry (Ed.), *Understanding digital humanities* (pp. 1–20). New York: Palgrave Macmillan.
Biesta, G. (2004). Education, accountability, and the ethical demand: Can the democratic potential of accountability be regained? *Educational Theory, 54*(3), 233–250.
Bishop, M., & Green, M. (2008). *Philanthrocapitalism: How giving can save the world*. London: Black.
Bouchard, P., Boily, I., & Proulx, M. (2003). *School success by gender: A catalyst for masculinist discourse*. Ottawa: Status of Women Canada.
Bourdieu, P. (1986). The forms of capital. In J. G. Richardson (Ed.), *Handbook of theory and research for the sociology of education* (pp. 241–258). Westport, CT: Greenwood Press.
Bourdieu, P. (2003). *Firing back: Against the tyranny of the market*. London: Verso.
Bowker, G. C., Baker, K., Millerand, F., & Ribes, D. (2010). Toward information infrastructure studies: Ways of knowing in a networked environment. In J. Husinger, L. Klastrup, & M.M. Allen (Eds.), *International handbook of internet research* (pp. 97–117). Dordrecht: Springer.
Boyd, D., & Crawford, K. (2012). Critical questions for big data: Provocations for a cultural, technological, and scholarly phenomenon. *Information, Communication & Society, 15*(5), 662–679. doi:10.1080/1369118X.2012.678878
Breakspear, S. (2012). *The policy impact of PISA: An exploration of the normative effects of international benchmarking in school system performance*. OECD Education Working Papers, No. 71. Paris: OECD.
Brenner, N. (2004). *New state spaces: Urban governance and the rescaling of statehood*. Oxford: Oxford University Press.
Brown, P., Halsey, A. H., Lauder, H., & Stuart Wells, A. (1997). The transformation of education and society: An introduction. In A. H. Halsey, H. Lauder, P. Brown, & A. Stuart Wells (Eds.), *Education: Culture, economy and society* (pp. 1–44). Oxford: Oxford University Press.
Brown, P., & Scase, R. (1997). Universities and employers: Rhetoric and reality. In A. Smith & F. Webster (Eds.), *The postmodern university? Contested visions of higher education in society* (pp. 85–98). London: SRHE and Open University Press.
Brown, P., & Tannock, S. (2009). Education, meritocracy and the global war for talent. *Journal of Education Policy, 24*(4), 377–392.
Brüggemann, C., & Bloem, S. (2013). The potential of international student assessments to measure educational outcomes of Roma Students. *Sociologia—Slovak Sociological Review, 45*(6), 519–541.
Burch, P. (2006). The new educational privatization: Educational contracting and high stakes accountability. *Teachers College Record, 108*(12), 2582–2610.
Burch, P. (2009). *Hidden markets: The new educational privatization*. New York: Routledge.
Caluya, G. (2010). The post-panoptic society? Reassessing Foucault in surveillance studies. *Social Identities, 16*(5), 621–633.

References

Carroll, P., & Head, B. (2009, September 28–30). *Comparing the second and third waves of regulatory reform in Australia*. Paper presented at the Australian Political Studies Association Conference, Sydney, Australia.

Carroll, P., & Kellow, A. (2011). *The OECD: A study of organizational adaptation*. Cheltenham: Edward Elgar.

Carvalho, L.M., & Costa, E. (2014). Seeing education with one's own eyes and through the PISA lenses: Considerations of the reception of PISA in European countries. *Discourse: Studies in the Cultural Politics of Education*. doi:10.1080/01596306.2013.871449

Chan, P.W.K., & Seddon, T. (2014). Governing education in China: PISA, comparison and educational regions. In T. Fenwick, E. Mangez, & J. Ozga (Eds.), *Governing knowledge: Comparison, knowledge-based technologies and expertise in the regulation of education (World Yearbook of Education 2014)* (pp. 200–217). London: Routledge.

Chen, X. (2009). A globalizing city on the rise: Shanghai's transformation in comparative perspective. In X. Chen (Ed.), *Shanghai rising: State power and local transformations in a global megacity* (pp. xv–xxxv). Minneapolis: University of Minnesota Press.

Cheng, K. (2011). Shanghai: How a big city in a developing country leaped to the head of the class. In M. Tucker (Ed.), *Surpassing Shanghai: An agenda for American education built on the world's leading systems* (pp. 21–50). Cambridge, MA: Harvard Education Press.

Chua, A. (2011). *Battle hymn of the tiger mother*. New York: Penguin.

CMEC (Council of Ministers of Education, Canada). (2011). *PCAP— 2010: Report on the Pan-Canadian Assessment Program of Mathematics, Science, and Reading*. Toronto: Author.

CMEC (Council of Ministers of Education, Canada). (2013a). *Measuring up: Canadian results of the OECD PISA study*. Toronto: Author.

CMEC (Council of Ministers of Education, Canada). (2013b). What is the potential for boys to catch up to girls in reading? Results from PISA 2009. *Assessment Matters, 5*. Available www.cmec.ca/9/Publications/index.html?searchCat=6 (accessed November 16, 2014).

COAG Reform Council. (2011). *National Partnership Agreement on literacy and numeracy: Performance report for 2010*. Sydney: Author.

Coffield, F. (2012). Why the McKinsey reports will not improve school systems. *Journal of Education Policy, 27*(1), 131–149.

Collin, R. (2012). Mapping the future, mapping education: An analysis of the 2011 State of the Union Address. *Journal of Education Policy, 27*(2), 155–172.

Collins, C., Kenway, J., & McLeod, J. (2000). *Factors influencing the educational performance of males and females in school and their initial destinations after leaving school*. Canberra: Department of Education, Training and Youth Affairs.

Commonwealth of Australia. (2008). *Quality education: The case for an education revolution in our schools*. Canberra: Author.

Condron, D. (2011). Egalitarianism and educational excellence: Compatible goals for affluent societies? *Educational Researcher, 40*(2), 47–55.

Connolly, P. (2008). A critical review of some recent developments in quantitative research on gender and achievement in the United Kingdom. *British Journal of the Sociology of Education, 29*(3), 249–260.

Cowley, P., Easton, S., & Thomas, M. (2012). Report card on Ontario's secondary schools. *Fraser Institute*. Available http://ontario.compareschoolrankings.org/pdfs/Fraser_Institute_Report_Card_on_Ontario%E2%80%99s_Secondary_Schools_2012.pdf (accessed October 14, 2014).

Creagh, S. (2014). A critical analysis of the problems with the LBOTE category on the NAPLAN test. *Australian Educational Researcher, 41*, 1–23.

Darling-Hammond, L. (2010). *The flat world and education: How America's commitment to equity will determine our future.* New York: Teachers College Press.

Darling-Hammond, L. (2011). Foreword. In M. Tucker (Ed.), *Surpassing Shanghai: An agenda for American education built on the world's leading systems* (pp. ix–xii). Cambridge, MA: Harvard Education Press.

Dei, G., & Karumanchery, L. (1999). School reforms in Ontario: The 'marketization of education' and the resulting silence on equity. *Alberta Journal of Educational Research, 45*(2), 111–131.

Deleuze, G. (1995). *Negotiations.* New York: Columbia University Press.

Deleuze, G., & Guattari, F. (1987). *A thousand plateaus: Capitalism and schizophrenia* (B. Massumi, Trans.). Minneapolis: University of Minnesota Press.

de Sousa Santos, B. (2006). Globalizations. *Theory, Culture & Society, 23*(2/3), 393–399.

Desrosieres, A. (1998). *The politics of large numbers.* Cambridge, MA: Harvard University Press.

DfE (Department for Education). (2010). *The importance of teaching: The schools white paper 2010.* Norwich: HMSO.

Dimitriadis, G. (2012). *Critical dispositions: Evidence and expertise in education.* New York: Routledge.

Dohn, B. N. (2007). Knowledge and skills for PISA: Assessing the assessment. *Journal of Philosophy of Education, 41*(1), 1–16.

Dronkers, J., & de Heus, M. (2013). Immigrant children's academic performance: The influence of origin, destination and community. In H. Meyer & A. Benavot (Eds.), *PISA, power and policy: The emergence of global educational governance* (pp. 247–265). Oxford: Symposium Books.

Dumas, M. (2009). Theorizing redistribution in urban education research: 'How do we get dictionaries at Cleveland?' In J. Anyon (Ed.), *Theory and educational research* (pp. 81–107). New York: Routledge.

Easton, D. (1953). *The political system: An inquiry into the state of political science.* New York: Alfred A. Knopf.

Eccleston, R. (2011). The OECD and global economic governance. *Australian Journal of International Affairs, 65*, 243–255. doi:10.1080/10357718.2011.550106

Educational Quality and Accountability Office (EQAO) (2010). Programme for International Student Assessment (PISA), 2009: Highlights of Ontario Student Results. Available www.eqao.com/pdf_e/10/2009_PISA_Highlights_en.pdf (accessed October 3, 2013).

Engels, Laura C. and Frizzell, Matthew O. (2015) Competitive comparison and PISA bragging rights: Sub-national uses of the OECD's PISA in Canada and the USA. *Discourse: Studies in the Cultural Politics of Education.* DOI: 10.1080/01596306.2015.1017446.

Epstein, D. (1996). Defining accountability in education. *British Educational Research Journal, 19*(3), 243–257.

Ertl, H. (2006). Educational standards and the changing discourse on education: The reception and consequences of the PISA study in Germany. *Oxford Review of Education, 32*(5), 619–634.

Espland, W. (2000). Commensuration and cognition. In K. A. Cerulo (Ed.), *Culture in mind: Toward a sociology of culture and cognition* (pp. 63–88). London: Routledge.

Fairclough, N. (2000). *New Labour, new language.* London: Routledge.
Fine, M., & Weis, L. (1998). *The unknown city: The lives of poor and working-class young adults.* Boston, MA: Beacon Press.
Foucault, M. (1980). The confession of the flesh (C. Gordon, L. Marshall, J. Mepham, & K. Soper, Trans.). In C. Gordon (Ed.), *Power/knowledge: Selected interviews and other writings, 1972–1977* (pp. 194–228). New York: Vintage Books.
Foucault, M. (1995). *Discipline and punish: The birth of the prison.* New York: Vintage Books.
Foucault, M. (1998). *The history of sexuality* (R. Hurley, Trans.). New York: Vintage Books.
Fraser, N. (1997). *Justice interruptus.* New York: Routledge.
Gillborn, D. (2008). *Racism and education: Coincidence or conspiracy?* London: Routledge.
Gillborn, D., & Youdell, D. (2000). *Rationing education: Policy, practice, reform, and equity.* Buckingham: Open University Press.
Goldberg, D. (2009). *The threat of race: Reflections on racial neoliberalism.* Malden, MA: Wiley-Blackwell.
Gordon, I., Lewis, J., & Young, R. (1977). Perspectives on policy analysis. *Public Administration Bulletin, 25,* 26–35.
Gorur, R. (2013). My school, my market. *Discourse: Studies in the Cultural Politics of Education, 34*(2), 214–230.
Gove, M. (2010a). Speech to the National College Annual Conference, Birmingham. Available www.education.gov.uk/inthenews/speeches/a0061371/michael-gove-to-the-national-college-annual-conference-birmingham (accessed July 16, 2012).
Gove, M. (2010b, December 28). My revolution for culture in the classroom: Why we must raise standards so children can compete with the rest of the world. *Telegraph.* Available www.telegraph.co.uk/education/8227535/Michael-Gove-my-revolution-for-culture-in-classroom.html (accessed July 16, 2012).
Gove, M. (2011a). *Education for economic success.* Speech to the 2011 Education World Forum, London. Available www.education.gov.uk/inthenews/speeches/a0072274/michael-gove-to-the-education-world-forum (accessed July 16, 2012).
Gove, M. (2011b). Speech to the Policy Exchange on Free Schools, London. Available www.education.gov.uk/inthenews/speeches/a0077948/michael-goves-speech-to-the-policy-exchange-on-free-schools (accessed July 16, 2012).
Gove, M. (2012). *A coalition for good—how we can all work together to make opportunity more equal.* Speech to Brighton College. Available www.education.gov.uk/inthenews/speeches/a00208822/brighton-college (accessed July 16, 2012).
Grek, S. (2009). Governing by numbers: The PISA 'effect' in Europe. *Journal of Education Policy, 24*(1), 23–27.
Grek, S., Lawn, M., Lingard, B., Ozga, J., Rinnie, R., Segerholm, C., & Simola, H. (2009a). National policy brokering and the construction of the European Education Space in England, Sweden, Finland and Scotland. *Comparative Education, 45*(1), 5–21.
Grek, S., Lawn, M., Lingard, B., & Varjo, J. (2009b). North by northwest: Quality assurance and evaluation processes in European education. *Journal of Education Policy, 24*(2), 121–133.
Grubb, W. (2007). Dynamic inequality and intervention: Lessons from a small country. *Phi Delta Kappan, 89*(2), 105–114.
Grubel, H. (2013). Canada's immigrant selection policies: Recent record, marginal changes and needed reforms. *Fraser Institute.* Available www.fraserinstitute.org/research-news/display.aspx?id=20300 (accessed February 27, 2015).

References

Gulson, K. (2011). *Education, policy, space and the city: Markets and the (in)visibility of race.* New York: Routledge.
Gulson, K., & Symes, C. (Eds.). (2007). *Spatial theories of education: Policy and geography matters.* London: Routledge.
Hacking, I. (1986). Making up people. In T. L. Heller, M. Sosna, & D. E. Wellbery (Eds.), *Reconstructing individualism: Autonomy, individuality, and the self in Western thought* (pp. 222–236). Stanford, CA: Stanford University Press.
Hacking, I. (1990). *The taming of chance.* Cambridge: Cambridge University Press.
Hacking, I. (2006). Making up people. *London Review of Books, 28*(16), 23–26.
Hammer, K. (2011). Boys poor results in reading feared to be spreading to math, science. *Globe and Mail.* Available www.theglobeandmail.com/news/national/education/primary-to-secondary/boys-poor-results-in-reading-feared-to-be-spreading-to-math-science/article2254436/?utm_medium=Feeds%3A%20RSS%2FAtom&utm_source=Home&utm_content=2254436 (accessed August 19, 2014).
Hargreaves, A., & Shirley, D. (2012). *The global fourth way: The quest for educational excellence.* Thousand Oaks, CA: Corwin-Sage.
Harvey, C. (2010). Making hollow men. *Educational Theory, 60*(2), 189–201.
Head, B. W. (2008). Three lenses of evidence-based policy. *Australian Journal of Public Administration, 67*(1), 1–11.
Henig, J. R. (2013). Foreword. In D. Anagnostopoulos, S. Rutledge, & R. Jacobsen (Eds.), *The infrastructure of accountability: Data use and the transformation of American education* (pp. vii–xiii). Cambridge, MA: Harvard Education Press.
Henry, M., Lingard, B., Rizvi, F., & Taylor, S. (2001). *The OECD, globalization and education policy.* Oxford: Pergamon.
Hill Collins, P. (1990). *Black feminist thought: Knowledge, consciousness, and the politics of empowerment.* Boston, MA: Unwin Hyman.
Hirschmann, A. O. (1970). *Exit, voice, and loyalty: Responses to decline in firms, organizations, and states.* Cambridge, MA: Harvard University Press.
Hogan, A. (2014). NAPLAN and the role of edu-business: New governance, new privatisations and new partnerships in Australian education policy. *Australian Educational Researcher.* doi:10.1007/s13384-014-0162-z
Hogan, A., Sellar, S., & Lingard, B. (2015). Network re-structuring of global edu-business: The case of Pearson's Efficacy Framework. In W. Au & J. Ferrare (Eds.), *Mapping corporate education reform: Power and policy networks in the neoliberal state* (pp. 43–62). New York: Routledge.
Holland, D. C., Lachicotte, W., Jr., Skinner, D., & Cain, C. (1998). *Identity and agency in cultural worlds.* Cambridge, MA: Harvard University Press.
Human Resources and Skills Development Canada, CMEC and Statistics Canada (2010). *Measuring up: Canadian results of the OECD PISA study: The performance of Canada's youth in Reading, Mathematics and Science.* Ottawa: Statistics Canada.
Istance, D. (1996). Education at the Chateau de la Muette. *Oxford Review of Education, 22,* 91–96.
Jacques, M. (2012). *When China rules the world* (2nd ed.). London: Penguin.
Jakobi, A., & Martens, K. (2010). Expanding and intensifying governance: The OECD in education policy. In K. Martins & A. P. Jakobi (Eds.), *Mechanisms of OECD Governance: International incentives for national policy-making?* (pp. 163–176). Oxford: Oxford University Press.

Jakobi, A. P., & Martens, K. (2010). Introduction: The OECD as an actor in international politics. In K. Martins & A. P. Jakobi (Eds.), *Mechanisms of OECD governance: International incentives for national policy-making?* (pp. 1–25). Oxford: Oxford University Press.

James, C. (2012). *Life at the intersection: Community, class and schooling.* Halifax, NS: Fernwood.

Jensen, B., Hunter, A., Sonneman, J., & Burns, T. (2012). *Catching up: Learning from the best school systems in East Asia.* Melbourne: Grattan Institute.

Johnson, C., & Tonkiss, F. (2002). The third influence: The Blair government and Australian Labor. *Policy and Politics, 30*(1), 5–18.

Jones, M. G., Jones, B. D., Hardin, B., Chapman, L., Yarbrough, T., & Davis, M. (1999). Impact of high-stakes testing on teachers and students in North Carolina. *Phi Delta Kappan, 81*(3), 199–203.

Jordan, W. (2010). Defining equity: Multiple perspectives to analyzing the performance of diverse learners. *Review of Research in Education, 34*(1), 142–178.

Kallo, J. (2009). *OECD education policy: A comparative and historical study focusing on the thematic reviews of tertiary education.* Helsinki: Finnish Educational Research Association.

Kamens, D. (2013). Globalization and the emergence of an audit culture: PISA and the search. In H. Meyer & A. Benavot (Eds.), *PISA, power and policy: The emergence of global educational governance* (pp. 117–139). Oxford: Symposium Books.

Kaplan, D., & Turner, A. (2012). *Statistical matching of PISA 2009 and TALIS 2008 data in Iceland. OECD Education Working Papers No. 78.* Paris: OECD.

Kirsch, I., Lennon, M., von Davier, M., Gonzalez, E., & Yamamoto, K. (2013). On the growing importance of international large-scale assessments. In M. von Davier, E. Gonzalez, I. Kirsch, & K. Yamamoto (Eds.), *The role of international large-scale assessments: Perspectives from technology, economy and educational research* (pp. 1–11). Dordrecht: Springer.

Kitchin, R. (2014). Big data, new epistemologies and paradigm shifts. *Big Data & Society, 1*(1), 1–12. doi:10.1177/2053951714528481

Knodel, P., & Walkenhurst, H. (2010). What's England got to do with it? British underestimation of international initiatives in education policy. In K. Martens, A.-K. Nagel, M. Windzio, & A. Weymann (Eds.), *Transformation of education policy* (pp. 132–152). London: Palgrave Macmillan.

Koh, A. (2009). The visualization of education policy: A videological analysis of learning journeys. *Journal of Education Policy, 24*(3), 283–315.

Ladson-Billings, G. (2006). From the achievement gap to the education debt: Understanding achievement in U.S. schools. *Educational Researcher, 35*(7), 3–12.

Larose, F., Bourque, J., Terisse, B., & Kurtness, J. (2001). La résilience scolaire comme indice d'acculturation chez les Autochtones. *Revue des sciences de l'éducation, 27*(1), 151–180.

Lather, P. (2013). Methodology-21: What do we do in the afterward? *Qualitative Studies in Education, 26*(6), 634–645.

Latour, B. (1987). *Science in action: How to follow scientists and engineers through society.* Cambridge, MA: Harvard University Press.

Latour, B. (1999). *Pandora's hope: Essays on the reality of science studies.* Cambridge, MA: Harvard University Press.

Lawn, M. (2013). A systemless system: Designing the disarticulation of English state education. *European Educational Research Journal, 12*(2), 231–241. doi:10.2304/eerj.2013.12.2.231

Lawn, M., & Grek, S. (2012). *Europeanizing education: Governing a new policy space.* Oxford: Symposium Books.

Lawn, M., & Lingard, B. (2002). Constructing a European policy space in educational governance: The role of transnational policy actors. *European Educational Research Journal, 1*(20), 290–307.

Lefstein, A., & Feniger, Y. (2014). How not to reason with PISA: An ironic investigation. *Journal of Education Policy, 29*(6), 845–855.

Leonardo, Z. & Grubb, N. (2014) *Education and racism: A primer on issues and dilemmas.* New York: Routledge.

Levin, H. M. (2013). The utility and need for incorporating noncognitive skills into large-scale educational assessments. In M. von Davier, E. Gonzalez, I. Kirsch, & K. Yamamoto (Eds.), *The role of international large-scale assessments: Perspectives from technology, economy, and education research* (pp. 67–86). Dordrecht: Springer.

Lingard, B. (2010). Policy borrowing, policy learning: Testing times in Australian schools. *Critical Studies in Education, 51*(2), 129–147.

Lingard, B. (2011). Policy as numbers: Ac/counting for educational research. *Australian Educational Researcher, 38*(4), 355–382.

Lingard, B., Creagh, S., & Vass, G. (2012). Education policy as numbers: Data categories and two Australian cases of misrecognition. *Journal of Education Policy, 27*(3), 315–333.

Lingard, B., & Douglas, P. (1999). *Men engaging feminisms: Pro-feminism, backlashes and schooling.* Buckingham: Open University Press.

Lingard, B., Martino, W., & Rezai-Rashti, G. (2013). Testing regimes, accountabilities and education policy: Commensurate global and national policy developments. *Journal of Education Policy, 28*(5), 539–556.

Lingard, B., & McGregor, G. (2014). Two contrasting Australian curriculum responses to globalisation: What students should learn or become. *Curriculum Journal.* doi:10.1080/09585176.2013.872048

Lingard, B., & Rawolle, S. (2004). Mediatizing educational policy: The journalistic field, science policy, and cross-field effects. *Journal of Education Policy, 19*(3), 361–380.

Lingard, B., & Rawolle, S. (2009). Understanding quality and equity of schooling in Scotland: Locating educational traditions globally. *Education in the North, 17*(1), 1–25.

Lingard, B., & Rawolle, S. (2011). New scalar politics: Implications for education policy. *Comparative Education, 47*(4), 489–502.

Lingard, B., & Sellar, S. (2013a). 'Catalyst data': Perverse systemic effects of audit and accountability in Australian schooling. *Journal of Education Policy, 28*(5), 634–656.

Lingard, B., & Sellar, S. (2013b). Globalization, edu-business and network governance: The policy sociology of Stephen J. Ball and rethinking education policy analysis. *London Review of Education, 11*(3), 265–280.

Lingard, B., & Sellar, S. (2014). Representing your country: Scotland, PISA and new spatialities of educational governance. *Scottish Educational Review, 46*(1), 5–18.

Lingard, B., Sellar, S., & Baroutsis, A. (2015). Researching the habitus of global policy actors in education. *Cambridge Journal of Education, 45*(1), 25–42. doi:10.1080/0305764X.2014.988686

Lingard, B., Sellar, S., & Savage, G. (2014). Rearticulating social justice as equity in schooling policy: The effects of testing and data infrastructures. *British Journal of Sociology of Education, 35*(5), 710–730.

Lipman, P. (2004). *High stakes education: Inequality, globalization, and urban school reform.* New York: RoutledgeFalmer.
Lipman, P. (2011). *The new political economy of urban education: Neoliberalism, race and the right to the city.* New York: Routledge.
Loveless, T. (2013a). *PISA's China problem.* Available www.brookings.edu/research/papers/2013/10/09-pisa-china-problem-loveless (accessed January 19, 2015).
Loveless, T. (2013b). *Attention OECD-PISA: Your silence on China is wrong.* Available www.brookings.edu/research/papers/2013/12/11-shanghai-pisa-scores-wrong-loveless (accessed January 19, 2015).
Loveless, T. (2014). *PISA's China problem continues: A response to Schleicher, Zhang, and Tucker.* Available www.brookings.edu/research/papers/2014/01/08-shanghai-pisa-loveless (accessed January 19, 2015).
Loya, T. A., & Boli, J. (1999). Standardization in the world polity: Technical rationality over power. In J. Boli & G. M. Thomas (Eds.), *Constructing world culture: International nongovernmental organizations since 1875* (pp. 169–197). Stanford, CA: Stanford University Press.
Lucas, S., & Beresford, L. (2010). Naming and classifying: Theory, evidence, and equity in education. *Review of Research in Education, 34*(1), 25–84.
Luke, A. (2011). Generalizing across borders: Policy and the limits of educational science. *Educational Researcher, 40*(8), 367–377.
Luke, A., Green, J., & Kelly, G. (2010). What counts as evidence and equity? *Review of Research in Education, 34*(1), vii–xvi.
Luke, A., & Hogan, D. (2006). Redesigning what counts as evidence in educational policy: The Singapore model. In J. Ozga, T. Seddon, & T. Popkewitz (Eds.), *World yearbook of education 2006: Educational research and policy: Steering the knowledge-based economy* (pp. 170–184). London: Routledge.
Lury, C., Luciana P., & Tiziana T. (2012). Introduction: The becoming topological of culture. *Theory, Culture & Society, 29*(4–5), 3–35. doi:10.1177/0263276412454552
Lyotard, J.-F. (1984). *The postmodern condition: A report on knowledge.* Minneapolis: University of Minnesota Press.
Mahony, P., Hextall, I., & Menter, I. (2004). Building dams in Jordan, assessing teachers in England: A case study in edu-business. *Globalisation, Societies and Education, 2*(2), 227–296.
Martens, K. (2007). How to become an influential actor—the 'comparative turn' in OECD education policy. In K. Martens, A. Rusconi, & K. Leuze (Eds.), *New arenas of education governance—the impact of international organizations and markets on educational policy making* (pp. 40–56). New York: Palgrave Macmillan.
Martens, K., & Niemann, M. (2013). When do numbers count? The differential impact of the PISA ranking and rating on education policy in Germany and the US. *German Politics, 22*, 314–332. doi:10.1080/09644008.2013.794455
Martino, W. (2001). Boys and literacy: Investigating boys' reading preferences and involvement in literacy. *Australian Journal of Language and Literacy, 24*(1), 61–74.
Martino, W. (2008). *Boys' underachievement: Which boys are we talking about?* Toronto: Ontario Ministry of Education.
Martino, W., & Rezai-Rashti, G. (2012). Neo-liberal accountability and boys' underachievement: Steering education policy by numbers in the Ontario context. *International Journal of Inclusive Education, 16*(4), 423–440.
Massumi, B. (2005). Fear (the spectrum said). *Positions, 13*(1), 31–48.
Masters, G. N. (2009a). *Improving literacy, numeracy and science learning in Queensland primary schools, preliminary advice.* Melbourne: Australian Council for Educational Research.

References

Masters, G. N. (2009b). *Improving literacy, numeracy and science learning in Queensland primary schools*. Melbourne: Australian Council for Educational Research.

Mayer-Schonberger, V., & Cukier, K. (2013). *Big data: A revolution that will transform how we live, work and think*. Boston, MA: Eamon Dolan/Houghton Mifflin Harcourt.

Mayer-Schonberger, V., & Cukier, K. N. (2014). *Learning with big data: The future of education*. Boston, MA: Houghton Mifflin Harcourt.

McCarthy, C. (1998). *The uses of culture: Education and the limits of ethnic affiliations*. New York: Routledge.

McCaskell, T. (2011). The TDSB achievement gap report: What's missing? Available http://educationactiontoronto.com/home/the-tdsb-achievement-gap-report-what-s-missing (accessed October 19, 2014).

McKinsey & Co. (2007). *How the world's best-performing school systems come out on top*. London: Author.

McKinsey & Co. (2010). *How the world's most improved school systems keep getting better*. London: Author.

Mead, S. (2006). *The truth about boys and girls*. New York: Education Sector.

Mehta, J. D., & Schwartz, R. B. (2011). Canada looks a lot like us but gets much better results. In M. S. Tucker (Ed.), *Surpassing Shanghai: An agenda for American education built on the world's leading systems* (pp. 141–165). Cambridge, MA: Harvard Education Press.

Meyer, H., & Benavot, A. (2013). *PISA, power and policy: The emergence of global educational governance*. Oxford: Symposium Books.

Meyer, H.-D., & Schiller, K. (2013). Gauging the role of non-educational effects in large-scale assessments: Socio-economics, culture and PISA outcomes. In H.-D. Meyer & A. Benavot (Eds.), *PISA, power, and policy: The emergence of global educational governance* (pp. 207–224). Oxford: Symposium Books.

Meyer, J., Boli, J., Thomas, G. M., & Ramirez, F. O. (1997). World society and the nation state. *American Journal of Sociology, 103*, 144–181. doi:10.1086/231174

Miller, P., & Rose, N. (2008). *Governing the present*. Cambridge: Polity.

Mollenhauer, K. (2014). Forgotten connections: On culture and upbringing (N. Friesen, Ed. & Trans.). Abingdon: Routledge.

Mourshed, M., Chijioke, C., & Barber, M. (2010). *How the world's most improved school systems keep getting better*. London: McKinsey.

Mukerji, C. (2010). The territorial state as figured world of power: Strategies, logistics and impersonal rule. *Sociological Theory, 28*, 402–424. doi:10.1111/j.1467–9558.2010.01381

Mundy, K., & Farrell, J. (2008). International educational indicators and assessment: Issues for teachers. In K. Mundy, K. Bickmore, R. Hayhoe, M. Madden, & K. Madjidi (Eds.), *Comparative and International Education: Issues for Teachers* (pp. 189–213). New York: Teachers College Press.

Nichols, S. L., & Berliner, D. C. (2007). *Collateral damage: How high-stakes testing corrupts America's schools*. Cambridge, MA: Harvard Education Press.

Noguera, P. (2008). *The trouble with black boys: And other reflections on race, equity and the future of public education*. San Francisco, CA: Jossey-Bass.

Nous Group. (2011). *Schooling challenges and opportunities: A report for the Review of Funding for Schooling Panel*. Melbourne: Nous Group.

Novoa, A., & Yariv-Mashal, T. (2003). Comparative research in education: A mode of governance or a historical journey? *Comparative Education, 39*(4), 423–438.

Nye Jr, J. S. (2004). *Soft power: The means to success in world politics*. New York: PublicAffairs.

O'Neill, O. (2002). *A question of trust (The BBC Reith Lectures 2002)*. Cambridge: Cambridge University Press.

O'Neill, O. (2013). Intelligent accountability in education. *Oxford Review of Education*, *39*(1), 4–16.
OECD. (1995). *Governance in transition: Public management reforms in OECD countries.* Paris: Author.
OECD. (1996). *The knowledge-based economy.* Paris: Author.
OECD. (1999). *Measuring student knowledge and skills: A new framework for assessment.* Paris: Author.
OECD. (2002). *Education policy analysis.* Paris: Author.
OECD. (2010a). *PISA 2009 results: Overcoming social background* (Vol. 2). Paris: Author.
OECD. (2010b). *PISA 2009 results: Learning to learn* (Vol. 3). Paris: Author.
OECD. (2010c). Programme for International Student Assessment (PISA): Strong performers and successful reformers in education. Available www.oecd.org/edu/school/programmeforinternationalstudentassessmentpisa/strongperformersandsuccessfulreformersineducation.htm (accessed February 26, 2015).
OECD. (2010d). *Making reform happen: Lessons from OECD countries.* Paris: Author.
OECD. (2011a). *Lessons from PISA for the United States, strong performers and successful reformers in education.* Paris: Author.
OECD. (2011b). *Education at a glance 2011: OECD indicators.* Paris: Author.
OECD. (2012). *Better skills, better jobs, better lives: A strategic approach to skills policy.* Paris: Author.
OECD. (2013a). PISA 2012 results: Excellence through equity. Paris: Author.
OECD. (2013b). PISA 2012 results in focus: What 15-year-olds know and what they can do with what they know. Paris: Author. Available www.oecd.org/pisa/keyfindings/pisa-2012-results-overview.pdf (accessed January 8, 2014).
OECD. (2013c). What the survey of adult skills (PIAAC) measures. In *The survey of adult skills: Reader's companion.* Paris: Author.
OECD. (2013d). *PISA 2012 results: Ready to learn: Students' engagement, drive and self-beliefs* (Vol. 3). PISA. Paris: Author.
OECD. (2015). *Education policy outlook 2015: Making reforms happen.* Paris: Author.
Ontario Ministry of Education. (2009). *Ontario's equity and inclusive education strategy.* Toronto: Queen's Printer for Ontario.
Ozga, J. (1987). Studying education policy through the lives of policy makers. In S. Walker & L. Barton (Eds.), *Changing policies, changing teachers: New directions for schooling?* Philadelphia, PA: Open University Press.
Ozga, J. (2009). Governing education through data in England: From regulation to self-evaluation. *Journal of Education Policy*, *24*(2), 149–162.
Ozga, J., Dahler-Larsen, P., Segerholm, C., & Simola, H. (Eds.). (2011). *Fabricating quality in education: Data and governance in Europe.* London: Routledge.
Ozga, J., & Lingard, B. (2007). Globalisation, education policy and politics. In B. Lingard & J. Ozga (Eds.), *The RoutledgeFalmer reader in education policy and politics* (pp. 65–82). Oxford: Routledge.
Papadopoulos, G. S. (1994). *Education 1960–1990: The OECD perspective.* Paris: OECD.
Pearson plc. (2012). Annual report and accounts 2012. Available www.pearson.com/content/dam/pearsoncorporate/files/cosec/2013/15939_PearsonAR12.pdf (accessed March 2, 2015).
Phillips, D., & Ochs, K. (Eds.). (2004). *Educational policy borrowing: Historical perspectives.* Oxford: Symposium.
Phillips, J. W. P. (2013). On topology. *Theory, Culture & Society*, *30*(5), 122–152.

Piketty, T. (2014). *Capital in the twenty-first century* (A. Goldhammer, Trans.). Cambridge, MA: Belknap Press.
Pons, X. (2011). What do we really learn from PISA? The sociology of its reception in three European countries (2001–2008). *European Journal of Education, 46*(20), 540–548.
Porter, T. (1995). *Trust in numbers: The pursuit of objectivity in science and public life*. Princeton, NJ: Princeton University Press.
Poster, M. (1990). *The mode of information*. Cambridge: Polity Press.
Power, M. (1997). *The audit society: Rituals of verification*. Oxford: Oxford University Press.
Power, M. (2000). The audit society—second thoughts. *International Journal of Auditing, 4*, 111–119.
Power, M. (2004). Counting, control and calculation: Reflections on measuring and management. *Human Relations, 57*(6), 765–783.
Power, M. (2007) The theory of the audit explosion. In Ferlie, L., Lynn Jr, .L.E., and Pollittt, C. (Eds.) *The Oxford Handbook of Public Management*. Oxford: Oxford University Press.
Power, S., & Frandji, D. (2010). Education markets, the new politics of recognition and the increasing fatalism towards inequality. *Journal of Education Policy, 25*(3), 385–339.
Protevi, J. (2009). *Political affect: Connecting the social and the somatic*. Minneapolis: University of Minnesota Press.
Ranson, S. (2003). Public accountability in the age of neo-liberal governance. *Journal of Education Policy, 18*(5), 459–480.
Ranson, S. (2012). Schools and civil society: Corporate or community governance. *Critical Studies in Education, 53*(1), 29–45.
Ravitch, D. (2011). *The death and life of the great American school system: How testing and choice are undermining education*. New York: Basic Books.
Rezai-Rashti, G. (2003). Equity education and educational restructuring in Ontario: Global and local policy and practice. *World Studies in Education, 4*(1), 29–44.
Rezai-Rashti, G. (2009). The assault of neo-liberalism on education reform, restructuring, and teaching in Ontario secondary schools. In C. Levine-Rasky (Ed.), *Canadian perspectives on the sociology of education* (pp. 307–321). Toronto: Oxford University Press.
Rezai-Rashti, G., Segeren, A. & Martino, W. (in press). Race and racial justice in Ontario education: Neoliberalism and strategies of racial invisibility. In Majhonvic, S. & Malet, R. (Eds.) *Education for democracy in diversity*. Rotterdam: Sense.
Rhodes, R.A.W. (1997). *Understanding governance policy networks, governance, reflexivity and accountability*. Buckingham: Open University Press.
Riddile, M. (2010). PISA: It's poverty not stupid. Available http://nasspblogs.org/principaldifference/2010/12/pisa_its_poverty_not_stupid_1.html (accessed October 22, 2014).
Rinne, R., Kallo, J., & Hokka, S. (2004). Too eager to comply? OECD education policies and the Finnish response. *Educational Research Journal, 3*(2), 454–485. doi:10.2304/eerj.2004.3.2.3
Rizvi, F., & Lingard, B. (2010). *Globalizing education policy*. London: Routledge.
Robertson, S.L., Bonal, X. and Dale, R. (2002) GATS and the education service industry. *Comparative Education Review*. 6(4): 472–497.
Rose, N. (1988). Calculable minds and manageable individuals. *History of the Human Sciences, 1*(2), 179–200.
Rose, N. (1991). Governing by numbers: Figuring out democracy. *Accounting Organizations and Society, 16*(7), 673–692.

Rose, N. (1999). *Powers of freedom: Reframing political thought*. Cambridge: Cambridge University Press.
Rothstein, R. (2004). *Class and schools: Using social, economic, and educational reform to close the black–white achievement gap*. Washington, DC: Economy Policy Institute.
Ruppert, E. (2012). The governmental topologies of database devices. *Theory, Culture & Society, 29*(4–5), 116–136. doi:10.1177/0263276412439428
Rutkowski, D. (2014). The OECD and the local: PISA-based test for schools in the US. *Discourse: Studies in the Cultural Politics of Education*. doi:10.1080/01596306.2014.943157
Sahlberg, P. (2010). Rethinking accountability in a knowledge society. *Journal of Educational Change, 11*(1), 45–61.
Sahlberg, P. (2011). *Finnish lessons: What can the world learn from educational change in Finland?* New York: Teachers College Press.
Santiago, P., Donaldson, G., Herman, J., & Shewbridge, C. (2011). *OECD Reviews of Evaluation and Assessment in Education: Australia*. Paris: OECD.
Sassen, S. (2001). *The global city: New York, London, Tokyo* (2nd ed.). Princeton, NJ: Princeton University Press.
Sassen, S. (2007). *A sociology of globalization*. New York: W.W. Norton.
Sassen, S. (2009). The global city perspective: Theoretical implications for Shanghai. In X. Chen (Ed.), *Shanghai Rising: State power and local transformations in a global megacity* (pp. 3–30). Minneapolis: University of Minnesota Press.
Savage, G., & O'Connor, K. (2014). National agendas in global times: Curriculum reforms in Australia and the USA since the 1980s. *Journal of Education Policy*. doi:10.1080/02680939.2014.969321.
Savage, M., & Burrows, R. (2007). The coming crisis of empirical sociology. *Sociology, 41*(5), 885–899. doi:10.1177/0038038507080443
Schleicher, A. (2013, July 22). Big data and PISA. *Huffington Post*. Available www.huffingtonpost.com/andreas-schleicher/big-data-and-pisa_b_3633558.html (accessed February 27, 2015).
Schriewer, J. (1990). The method of comparison and the need for externalization: Methodological criteria and sociological concepts. In J. Schriewer & B. Holmes (Eds.), *Theories and methods in comparative education* (pp. 25–83). Frankfurt: Peter Lang.
Schriewer, J. (2000). World system and interrelationship networks: The internationalization of education and the role of comparative inquiry. In T.S. Popkewitz (Ed.), *Educational knowledge* (pp. 305–343). Albany: State University of New York Press.
Schriewer, J., & Martinez, C. (2004). Constructions of internationality in education. In G. Steiner-Khamsi (Ed.), *The global politics of educational borrowing and lending* (pp. 29–53). New York: Teachers College Press.
Schwartz, R., & Mehta, J. (2011). Finland: Superb teachers—How to get them, how to use them. In M. S. Tucker (Ed.), *Surpassing Shanghai: An agenda for American education built on the world's leading systems* (pp. 51–78). Cambridge, MA: Harvard Education Press.
Scott, J. C. (1998). *Seeing like a state: How certain schemes to improve the human condition have failed*. New Haven, CT: Yale University Press.
Sellar, S. (2014). Data infrastructure: A review of expanding accountability systems and large-scale assessments in education. *Discourse: Studies in the Cultural Politics of Education*. doi:10.1080/01596306.2014.931117
Sellar, S., & Lingard, B. (2013a). Looking East: Shanghai, PISA 2009 and the reconstitution of reference societies in the global policy field. *Comparative Education, 49*(4), 464–485. doi:10.1080/03050068.2013.770943

Sellar, S., & Lingard, B. (2013b). PISA and the expanding role of the OECD in global educational governance. In H.-D. Meyer & A. Benavot (Eds.), *PISA, power, and policy: The emergence of global educational governance* (pp. 185–206). Oxford: Symposium Books.

Sellar, S., & Lingard, B. (2014). The OECD and the expansion of PISA: New global modes of governance in education. *British Educational Research Journal, 40*(6), 917–936.

Seth, S. (2007). *Subject lessons: The western education of colonial India*. Durham, NC: Duke University Press.

Silander, T., & Välijärvi, J. (2013). Practice of building pedagogical skill in Finnish teacher education. In. H. Meyer & A. Benavot (Eds.), *PISA, power and policy: The emergence of global educational governance* (pp. 77–97). Oxford: Symposium Books.

Simola, H. (2005). The Finnish miracle of PISA: Historical and sociological remarks on teaching and teacher education. *Comparative Education, 41*(4), 455–470.

Simola, H., Rinnie, R., Varjo, J., & Kauko, J. (2013). The paradox of the education race: How to win the ranking game by sailing to headwind. *Journal of Education Policy, 28*(5), 612–633.

Simons, M. (2014). Governing education without reform: The power of the example. *Discourse: Studies in the Cultural Politics of Education*. doi:10.1080/01596306.2014.892660

Sobe, N. (2015). All that is global is not world culture: Accountability systems and educational apparatuses. *Globalisation, Societies and Education, 13*(1), 135–148.

Spivak, G. (2012). *An aesthetic education in the era of globalization*. Cambridge, MA: Harvard University Press.

Star, S. L., & Ruhleder, K. (1996). Steps toward an ecology of infrastructure: Design and access for large information spaces. *Information Systems Research, 7*, 111–134.

Steiner-Khamsi, G. (Ed.). (2004). *The global politics of educational borrowing and lending*. New York: Teachers College Press.

Stengers, I. (2011). Comparison as a matter of concern. *Common Knowledge, 17*(1), 48–63.

Stobart, G. (2008). *Testing times: The uses and abuses of assessment*. London: Routledge.

Strathern, M. (1995). New accountabilities: Anthropological studies in audit, ethics and the academy. In M. Strathern (Ed.), *Audit cultures: Anthropological studies in audit, ethics and accountability*. London: Routledge.

Stronach, I. (2010). *Globalizing education, educating the local. How method made us mad*. London: Routledge.

Suspitsyna, T. (2010). Accountability in American education as a rhetoric and a technology of governmentality. *Journal of Education Policy, 25*(5), 567–586.

Takayama, K. (2007). 'A Nation at Risk' crosses the Pacific: Transnational borrowing of the U.S. crisis discourse in the debate on education reform in Japan. *Comparative Education Review, 51*(4), 423–446.

Takayama, K. (2008). The politics of international league tables: PISA in Japan's achievement crisis debate. *Comparative Education, 44*(4), 387–407.

Takayama, K. (2011). Other Japanese educations and Japanese education otherwise. *Asia Pacific Journal of Education, 31*(3), 345–359.

Takayama, K. (2015). Provincialising the world culture theory debate: Critical insights from a margin. *Globalisation, Societies and Education, 13*(1), 34–57.

Tan, C. (2012). The culture of education policy making: Curriculum reform in Shanghai. *Critical Studies in Education, 53*(20), 153–167.

Tan, C. (2013). *Learning from Shanghai: Lessons on achieving educational success*. Dordrecht: Springer.

Taubman, P. M. (2009). *Teaching by numbers*. New York: Routledge.
TDSB (Toronto District School Board). (2006). Research report: The TDSB Grade 9 cohort study: A five-year analysis, 2000–2005. Toronto: Author.
Thrift, N. (2005). *Knowing capitalism*. London: Sage.
Titus, J. (2004). Boy trouble: Rhetorical framing of boys' underachievement. *Discourse: Studies in the Cultural Politics of Education, 25*(2), 145–169.
Torrance, H. (2006). Globalizing empiricism: What, if anything, can be learned from international comparisons of educational achievement? In H. Lauder, P. Brown, J.A. Dillabough, & A. Halsey (Eds.), *Education, globalization and social change* (pp. 824–834). Oxford: Oxford University Press.
Tucker, M. (Ed.). (2011). *Surpassing Shanghai: An agenda for American education built on the world's leading systems*. Cambridge, MA: Harvard Education Press.
Urry, J. (2007). *Mobilities*. Cambridge: Polity Press.
Varjo, J., Simola, H., & Rinnie, R. (2013). Finland's PISA results: An analysis of dynamics in education politics. In. H. Meyer & A. Benavot (Eds.), *PISA, power and policy: The emergence of global educational governance* (pp. 51–76). Oxford: Symposium Books.
Verger, T., Novelli, M., & Altinyelken, H. (Eds.). (2012). *Global education policy and international development: New agendas, issues and policies*. London: Continuum.
Waldow, F. (2012). Standardisation and legitimacy. In G. Steiner-Khamsi & F. Waldow (Eds.), *World yearbook of education: Policy borrowing and lending in education* (pp. 411–427). New York: Routledge.
Wang, L., & Holland, T. (2011). In search of educational equity for the migrant children of Shanghai. *Comparative Education, 47*(20), 471–487.
Webb, P. T. (2011). The evolution of accountability. *Journal of Education Policy, 26*(6), 735–756.
Weis, L., & Fine, M. (2012). Critical bifocality and circuits of privilege: Expanding critical ethnographic theory and design. *Harvard Educational Review, 82*(2), 173–201.
Weiss, T. G. (2013). *Global governance: Why? What? Whither?* Cambridge: Polity Press.
Whatmore, S.J., & Landström, C. (2011). Flood apprentices: An exercise in making things public. *Economy and Society, 40*(4), 582–610.
Wilkinson, R., & Pickett, K. (2009). *The spirit level: Why greater equality makes societies stronger*. London: Penguin.
Williams, P. (2002). The competent boundary spanner. *Public Administration, 80*(1), 103–124.
Wiseman, A. (2010). The uses of evidence for educational policy-making: Global contexts and international trends. *Review of Research in Education, 34*(1), 1–24.
Wiseman, A. (2013). Policy responses to PISA in comparative perspective. In H.-D. Meyer & A. Benavot (Eds.), *PISA, power, and policy: The emergence of global educational governance* (pp. 303–322). Oxford: Symposium Books.
Woodward, R. (2009). *The Organization for Economic Co-operation and Development (OECD)*. Abingdon: Routledge.
Yar, M. (2003). Panoptic power and the pathologisation of vision: Critical reflections on the Foucauldian thesis. *Surveillance & Society, 1*(3), 254–271.
Zumbo, B. D. (2007). Three generations of DIF analyses: Considering where it has been, where it is now, and where it is going. *Language Assessment Quarterly, 4*, 223–233. doi:10.1080/15434300701375832

INDEX

Aboriginal populations 137
ACARA *see* Australian Curriculum Assessment and Reporting Authority
accountability/ies: in Australia 73, 74; Canadian 124; defined 38; external 38; framing of 1, 87; global 6, 15–16, 28, 38, 60, 125, 145; hierarchical modes of 146; infrastructure of 3; interventions 65; mutual 21–2, 29, 30, 36, 39, 42, 44–5, 61–3, 67, 90, 131, 146; national (state) 9, 70, 85; neoliberal 28, 64, 67, 91, 119, 123, 144; new modes of 151; of principals 9; public sector 13; rich 151–6; of schools 9, 153; in Shanghai 49; surveillance of 86; of teachers 9, 64, 89; test-based 1, 63, 67, 118, 122, 130; two-way horizontal 15; *see also* accountability systems; educational accountability/ies
accountability systems: development of 117; introduction of 154; mediation of 122; need for contextual flexibility in 153; performative 151; reconceptualization of 152
ACER *see* Australian Council for Educational Research
achievement gaps 100, 110, 122; black–white 129, 133–4; in Canada 138–43; class inequalities 128; in England 128; and ethnic background 128; and need for economic reform 134; racial 117, 128; *see also* gender achievement gap
achievement variations 108, 128, 133, 137
actor-network theory 12
actors: global 61; international 93; nodal 57, 61; philanthropic 13; policy 4, 13, 15, 20, 23, 24, 35, 38, 43–4, 61, 126; transnational 126
adaptive learning technologies 71
administration: amenability to 2, 43, 101, 125–6, 138, 144; "empowered" 49; system 154
advocacy groups 120
Alberta (Canada), PISA performance in 131; *see also* Canada
America Achieves 158
American Federation of Teachers (USA) 160
Amplify 58, 159
analytics: data 4, 10, 157, 160; of governmentality 94, 125; topological 12
answerability 14, 153
Asian century 16, 41, 46, 51
assessment 1; expanding scope of 32, 35; explanatory power of 34–5; international 29, 40; *see also* large-scale assessments; testing
audit culture(s) 3, 9, 14, 67, 123
audit explosion 3, 28, 70
austerity policies 147

Index

Australia: China as reference society for 60, 62; educational jurisdiction in 122; education reform in 58–9, 73; education system in 15, 60, 66, 72, 87, 89, 148; equity issues in 147; gender achievement gap in 127; global educational accountabilities in 8; LBOTE students in 95, 148–9; looking to England and USA for educational lessons 45; migrant students in 108; national curriculum in 6, 8, 73; National Education Agreement in 73; national testing in 69; Pearson's involvement in 15; PISA data regarding quality and equity in 123; PISA testing in 58–60; political structure of 72; reciprocal exchange of policy with England 58; response to Shanghai's PISA performance 16, 40, 42, 60; study of policy developments in response to NAPLAN 67–8; target setting in 74–5, 79, 84–6; test-based accountability in 63; vernacular expressions of globalized accountability in 16
Australia in the Asian Century 59
Australian Council for Educational Research (ACER) 58, 75, 81, 83
Australian Curriculum Assessment and Reporting Authority (ACARA) 58, 64, 73, 88
Australian Institute of Teaching and School Leadership (AITSL) 73
Australian Local Government Association 72

Barber, Michael 57, 159
Battle Hymn of the Tiger Mother (Tan) 48
Beijing, China, participation in PISA 33, 47
benchmarking 33, 50, 61, 69, 90–1, 117
benchmarks 17, 21, 46, 52, 83, 87
best practices 91, 96, 119
big data 2–5, 10, 12, 70, 113, 149–50
biopolitics 2
biopower 2, 123
black underachievement 101, 133
Blair, Tony 45, 56, 57, 159
Bligh, Anna 81
boundary spanners 4, 159
boy crisis hype *see* boys; "failing boys" discourse
boys: as disadvantaged category 18, 124, 143; literacy data on 103; motivation of 136; as objects of government 126, 129; reading skills of 135–6; underachievement of 135–6; *see also* "failing boys" discourse
Brazil, OECD's engagement with 33
BRICs, OECD's relationship with 24
Britain *see* England
British Columbia (Canada), PISA performance in 131
British students: black Caribbean 128; white 128
Bush, George W. 51, 52, 122, 158
business practices, transnational 14, 61

Canada: Aboriginal populations in 137; achievement gap in 138–43; education systems in 9, 67, 131; as example of high-performing schools 17, 56; failing boys discourse in 143; federalism in schooling 123; gender achievement gap in 128; global educational accountabilities in 8; high-quality education in 132; immigration policy in 107; importance of categories in 148; inequalities in 117; Ministry of Education in 129; performance on PISA 93–4; racial context in 92; as reference society 50, 92, 125
Canadian students: Aboriginal 106, 137–8, 143; Albanian 108; Asian 109–10; at-risk 106; Australian 108; Caribbean 103; Chinese 108; East Asian 103; Hispanic 106; immigrant 142; Latino 113; Middle Eastern 106; minority 113; Portuguese-speaking 142; Somali-speaking 103, 142; South Asian 103; Spanish-speaking 142; US migrant 108
capital 3, 26; cultural 134, 137; economic 137; finance 13; human 4, 5, 7, 8, 26–8, 32, 40, 51, 73, 107, 151; movement of 98; network 159; reputational 63, 66, 79, 81, 84, 87; socioeconomic 108, 137
capitalism 3, 23; knowing/knowledge 3, 7, 49, 61, 70, 149; neoliberal market 54
catalyst data 16, 17, 22, 63–71, 83, 86–8, 147–8
Centre for International Mobility and Cooperation (CIMO; Finland) 114
Centre for Research and Innovation (CERI) 26
CERI (Centre for Research and Innovation) 26

Charter of Human Rights (Canada) 141
charter schools 51, 56, 131
China: economic reform in 42; education in 42, 54, 131; educational accountability in 9; educational history in 47–9; as example of top-performing system 56–7; as inspiration for education in England 57; "market socialism" in 69; OECD's engagement with 24, 33; Pearson's involvement in 158; and the PISA assessment 33; as reference society 62; *see also* Shanghai (China)
CIMO *see* Centre for International Mobility and Cooperation
citizens, engagement of 151–2
Citizenship and Immigration Canada 107
class *see* social class
clouds 12
CMEC *see* Council of Ministers of Education in Canada
COAG *see* Council of Australian Governments
codeability, grid of 2, 125
collaboration 28, 32
commensurability 2, 17, 78, 125
commensuration 30, 43–4
Common Core (US) 9, 51, 67, 122
communication skills 32
community, relationships with schools 154
comparison, as mode of governance 148
competency groups 152
competition 6, 51, 52, 54, 118, 131, 157
computational capacities, increased 3, 28, 150, 151
Confucianism 48, 59
consulting firms 159–60
contextual factors 147; in PISA performance 47, 49
control societies 70, 72, 86, 150
corporate responsibility 119; social 158
Council of Australian Governments (COAG) 72; Reform Council 67, 73, 78
Council of Ministers of Education in Canada (CMEC) 9, 121–3; role and function of 138–41
CTB/McGraw-Hill 33, 34, 158
Cultural Revolution (China) 48, 57
culture 140, 143; "becoming-topological" of 5, 11–12; in China 59; constituents of 11; homogeneity of 113; and PISA performance 47–9, 54; of testing 61; theory of 11; topology as means of analyzing 11
curricula/um 1, 57; in Australia 58, 64; boys' performance in 140; common core 67, 122; edu-business involvement in 157; local contexts for 152; national 6, 8, 30, 58, 64, 73; in Ontario 141; as reason for school reform 92; reform of 48–9, 73, 114, 154; in Shanghai 48–9; standardized 51, 100; and structural inequality 147; test-driven

data: catalyst 16, 17, 22, 63–71, 83, 86–8, 147–8; as central to structuring the system 2; collection of 3; and contemporary governance 4; disaggregated 128–9, 132–3, 143, 149; educational 4, 155; flows of 44; on human capital 28; international 55–6; interpretation of 134–5; interview 5; management of 44, 65, 157; national 55; in new public management 1–2; performance 37; production of 21, 44, 65; representation of 4; social 3; sources and quantities of 3; test-driven 97; theorization of 161; use for accountability rather than reform 84; *see also* big data
data analysis 3, 21; contextualization of 143; in PISA 126
data infrastructure(s) 5, 11, 37, 39, 69, 150, 156
data talks 88
data walls 88
"datafication" 3, 5, 10, 149, 151; of education 61
DEELSA (Directorate for Education, Employment, Labour and Social Affairs) 26
democracy 2, 23, 151
Department for Education and Skills (DFES) 128
Department of Human Resources and Skills Development (Canada) 139
deracination 31, 90, 91, 94, 117, 119, 148
DFES (Department for Education and Skills) 128
differential item functioning 30
Directorate for Education 26–7
Directorate for Education and Skills 27, 34
Directorate for Education, Employment, Labour and Social Affairs (DEELSA) 26

Directorate for Scientific Affairs 26
Directorate for Social Affairs, Manpower and Education 26
disciplinary society 70, 150
Discipline and Punish (Foucault) 149
discrimination, racial 98, 109, 133; *see also* racism(s)
dispositif/dispositive (Foucauldian) 7, 8, 12, 94, 119–20
diversity 103; and immigrant vs. nonimmigrant minorities 106–11; of students 18, 98–9, 103, 106–11
dropout rates 103–4, 106–7, 137, 142
Duncan, Arne 52, 131

East Asia: education in 16; as reference societies 46; *see also* China; Shanghai (China)
economic redistribution *see* redistribution
economy: global 69; knowledge-based 51
edu-businesses 4, 5, 13, 14, 32–4, 58, 61, 70, 89, 93, 151, 156–61; *see also* CTB-McGraw Hill; Pearson
education: in China 42; comparative 45; datafication of 61; economics of 32; global infrastructure in 40; global space of equivalence in 43; marketization of 126; network governance in 33; and the OECD 25–6; quasi-market forces in 131; reconstruction of as business 70; socioeconomic aspects of 121, 124, 126
educational accountability/ies 5; and edu-businesses 14; examination of 14–15; framing of 1; and GERM 6; global 3, 4, 10–11, 14, 15, 22, 23, 39, 40, 146; information produced for 154, 156; literature on 70; national curriculum as 8; national testing as 8, 58; neoliberal 89, 140; new modes of 3, 66, 143, 147; new spatialities of 5; and OECD's role in global governance 35–9; performance-driven 140; rich forms of 18, 153, 155; shaping of 152; target setting as driver of 88; test-based modes of 122
educational testing services 61
Education and Skills Directorate 147
Education at a Glance 24, 28, 39, 51
Education Committee 26
Education International 161
education policy 5; colorblindness in 91; global 40, 43, 46, 57, 68, 123; "hypernarratives" in 6; inequality in 129;

mediatization of 128–9, 147; neoliberal 51, 55, 124; visualization of 95, 102, 119; *see also* policy; policy making
Education, Quality and Accountability Office (EQAO) tests 102–3, 106; unquantifiable aspects of 153
education race 6–7
education reform 2, 92; in Australia 16, 58–9; in Canada 100, 140; data as argument for 37; in Finland 113–14, 118; global 95; neoliberal 100, 118; representation of 109–10; in Shanghai 49; and success in PISA 106
Education Revolution (Australia) 73, 74
education system(s): in Australia 15, 60, 66, 87, 89, 148; in China 42, 54, 131; decentralized 114; in England 15, 45; in Finland 16, 131; hierarchical sorting of 91; high performing 132; inequalities in 92; international 131; national 15, 41; in USA 9, 17, 45
Education World Forum (2011) 57
Efficacy Framework (Pearson) 159
egalitarianism, in Finland 112
empiricism, globalizing 43, 144
engagement, analysis of 32
England: China as reference society for 62; data production and management in 65; Department of Education 55–6; educational accountability in 9; education reform in 49, 55; as example of successful education system 45; export of education to colonies by 54–5; gender achievement gap in 128; influence of Shanghai's PISA scores on 60; looking to USA for educational lessons 45; national curriculum in 6; national education system in 15; PISA testing in 55–7; response to Shanghai's PISA performance 16, 40, 42
English language learners (ELLs) 103–5
Enhanced Engagement program 33
entrepreneurship 18, 32, 51, 91, 93, 99, 131, 158, 160
epistemologies, neopositivist 4
equity: analysis of 30–1; educational 97–8, 147; and the "failing boys" discourse 126–31; issues of 147; and PISA results 47; policy 18; and redistribution 126–31; research on 144–5; and student diversity 109; in USA education 54

Equity and Inclusive Education policy (Ontario Ministry of Education) 143
equivalence 2, 43, 95, 97, 125, 131, 136
ethnicity 110, 122, 124, 136, 137, 143
Europe: alignment with OECD and UNESCO 43; financial crises in 7, 25; and the language of quantification 43
European Union (EU) 11; *see also* Europe
evaluation 157; *see also* assessment; testing
expectations, low 133
externalization 2, 45, 60, 62, 147

"failing boys" discourse 18, 31, 121, 136, 138–40, 143; misrecognition and displacement in 124; *see also* gender achievement gap
federalism, educational 9, 67, 72, 73, 88, 89, 122–3
feedback loops 70, 150–1
Finland: early intervention in 115; education system in 16, 131; educational reform in 118; egalitarianism in 112; as example of top-performing system 17, 19, 41, 56, 111; gender achievement gap in 127, 136; as inspiration to Australia 58; as reference society 46, 90–2, 95–6, 110–19, 125; teacher quality in 127; teaching profession in 114; video on 90, 111–19
Finn, Chester E., Jr. 52
flows: in Australia 65, 83; of borrowing 95; of control 150; of data 44, 67, 148; of expertise 53; of ideas 12, 26; of influence 13; of money 12, 26; of people 5, 12, 26; of policy 12, 26, 53
Foucault, Michel 6, 7, 149, 150
fractals 12
framing 41, 95, 127, 136, 138
Fraser Institute 102
free market strategies 131
Fullan, Michael 103

gap talk 121; *see also* achievement gaps; gender achievement gap
gender 136; outcomes by 18; *see also* gender achievement gap
gender achievement gap 18, 110, 121–2, 124, 127–8, 135–6, 137, 139, 141; in Ontario 141–3; and PISA 138–41
GERM *see* Global Education Reform Movement

Germany: as benchmark system 50; in the PISA rankings 19–20, 22
Gillard, Julia 59
Gini coefficient of inequality 54, 118
girls, reading skills of 135
global education policy field 6, 16, 17, 23, 39–44, 46, 50, 57, 60–1, 68, 94, 123, 124, 131, 144, 146, 148, 157
Global Education Reform Movement (GERM) 5–6, 51, 118, 159
global financial crisis 7, 25
globalization 5, 144, 151; as creation of global infrastructure 26, 69; economic 8, 46, 50, 95; of educational accountabilities 35; of educational policy 37; and educational statistics 28; of empiricism 43, 69, 144; and the "failing boys" discourse 124; neoliberal 23, 24; and new global infrastructures 146; new spatial relations of 11; of policy discourse 69; and the rescaling of governance 44; and schooling 112; and schooling in Australia 66; semantics of 45; vernacular 8
globalized localism 6, 89, 159
global panopticism 6–7, 21, 30, 61, 149, 150
global panopticon 45, 149
Going for Growth 27
Gove, Michael 56–7
governance: cognitive 25, 36, 38; by comparison 46, 92; educational 146; epistemological 7, 36, 38; global 25, 35; global geographies of 39; infrastructural 7, 26, 36, 38; legal 25, 36; neoliberal 91, 93, 95, 120, 123, 131; network (heterarchical) 4–5, 12–14, 25, 33, 44, 69, 70, 120, 131, 151, 156; new geographies of 129; new modes of 151, 160; normative 25, 36, 38; palliative 25, 36; rescaling of 44; role of data in 65; in schooling 5; technologies of 30, 124
governance turn 44, 65, 69, 124
governmentality/ies: analytics of 94, 125; contemporary 2; specificity of 109; technologies of 2
Grattan Institute 59, 60
"grey sciences" 2
Group of Eight (G8) 25
Group of Seven (G7) 25
Group of Twenty (G20) 25
Guangdong (China), participation in PISA 33, 47

habitus, global policy 61
Hague, William 57
Harris, Mike 100
health care: in Finland 116; lack of 91, 92; for students 111, 116, 130, 134
heterarchy 12
high-stakes testing *see* testing
homogeneity, racial and cultural 111, 113
Hong Kong (China): participation in PISA 33; reform agenda in 59; strong performance on PISA 47
housing issues 91, 92, 109, 111, 117, 130, 133–4, 142
How the World's Best-Performing Systems Come Out on Top 160
How the World's Most Improved School Systems Keep Getting Better 160
human capital 4–5, 7–8, 26–8, 32, 40, 51, 73, 107, 150

IAFFR *see* Intergovernmental Agreement on Federal Financial Relations
identity 12, 134
ideological closure 111
IEA *see* International Association for the Evaluation of Educational Achievement
immigrants: in Canada 95, 106–8; economically advantaged ; language proficiency of 107; *see also* minority populations
immigration policy, Canadian 107
Importance of Teaching, The 56
incentive systems 54, 71, 79, 87, 151
India: education in 54; OECD's engagement with 33
Indicators of Education Systems (INES) program 29, 39, 51; and global education policy 43
indigenization 62
Indonesia, OECD's engagement with 33
inequality/ies: class-based 93, 122–3, 128; economic 117; in educational policy 129; in education systems 97, 111, 123, 144; gender 135; Gini coefficient of 54, 118; locked-in 109, 137; in neoliberal market capitalism 54; race and income 117; racial 91–3, 97, 103, 109–11, 123, 135; socioeconomic 17, 54, 61, 118–20, 142, 144, 147, 151; structural 118, 119, 120, 142, 147, 151; systemic 121
INES *see* Indicators of Education Systems (INES) program

infrastructure: of accountability 3; of capitalism 3; data 3, 5, 7, 10–11, 24–6, 31, 35–7, 39, 61, 69, 86, 146, 148–9, 150, 153, 155–7; global 16, 26, 40, 44, 69, 146; information 3; pedagogical 130, 143; relational 12, 160; technical 21, 69; for testing, assessment and funding 88
inscription devices 2
interconnectivity 5
Intergovernmental Agreement on Federal Financial Relations (IAFFR) 73
International Association for the Evaluation of Educational Achievement (IEA) 3, 29, 39, 61, 146; data generated by 159; interviews with 68; study 19–20; statistical programs of 43, 45
international rankings 90
interventions: accountability 65; early 115–16; federal 50, 103–4, 109; pace of 95; policy 32, 100, 102, 108, 110, 115, 120, 122, 124, 129–30; school-based 136, 138, 144
isomorphism 30

Jackson, Marguerite 103
Japan: education reform in 49; as example of successful education system 45; influence in the OECD 23; PISA performance of 59; reaction to Shanghai's PISA scores 41; as reference society 50; strong performance on PISA 47
Japanese Education Today 50
Jiangsu (China), participation in PISA 33, 47

Keynesianism 72
key performance indicators (KPIs) 13
Klein, Joel 58, 160
knowing/knowledge capitalism 3, 7, 49, 61, 70, 149
knowledge workers 26
Korea: PISA performance of 59; as reference society 95

Language Background other than English (LBOTE) students 95, 148–9
Lankinen, Timo 114
large-scale assessments (LSA) 1, 2, 7; and accountability 146; data generated by 17, 123, 147, 152–4; and the IEA 29; international 3, 9, 10, 15–16, 19, 40, 51;

national 9, 40; of noncognitive skills 32; *see also* National Assessment Program—Literacy and Numeracy; Programme for International Student Assessment
LBOTE *see* Language Background other than English (LBOTE) students
Learning Curve reports (Pearson) 160
Learning from the Best 60
learning technologies, adaptive 71
Levin, Ben 103
lists 12
literacy 32; in Australia 73–7, 81, 85; of boys 103, 136–7, 143; data 156; declining 71; and the GERM movement 6, 51; government funding for 65; improvement of 16, 67, 88; reading, mathematic and scientific 30, 32; statistical 85–6; testing 17, 49, 63, 64, 66, 148; *see also* National Assessment Program—Literacy and Numeracy; Programme for International Student Assessment; Progress in International Reading and Literacy Study
localism, globalized 6, 89, 159
LSAs *see* large-scale assessments
Lyotard, J.-F. 2, 8, 148, 151, 155

Macau (China), participation in PISA 33
Mann, Horace 50
mapping 2, 11, 125, 128
market economics, neoliberal 24–5
market economy 23
marketizations 6; educational 93; education policy 133
markets: and governance 124; technologies of 125
Marshall Plan 23
massive open online courses (MOOCs) 10
Masters, Geoff 81
Masters Report 81–2, 83
mathematical literacy 30, 32; *see also* numeracy
math performance 26
McGaw, Barry 58
McGuinty, Dalton 100
McKinsey Reports 57, 159, 160
media: reporting of NAPLAN results by 80, 82, 84, 140; role of 129, 141
media spins 93
mediatization: of education policy 119, 147; of PISA results 93–4, 96, 109, 111; of policy production 140

meritocracy 98
merit pay, for teachers 51, 118
meta-narratives, death of 2
metrics mania 6
middle schools, coasting 85
minimum standards 85, 147
minority populations: achievement gap in 128; disadvantages of 140; immigrant vs. nonimmigrant 106–11; *see also* immigrants
modelling 11, 12, 27
Mollenhauer, Klaus 155
motivation 32, 136
Murdoch, Rupert 58, 160
My School website (Australia) 58, 69, 71, 73, 85

NAEC *see* New Approaches to Economic Challenges (NAEC) initiative
NAEP *see* National Assessment of Educational Progress
NAPLAN *see* National Assessment Program—Literacy and Numeracy
Nation at Risk, A 20, 29, 45, 50
National Assessment of Educational Progress (NAEP) 19, 29
National Assessment Program—Literacy and Numeracy (NAPLAN) 8, 16–17, 58, 61, 63, 148, 151, 159; correlation with Teaching and Learning Audits 84; data generated by 152; government focus on 66; as high-stakes test 79, 83, 87–8; intention of 151; mandated measures 76–7; media reporting of results 80, 82, 84; online administration of 71, 150; policy developments in response to 65; politicization of 86; reward frameworks for 76, 78; as selection device 64; setting targets for 74–5, 79, 84–6; shock 80–1
National Assessment Program—Literacy and Numeracy (NAPLAN) study: as catalyst data 82, 87–9; context of 72–3; federal funding based on NAPLAN performance 73–80, 82, 84, 87–8; policy developments in response to 67–8; situating the analysis 68–72; systemic effects of poor performance in Queensland 80–6
National Association of Secondary School Principals (NASSP) 132

National Centre on Education and the Economy (NCEE) 52
National Curriculum, in Australia 73
National Education Agreement (Australia) 73
National Minimum Standards (Australia) 85
National Partnership Agreements (Australia) 73, 74, 84
National Partnership for Literacy and Numeracy 73, 74–5, 80
NCEE see National Centre on Education and the Economy
NCLB see No Child Left Behind (NCLB) Act
NASSP see National Association of Secondary School Principals
neoliberalism 7–8, 23, 24, 44, 64, 68–9; detrimental effects of 118; and educational policy 112; and "racelessness" 94–8; and the silencing of race 90–1
neopositivism 4, 155
network governance 2, 12
networking 11, 12
New Approaches to Economic Challenges (NAEC) initiative 25
New Corps 159
new managerialism 6, 28, 44, 124
new public management (NPM) 1–2, 12, 13, 68, 70
New South Wales (Australia) 16–17; NAPLAN mandated measure 76; NAPLAN performance in 75, 77, 78, 79; NAPLAN reward frameworks in 76, 78
new spatialities 5, 11–12, 60, 66, 86, 131, 151
New Zealand, migrant students in 108
NGOs see nongovernmental organizations
No Child Left Behind (NCLB) Act 51, 118, 122, 158
nodal actors 57, 61
nongovernmental organizations (NGOs) 5, 14, 120; American 158; international 151
nonschool services 113, 117
North America, racism in 91; see also Canada; United States of America
Northern Ireland, PISA testing in 55
Nous Group 59
NPM see new public management

numbers, politics of 123, 125, 144
numeracy 32; in Australia 73–7, 81, 85; declining 71; and the GERM movement 6; government funding for 65; improvement of 16, 67; testing 17, 66, 149; see also mathematical literacy; National Assessment Program—Literacy and Numeracy; Programme for International Student Assessment

Obama, Barack 9, 16, 51–4, 67, 122, 158
OECD see Organisation for Economic Co-operation and Development
OECD Council 24
OECD Skills Strategy 25
Office for Scientific and Technical Personnel 26
online testing 32, 37, 71, 150
Ontario, Canada: as example of high-performing schools 17–18; "failing boys" narrative in 123; gender gap discourse in 140–3; immigrant populations in 98; multicultural population in 90; as reference society 95–6, 125, 144; secondary analysis of 100–1; video on 90, 98–111, 141
Ontario Ministry of Education 18, 102, 121, 143–4
Ontario Secondary School Literacy Test 102
ontologies, neopositivist 4
"opportunity to learn" standards 14
optics problems 71
ordering 11
Organisation for Economic Co-operation and Development (OECD) 1, 2, 7, 15; adaptation of 38–9; and articulations of misrecognition 18; Australia's participation in 58; brief history of 23–6; budget of 27; capacity to adapt 39; commensurative work of 4; data collection of 34, 35, 37, 159; educational assessments of 4, 34; education policy work in 29; emphasis on PISA by 61; and the end of the Cold War 24; and the European financial crises 25; and the expansion of PISA 32, 146, 223; and global educational accountability 15–16; and global education policy 20, 22; and global governance 25; and global policy discourse 69; and global politics of mutual accountability 146;

interviews with 68; involvement in national education systems 93; on issues of equity 126; marketization of education by 126; and the masking of racial inequality 97; mission and purpose 23–4; as node in network of relationships 24; organizational structure of 24; and the PISA data infrastructure 37; and PISA results 17, 19–20, 39; policies of 6; post–Cold War 23, 33, 39; production of statistics by 29–35; promotional videos produced by 17; relationship with BRICs 24; relationship with China 24; role of education in 26; role in global governance 4, 35–9; on school reforms 84; secretariat staff at 4; statistical programs of 24, 43, 45; as a technology of governance 124; videos produced by 90, 95; voluntary nature of participation in 35

Organisation for European Economic Cooperation 23

organizations, international 4, 5; *see also* nongovernmental organizations

out-of-school experiences, access to 133

oversampling 55

Pan-Canadian Assessment Program (PCAP) 18, 121; alignment with PISA 140; data generated by 152; as driver of policy 123; function and purpose of 139, 140

panoptic, global 95

panopticism, global 6–7, 21, 30, 61, 149, 150

panopticon, global 45, 149

parents, engagement of 151–2

path dependency 6, 91, 147

PCAP *see* Pan-Canadian Assessment Program

Pearson 32, 157, 158; interest in national and international testing 89

Pearson Affordable Learning Fund 158

Pearson Foundation 17, 57, 90, 95, 119, 157

Pearson plc 57, 119

pedagogy/ies 1, 2, 96, 115, 129, 154, 157

perception(s): effect of PISA on 20–3, 25, 31, 32, 34, 35, 38, 41, 42, 74–5, 92; influences on 21, 39, 74, 78–80, 87, 161

performance management systems 131

performance targets 66

performativity 8, 17, 25, 88, 89, 94, 126, 151, 154–5; comparative neoliberal 30; and governance 124

philanthrocapitalism 158

PIAAC *see* Programme for International Assessment of Adult Competencies

Pilot Twelve-Country Study 29

PISA *see* Programme for International Student Assessment

PISA for adults *see* Programme for International Assessment of Adult Competencies (PIAAC)

PISA for Development 33, 146

PISA Governing Board (PGB) 55

PISA in Focus 34

PISA shock(s): in Australia 41; created by Shanghai 9, 39, 42, 47, 52; defined 41–2; in England 41; in Germany 9, 41; global 42; in Japan 41; response to 63, 65; in USA 9, 41, 52

PISA Tests for Schools 15, 32–3, 146

PISA 2009 Results: Overcoming Social Background (Volume (II) 126policy: analysis of 5; evidence-informed 4, 43, 70, 123; formation of 4; global 40, 46, 61; globalized 69; Keynesian 12; neoliberal regime 123; as numbers 1–2, 13, 43, 44, 46, 70, 97, 111, 149, 153; reform 6, 147; research for 4; role of visual media in 91; *see also* education policy; immigration policy, Canadian; policy making

policy discourse, related to the gender gap 140

policy dispositif 108

policy making: in Canada 121, 123, 142–3; equity issues in 126, 135; evidence-based 4, 111, 154, 161; externalization in 45; and the "failing boys" narrative 123–4, 126, 138, 141; global 4, 44, 133, 138; mediatization of 119, 140; national 5; OECD/PISA influence on 20, 22, 24, 25, 35, 37, 38, 40, 55, 57, 120, 136, 138; respatialization of 3; and socioeconomic disadvantage 133

"policyscapes," global 5

policy sociology 3, 5, 18, 123, 143, 160

politics: global 146; interest group 151; of numbers 123, 125, 144; technicization of 120

poverty: effects of 54, 91, 110, 116, 117, 119, 131, 132; generational 130, 134; racialized 101, 113

power: different scales of 11; logistical 36–7; panoptic 30, 37, 39; soft 20, 25, 35–6, 39; strategic 36–7; topological configurations of 12–14
power relationships 11
principals: accountability of 1; firing of 131–2; self-government of 70; work of 5
privatizations 6, 13
professional learning communities 49
Programme for International Assessment of Adult Competencies (PIAAC) 4, 15, 31
Programme for International Student Assessment (PISA) 3, 4, 7, 9, 10, 15–16, 69; in Australia 150; changing perceptions by 20–3, 25, 31, 32, 34, 35, 38, 42, 74–5, 92; data generated by 26, 147, 152, 154; deconstruction of categories and data 148; development of 29–30; and the downplaying of contextual factors 92; effect on global education 20–2; explanatory power of 146; and the "failing boys" narrative 121; fee for participation in 27, 160; first results of 19–20, 23; focus on equity and achievement gaps 143; and the gender-achievement gap 138–41; and gendered reading performance 135–8; and global education policy 43; as governing device 131; growth and expansion of 32–3, 38; high stakes associated with 71; impact on national schooling systems 30–5; inception of 28–9; introduction of 22; as measure of national economic competitiveness 51; media dissemination of results 93–4; and the new reference societies 46; OECD's desire for China to participate 24; online administration of 32, 37, 71, 150; Pearson's involvement with 157; as policy dispositif 120; as policy steering technology 25, 37, 57, 61, 123, 131–5, 144; and race 90–3 (*see also* Ontario, Canada); scale of 146; scope of 146; Shanghai's strong performance on 40, 42; and social inequality 97; as technology of governance 124, 131, 136, 138, 143; USA influence on development of 23, 51
Progress in International Reading and Literacy Study (PIRLS) 3, 29, 30, 69;

fee for participation 160; and global education policy 43; high stakes associated with 71
psychometrics 30, 32, 37

quality of life 15, 26
Queensland (Australia) 16–17; advice and recommendations for improvement 81; audit and accountability in 88; NAPLAN mandated measure 77; NAPLAN performance in 75, 78, 79–86; NAPLAN reward frameworks in 76, 78, 82; performance on TIMSS 81; poor NAPLAN performance in 80–6; target setting in 84–6; Teaching and Learning Audits in 68, 86

race 136, 140, 143; achievement gap in 128; and education 124; invisibility of 100
racelessness 91, 120; of media spins 94; politics of 117
Race to the Top initiative 9, 51, 54, 58, 67, 118, 122, 158
racial homogeneity 111, 113
racism(s) 91–2, 98, 113, 120, 122, 133; *see also* discrimination, racial
rationalities 2, 4, 91, 94, 95, 108, 110, 112, 120, 125
Ravitch, Diane 159, 161
redistribution 111, 133, 134, 137; economic 92; and equity 126–31; and the "failing boys" narrative 126–31
reference societies 16, 45–6, 50, 51, 60–1, 95
reform: curriculum 48–9, 73, 114, 154; economic 42, 48, 134; policy 6, 147; in Shanghai 59
regulatory state 70
relationships: center-periphery 67; power 11; school-community 153
research projects: comparative 44; educational 4; on equity and social justice 144–5; government-funded 5; for policy 4; *of* policy vs. *for* policy 160; by private companies 4; social 4
resources: access to 130, 136; allocation of 101; cultural 130; educational 126, 130; financial 114, 129; human 14; intellectual 5; neighborhood 117; for schools 14, 99, 156; semiotic 113; social 129; theoretical 12

Review of Funding for Schooling (Australia) 59
rote learning, in China 47, 49, 59
Rudd, Kevin 72–3

Sahlberg, Pasi 114
sampling errors 79
Scandinavia, as example of top-performing system 56
scapes 12
Schleicher, Andreas 29, 52, 57, 60
Schneider, Mark 52
school choice policies 6
School Improvement Unit (Australia) 68
schooling: "datafication" of 3, 15; hierarchical modes of governance in 5; national system of 41, 87; socioeconomic contexts of 112–13; *see also* education; schools
Schooling Challenges and Opportunities: A Report for the Review of Funding for Schooling Panel 59
schooling systems *see* education system(s)
schools: accountability of 1, 8; charter 51, 56, 131; competition between 6; in developing nations 158; effectiveness of 17, 57, 91, 92, 111, 133; failing 130; middle schools 85; work of 5
science: constituents of 11; literacy in 30, 32; performance in 26
science, technology, engineering, and mathematics (STEM) teaching and research 52
Scotland: as benchmark system 50; PISA testing in 55
Secretariat of the OECD 7
self-responsibilizing 72
sexuality, and education 121, 124
Shanghai (China): analysis of education system in 60; as benchmark for educational development 46; as example of high-performing schools 17; as global city 46, 49; as internal reference 62; participation in PISA 33; as reference society 46, 60, 95; reform agenda in 59; 2009 PISA performance 9, 16, 40, 42, 46–50, 52, 59, 60
Shared Challenge Improving Literacy, Numeracy and Science Learning in Queensland Primary Schools 81–2, 83
Singapore: as example of top-performing system 56; PISA performance of 59; reaction to Shanghai's PISA scores 41, 42; as reference society 95; reform agenda in 59; teacher quality in 127
skills: cognitive 32; communication 32; development of 4, 49, 107; and the global economy 53, 59, 71; literacy 135; measurement of 7, 31, 35, 37; noncognitive 32; and the OECD/PISA 7, 23, 25, 27, 29, 30, 32, 35, 57, 126; 21st century 32
Skills Strategy 27
social analysis 2
social class 133, 136, 140, 143; disadvantage in 111; and inequality 128; privileged 136; *see also* socioeconomic factors
social equality 134; *see also* equity
social inclusion 147
social justice 15, 133; in education 31, 147; research on 144–5
social science theories 5
society: computerization of 156; of control 149–50; disciplinary 70, 149; as statistical construct 43
socioeconomic factors 47, 124, 126, 130, 133–4, 148; advantages 109; background 30–1; differences 113–34; disadvantage(s) 121, 133–4, 144; *see also* social class
sociology: empirical 3; policy 3, 5, 18, 123, 143, 161; visual 17
sound bites 93
South Africa, OECD's engagement with 33
South Korea: as example of top-performing system 56; reaction to Shanghai's PISA scores 41, 42; strong performance on PISA 47
Soviet Union 16
space(s), global 12; policy 5; topological 11, 148, 149; *see also* space of measurement
space of measurement 4, 7, 16, 23, 30, 40, 43, 44, 46, 65, 69, 87, 146
space race 16, 52
spatialities, post-Euclidian 5
Sputnik moment (1957) 16, 52
stakeholders, local 152–3, 154
standardization: in global education policy 133; of teaching and learning 118
Standing Council on School Education and Early Childhood (SCSEEC) 72
statistical analysis 138
statistical literacy, of school leaders 86

statistics: comparative educational 27–8; and the construction of state 43; produced by OECD 27–9
Statistics Canada 139
Stengers, Isabelle 155
Strong Performers and Successful Reformers: Lessons from PISA for the United States 47
Strong Performers and Successful Reformers in Education 57, 90, 92, 98, 119, 158; Finland 90, 111–19; Ontario 90, 98–111
student achievement, variations in 133
students: Aboriginal 137–8, 143; at-risk 137; black 133–4; British 128; diversity of 17–18, 98–9, 103, 106–11; ELL 103–5; immigrant 92, 95, 103, 142, 148; Latino 113, 133; LBOTE 95, 148–9; living in poverty 132; migrant 108; minority 113, 117, 142; nonimmigrant minority 97; Roma 97; self-reports of 32; socioeconomic background of 126–7; variations in achievement 108, 128, 133, 137; *see also* Canadian students
Students First policy (Australia) 66
Student Success Strategy (Canada) 104–5
Student Success Teachers 104–5
Student Welfare Team (Finland) 115
Surpassing Shanghai: An Agenda for American Education Built on the World's Leading Systems (ed. Tucker) 52
surveillance 45, 61, 86, 150
Sweden, as example of top-performing system 56
systems, work of 5; *see also* accountability systems; education system(s)

TALIS *see* Teaching and Learning International Survey
teachers: accountability of 1, 8; employment of 9; firing of 131–2; improving quality of 112–15, 117; low expectations of 13; merit pay for 51, 118; performance pay for 70; quality of 127; as reason for school reform 92; self-government of 70; using test scores to evaluate 131; work of 5
teachers' unions 34, 100, 160
teacher tenure 51
teaching: alternative routes into 51; in Finland 114; standardization of 118
Teaching and Learning Audits 17, 68, 83–4; in Queensland 86

Teaching and Learning International Survey (TALIS) 4, 34, 146
technologies: adaptive learning 71; constituents of 11; cultural 93; of governance 30, 124; of governmentality 2; of markets 125
test-data performance 14
testing: and accountability 1; culture of 61; high-stakes 1, 66, 71–2, 130; international 4–6, 45, 63, 69; national 4, 6, 8, 45, 63, 67, 69; online 10, 32, 37, 71, 150; standardized 51, 100, 141–2; as systemic meta-policy 2; in the USA 51; *see also* assessment
testing literacy 17, 49, 63, 64, 66, 149
test scores: disaggregation of 139; factors influencing interpretation of 134–5
think tanks 120
"Tiger Mother" phenomenon 48, 59
TIMSS *see* Trends in International Mathematics and Science Study
Tirozzi, Gerald 132
topological analytics 12
topological space 11, 148, 149
topological turn 11–12
topologies, governmental 12
Toronto District School Board (TDSB) 100, 106, 142
Trade Union of Education (Finland) 114
transformations, incorporeal 22
transparency: in Australia 73, 74; in Shanghai 49
Transparency International 151
trend analyses 35
Trends in International Mathematics and Science Study (TIMSS) 3, 29, 30, 61, 69; fee for participation 160; and global education policy 43; high stakes associated with 71; Queensland performance on 81
truth telling 94
Tucker, Marc 52
21st century skills 32

UK Department of Education 55–6
UNESCO 6, 19, 28, 29
unions, teachers' 34, 100, 161
Unionville High School (Ontario, Canada) 99, 101–6, 141
United Kingdom (UK) *see* England
United States of America (USA): disaggregation of test scores in 110;

education in 9, 17; educational reform in 49–1; educational segregation in 116; as example for Australia 58, 60; as example of successful education system 45; federal education system in 51, 122, 148; gender achievement gap in 128; inequalities in 54, 117; influence in the OECD 23, 51; influence of Shanghai's PISA scores on 16, 40, 42, 60, 62; looking to Japan for educational lessons 45; and measure of national schooling system performance 28–9; PISA in 33; racial context in 92; school-level assessments in 34

UN Millennium Development Goals 33

values: of accountability systems 152–6; Canadian 141; Confucian 48; consensus 8; educational 4, 154, 161; of global governance 35; local 153; neoliberal 94; of the OECD 23, 25, 38; political 4; shared 23, 37–8; social 29

Victoria (Australia) 16; NAPLAN mandated measure 77; NAPLAN performance in 73–4, 78; reward frameworks in 76, 78
Vietnam, "market socialism" in 69
Virkkunen, Henna 112
visibility, regime of 2, 125
visual media, and policy 91
vocabularies, new conceptual 11–12
voices, accessed 96, 98, 101, 104, 106, 113, 115, 116
voluntarism 30

Wales, PISA testing in 55
welfare state: in Finland 111–13, 115–16, 118; withdrawal of 118
white failure, discourse of 128
workplace skills 32
World Bank 6, 93
world class standards 124
World Trade Organization (WTO) 25

#0091 - 250816 - C0 - 229/152/11 [13] - CB - 9780415710244